The Man Who Climbs Trees

The Man Who Climbs Trees

James Aldred

WH
ALLEN

1 3 5 7 9 10 8 6 4 2

WH Allen, an imprint of Ebury Publishing,
20 Vauxhall Bridge Road,
London SW1V 2SA

WH Allen is part of the Penguin Random House group of companies
whose addresses can be found at global.penguinrandomhouse.com

Penguin
Random House
UK

First published in the United Kingdom by WH Allen in 2017

www.penguin.co.uk

A CIP catalogue record for this book is available from the British Library

ISBN 9780753545874

Printed and bound in Great Britain by Clays Ltd, St Ives PLC

Penguin Random House is committed to a sustainable future for
our business, our readers and our planet. This book is made from
Forest Stewardship Council® certified paper.

For you, Yogita
Mera pehla, mera aakhiree, mera sachcha pyaar.

Never before had he been so suddenly and so keenly aware of the feel and texture of a tree's skin and of the life within it. He felt a delight in the wood and the touch of it, neither as forester nor as carpenter; it was the delight of the living tree itself.
(J.R.R. Tolkien, *The Lord of the Rings*)

Trees are poems that the earth writes upon the sky.
(Kahlil Gibran, *Sand and Foam*)

Prologue
Beginnings

1988

The bog sucked at my left boot, pulling me off balance. Straight-away, I could feel the earthy soup seep in through the lace holes. I spied a solid tussock of grass ahead of me and pitched myself onto it. Stretching up to grab an overhanging branch, I dragged my leg free, hauled myself forward and crawled across to solid ground. I was back in the woodland, the bone-dry leaf litter sticking to the black, muddy glue on my legs.

Treacherous bogs are a real speciality of the New Forest. Earlier that day I'd placed my foot on seemingly solid ground only to feel it wobble and bounce like the thin hull of a rubber dinghy. If you break through the mat of moss and weed on the surface of a blanket bog, you can be up to your neck in seconds. I'd already seen plenty of green-stained animal bones jutting out of these mires – a gruesome reminder to give them a wide berth. But at thirteen years old I was still learning how to read the landscape, and impatience sometimes got the better of me. I took a deep breath, and wiped off my hands. Next time, I wouldn't resent taking an extra ten minutes to walk around a bog, that was for sure.

I pulled out my map: Stinking Edge Wood. It figured. As I sat down to clean the gunk from between my toes with a sock, distant heavy thuds and the sharp crack of branches echoed through the forest. I had been following a herd of fallow deer but these noises were too violent and big to be coming from them. Tugging my boot back on I started slowly forward through the trees. The ground was littered with huge dead branches dropped from the dense canopy above. The afternoon sun streamed into the open space between the trees and a thin veil of dust hung in the air.

The thuds were louder now and I could hear whinnying. A low drumbeat shook the ground briefly before a long stream of ponies came barrelling out of the trees towards me. A dozen mares with nostrils flared, their long manes wild and ragged with tangled bracken.

There was a crazed excitement to them, a dangerous energy in the air. They galloped round in a spiral to face inwards and beyond them I could see two white stallions reeling together in a violent storm of teeth, hooves and spittle. Eyes rolling, pink nostrils open wide, lips curled back to expose savage teeth. They bucked, kicked and reared up to land heavy blows on

each other with their hooves. The mares were almost scream-
ing with excitement, giving out long intense whinnies. The
ground shook again and it suddenly struck me that despite
being so close, the whole herd was still completely oblivious
of me. The air was thick with their pungent smell and I was
in very serious danger of getting caught up in the fray, over-
run and trampled. I suddenly panicked, realising I had only
moments to find somewhere to hide.

The mares were running again – circling the two stallions in
wild flurries and closing fast. I couldn't outrun them. Stepping
back, I felt a tree trunk behind me. A big oak, but there were
too many ponies for it to offer any real protection. Its first
branch was out of reach high above, and my heart raced as my
legs began to shake. Desperately running my hands along its
rough bark, I felt an ancient iron peg jutting out of the trunk.
It had been there so long the tree had almost engulfed it, but
there was just enough still protruding to grip. Above it I found
a second, then a third, fourth and fifth – and before I knew
it I was lying flat on my stomach on a wide branch looking
straight down onto the muscular backs of the stallions roiling
five feet below. The oak and I were at the centre of a swirling
mass of ponies beside themselves in a weltering frenzy.

Dust and noise filled the air and I was gripping the corrugated bark hard, my head spinning and my heart racing as
adrenaline coursed through me. One of the stallions broke
away and the herd rolled after him through the trees. I listened
to the fading drumming of hooves on dry earth and took
another deep breath in gratitude for being given such a timely

escape. Silence returned to the forest and the dust began to settle.

Looking at the branches around me, I was sitting in an ancient oak pollard. The iron pegs were testimony that someone, perhaps a forest-keeper, verderer or even poacher, had used it regularly many years ago. Perhaps it had been a lookout, or a place to hide long before I had sought refuge there myself.

The wide horizontal branches stretched away from me to curl up like the giant fingers of an enormous cupped hand. I slid back into the centre of its protective palm and waited for my heart to slow. After a while the small herd of fallow deer I had been following emerged from the trees, carefully picking their way through the churned-up leaf litter to pass beneath me in the wake of the ponies. They had been there all along and I was immediately struck that not one of them appeared to have seen or smelt me as I crouched in the arms of the oak directly above.

The relief I felt, once in the branches of that tree, had been immediate. I had instantly known I was safe from the violent turmoil below, and seeing the fallow deer pass by had only reinforced my feeling of sanctuary and removal. But beyond that, I also felt an ancient connection to whoever had placed those iron pegs and sat in these same branches where I was now sitting, as if the intervening time had collapsed completely.

I've revisited that same oak on the edge of Stinking Edge Wood many times since. Those iron pegs are a tangible reminder that trees inhabit a different timescale to us and that the life of one tree can easily span dozens of human generations. Climbing up into its giant arms always takes me back to that exciting day in 1988 when as a thirteen-year-old boy I first discovered that trees were places of refuge and offered new vantage points from which to view our world. Even now, almost thirty years later, I still find myself puzzling over the way it just happened to be there for me. In the right place at the right time, when I had needed it most.

Introduction

How I Got Here

I had been woken by a sudden downdraft of air that left my hammock gently swaying. Lying on my side, I stared in drowsy amazement at the huge prehistoric-looking bird that had just landed next to me. The two of us were 200 feet off the ground in the top of a tree in Borneo, and I'd never seen a rhinoceros hornbill so close-up before. It hadn't noticed me yet and was using its long beak to preen its breast feathers. A huge colourful casque curled up from the top of its head like a flamboyant Turkish slipper – fiery reds and yellows glowing brightly in the half-light of dawn. I was entranced.

A few seconds later it froze, then raised its pterodactyl head to peer at me with a ruby-red eye before launching off the branch into space. Immense black wings unfurled to catch its weight and it was gone. Swallowed in an instant by the thick morning mist.

Rolling onto my back I lay staring up into the giant branches above. It had been a long night. The sweat from yesterday's climb had long since congealed into a clammy grime all over me. My clothes were dank, gritty and torn and my skin crawled with biting ants. I had a burning rash on my chest from who knows what, and I'd been stung twice on the face by a night wasp sometime around midnight. But it was worth it – all of it. Encountering a hornbill like that was what it was all about. I was immersed in my very own dreamworld of swirling mists and fairy-tale creatures. There was nowhere else I'd rather be.

The sun hadn't yet risen and I was cold for the first time since arriving in Borneo, a welcome change from the usual stifling heat of the rainforest. Sunrise couldn't be far off, but for now I was happy to lie back and watch the individual droplets of water drift past. They swirled in the visible currents of air, condensing as shiny beads on the metal of my climbing gear. I had slept in my safety harness attached to a rope, my only direct link to the other world far below.

• • •

Yesterday's climb had been nothing short of a mission. Borneo is home to the tallest tropical rainforest on the planet and many of the hardwood trees here are well over 250 feet tall, frequently with no branches for at least the first 150 feet. Tall, straight columns of wood that support enormous parasols of branches high above. Just getting a rope up into them was often near impossible.

Experience had taught me that my catapult could propel a 200-gram throw-bag 170 feet into the air. But time and again the bag fell short of its target branch, the thin line it towed floating back down to tangle in the understorey, slack and lifeless. The branch was clearly much higher than I had realised. In exasperation, I attached the catapult to the top of a ten foot pole and used my bodyweight to pull the creaking elastic right down to the ground. My muscles shuddered as I crouched, taking aim at the branch high above me. As I let go, the catapult's elastic cracked like a whip and tangled into a limp coil. Its job done, I dropped it to the floor. The bag powered up through the gap in the dense understorey to skim over the top of the target branch with barely inches to spare. Then down it came, the line accelerating into a high-pitched whine as the bag finally embedded itself in the leaf litter with a dull thud. All was quiet again. I squinted up through my fogged binoculars, tracing the thin line against the bright tropical sky high above. It was a good shot, at last.

I used the line to thread my climbing rope up over the top branch and back down to the forest floor, where I anchored it securely around the base of a neighbouring tree.

The start of a climb up into a monster like this is always a slow, laborious affair. Most of your energy is soaked up by the elasticity in such a long rope. There was around 400 feet of it in the system, so I bounced erratically as the nylon stretched and contracted. It was impossible not to career into the huge buttress roots and it wasn't until I was a good way up that I was finally able to brace both feet against the trunk and get stuck into it properly. I inch-wormed my way upwards, using two rope-clamps, or 'jumars', to haul myself up the thin nylon line. Rhythm is key in climbing, and it always pays to synchronise yourself with the rope's natural bounce. But it was going to be a long haul regardless. My arms were already knackered from the struggle to get a line up in the first place, so I used my legs to push myself up in an attempt to take the strain off my biceps.

The next challenge was to get up through the forest's tangled understorey. Vines grappled me like tentacles and leaves brushed across my sweaty face, depositing dust and algae in my eyes and ears. The sheer amount of organic debris hanging around in these lower levels beggars belief. Decades of accumulated dirt, dead branches and rotting vegetation is hanging there, snagged in a web of foliage just waiting to be dislodged. This first fifty feet was a filthy fight. Debris rained down in mini avalanches to cling to my sweat-soaked clothes and every twitch of my rope showered me with fine black compost from above. But there was no alternative route; all I had was the straight line of the rope above me. By the time I emerged into the open space above I was caked in dirt.

Although it was late afternoon I was hit by the full force of the tropical sun as soon as I poked my head above the understorey. For the next 100 feet there was nothing except open space and the monolithic tree trunk next to me. This branchless region is a strange limbo world where climbers are fully exposed to the precariousness of dangling on a nylon thread high aboveground. Concentrating on the brown, flaky bark in front of me, I slowly pressed on towards the sanctuary of the canopy.

Ten storeys aboveground I was halfway up and the tree trunk still measured five feet in diameter. These Borneo trees are on a different scale to any other hardwoods in the world. I span round to take a look at the view. I had been saving this moment until I was way above the understorey, in a place that would do it justice. But I had felt its presence lurking behind me the whole time as I climbed. An almost palpable, brooding watchfulness, as if a thousand pairs of hidden eyes were boring into me from the surrounding jungle.

As I twisted round, I was greeted by one of the most breath-taking views I'd ever seen. Dense rainforest swept away from me, cascading steeply down from the ridge to merge into an enticing landscape of giant trees far below. Many miles away on the horizon the forest rose back up to swarm over a ridge of tall, rugged hills. A vast ocean of unexplored, virgin jungle. What hidden wonders lay out there in those trees?

I was now hanging in the full glare of the sun and could feel the sweat trickling down my spine between my shoulder blades. The air was heavy with humidity and I could hear thunder in the distance. By the time I raised my arms to take the next step, my shirt was soaked through and sticking like cling film. I pushed on, up into the dappled shade of the canopy above. Soon I reached my branch 200 feet above the ground, and panting as I slung myself over it, I removed my helmet to reduce excess body heat.

The next twenty minutes were spent rigging my hammock between two horizontal branches. By the time I rolled into it, slumping in an exhausted heap, the light was fading fast. The peals of thunder, distant at first, started rumbling louder and faster. Before long, the heavens opened and sweet, heavy rain fell into my cupped hands as I washed the grime from my face. The water tasted metallic and zingy. Almost electric, it was so pure and fresh. The rain only lasted half an hour or so but by the time it stopped there were several inches of water swilling around in my hammock with me. So I rolled to one side and tipped it glistening over the edge to the forest floor far below. Even before it was dark I had slipped into an exhausted, deep sleep devoid of dreams.

Apart from the incident with the wasps at midnight I had slept well. The mist was thinning and high above I could see the first hint of blue. It was going to be a clear sunrise. I felt decadent, lying back with nothing to do but wait for the slow arrival of the new day. Cocooned in my misty world, I found myself asking why I had felt the urge to sleep a night in this tree, of all places.

It certainly wasn't for comfort. I'd slept in my climbing harness, and eaten all my food ages ago so was now ravenous. I'd also been bitten and stung by so many insects I felt like one big lump of histamine. And yet I was at peace. Completely at peace with myself and the world around me. But why? What was it about climbing trees that was so appealing and resonated so deeply? And how on earth had I managed to make a living from doing it?

• • •

The reason I was in Borneo was to teach scientists how to climb trees, showing them the ropes – literally – and going over the drills until they could climb safely under their own supervision. They were out here to study the relationship between our planet and its atmosphere, doing incredibly valuable work mining the forest for data to fight climate change. Their research was inspiring and important.

But although I enjoyed teaching them, it wasn't really why I was here. I hadn't needed a reason to come and climb. My own passion for climbing trees was harder to define, born from something I had felt the first time I'd climbed into the canopy of that oak in the New Forest as a boy. There's just something about trees that enthrals me and keeps me coming back to spend time with them.

In many ways, I feel that they embody the very essence of nature. Providing us with a living connection to our planet, somehow bridging the gap between our own fleeting lives and the world around us. I feel I'm being offered a glimpse of a half-remembered ancestral world when I climb into them, and for some reason this makes me feel good. It helps me remember my place in the scheme of things.

But above all, my enjoyment flows from a deeply rooted belief that every tree has a unique personality that speaks to the climber if they're willing to listen. The soft shimmering glow of a beech canopy in springtime, or the vast sun-blasted canopy of a tropical giant, each tree has a unique character, and it is the privileged feeling of getting to know them a little better – of physically connecting with them, if only for a short while – that draws me back into their branches time and time again. As living ambassadors from the past, I believe they deserve our deep, abiding respect, and I'm willing to bet that most of us have experienced an emotional connection to them at some point in our lives.

• • •

My passion for tree-climbing was also born of a keen desire to discover the wonderful things held in their branches. There are entire worlds within worlds hidden in even the smallest of trees, let alone the huge forest giants like the one in Borneo I was currently lying in. The canopy is home to myriads of creatures that never touch the ground, spending their entire lives up here. Hunting, feeding, breeding, living and dying in an unseen treetop realm. Immersed in an endless cycle of secret dramas that have played out over and over again for millions of years.

A face-to-face encounter with an orangutan twenty storeys above the rainforest floor can be a humbling experience. But the branches of trees closer to home hold just as much fascination for me now as they ever did. I still vividly recall the delicate translucent green of the first bush cricket I saw in the canopy of the New Forest, marvelling at the way it leapt off a leaf to float down through the void, with its impossibly long antennae spread like the arms of a tiny skydiver.

It was a desire to share these experiences and help reveal this unknown treetop world to others that led me into natural-history filmmaking. Photography and tree-climbing went hand in hand, and by the time I was sixteen I was determined to be a wildlife cameraman.

But when I eventually left college and university it quickly became clear that a degree was no substitute for practical camera skills, and I still had a lot of learning to do. So I took whatever camera assistant jobs were offered, and worked for free in exchange for experience, doing night-shifts in factories and anything else I could find to tide me over. There can be few jobs quite as demoralising as collecting the wind-blown litter from fences around landfills, so I was extremely relieved to eventually be offered my first paid assistant role on a production in Morocco. A couple of years later I'd saved enough cash to make a tentative move to Bristol – home of the BBC Natural History Unit – where I began to find demand for my tree-rigging and assistant skills. My eventual transition from assistant to cameraman took a long time – about ten years – but it was an incredible journey, and I enjoyed every step of the way.

So even though I now struggle to figure out how on earth I ended up where I am, the bottom line is that I am profoundly grateful and simply can't imagine doing anything else. And whenever I feel the inclination to grumble to myself while getting stung and bitten by insects as I film from a camera hide a hundred feet aboveground in the jungle, I consider it a duty to give myself a metaphorical slap around the face just in case I'm tempted to grow complacent and take things for granted.

As much as I love the camera work, beneath it all still lies my enduring passion for trees. Deep down I know that however I had chosen to make my living I would still be out climbing trees in an effort to get as close to them as possible.

I climbed my first big tree with ropes when I was sixteen. The intervening years have raced past in a tangle of branches and foliage and I must have climbed enough trees to fill an entire forest by now. But although many have blurred together, there are others that rise above the fog of memory. Special trees that I remember spending time in as if it were yesterday. The touch of their bark, the smell of their timber and the shape of their branches, not to mention the wonderful animals and people I've encountered in their canopies.

• • •

Back in the Borneo canopy, the air had warmed with the coming of the sun and in the space of a few short minutes the mist had been pushed down into the valley to pool in one vast ocean of white. To my right the sun had just risen above the hills to set the valley on fire. The mist instantly began to rise in tendrils, glowing pink, orange and gold for a brief instant before evaporating altogether.

Within fifteen minutes the sun was high in a clear tropical sky and swifts were trawling for insects over the canopy. The new day had begun and I prepared to descend back to earth, back down into the gloom of the forest floor where night still lingered.

Chapter 1

Goliath – England

1859

It is a grey, damp winter's day in the heart of the New Forest. Pillows of limp copper bracken fringe the edge of a muddy track. Two men dressed in simple forester clothing, wearing heavy hobnailed boots, stand to one side of the trail. The first leans on a tall, straight-handled shovel next to a freshly dug hole. His companion kneels down next to a bushy four-foot-tall sapling lying at his feet. Its root ball is wrapped in hessian sacking tied with string, which he removes to reveal a compact clod of dark earth containing the young tree's soft, fragile roots. Lifting the sapling by its stem, he brushes some of the soil free to expose the root tips. The sapling is then gently lowered into the waiting hole and held straight as the first man backfills it, gently bouncing the shovel to help break the dense loam to evenly fill the gaps between earth and roots. He gently heals in the surface soil, compacting it just enough to hold the sapling steady, but leaving it spongy enough to allow air and rain to penetrate.

As the two men move off to repeat the process with a second identical sapling, which is resting on bracken on the other side of the track, a third man carrying two pails of water approaches from the direction of a stream. He kneels down next to the newly planted sapling and his rough hands sculpt a crude moat in the soil around its base, before slowly filling it with water. He waits for the soil to suck it all down and the moat to drain, before filling and refilling until the water sits on the surface of the earth, and he can see his face reflected against the sky.

By the time he returns again with replenished buckets, the others have finished planting the second sapling. He carefully waters it while his companions carry bundles of cleft chestnut palings from a nearby cart. Within a couple of hours both saplings are circled by five-foot-tall fences, protecting the soil at their feet and shielding their foliage from winter-hungry deer. The men know all too well that the first few years will be crucial for these young trees, and satisfied that they have given them the best chance they can, they collect their tools and head back to the cart. The sound of their voices and the crack and lurch of the carts gradually fade away, and the two trees are left alone in silence to guard the track.

Behind them lies an enormous plantation of young English oak trees. But unlike the anonymous, leafless rank and file stretching away into the drizzle, these two saplings are New World ambassadors fresh from California. Nurtured and raised from seeds collected in the Sierra Nevada mountains six years earlier, they hail from an exotic tribe of giant trees that will change the face of the British landscape for hundreds, if not thousands of years to come.

The drizzle soon turns to rain but as the skeleton army of young winter oaks grows dark in the wet, the verdant emerald foliage of the young evergreens begins to shine.

1991

It was back-to-back AC/DC and Aerosmith on the stereo as we sped round the single-lane bends of the New Forest in Paddy's beaten-up old Vauxhall. I was sixteen years old and feeling pretty rough. It was too early in the morning after the night before, and Steve Tyler's singing wasn't helping, nor was Paddy's driving. Apart from the occasional pony standing in the middle of the road, the empty tarmac seemed to demand Paddy gun his long-suffering car as hard as he could. Matt was crashed out on the backseat behind me. I turned away from the road ahead, opened the window and gazed out at the trees flashing by. The closest were moving too fast to focus on but behind them, in the depths of the forest, I could see the huge, silver-smooth pillars of ancient beech.

Paddy was in his element on these roads, but just as I was about to ask him to slow down, for the sake of his car's interior, he span the steering wheel to the right, yanked the handbrake and catapulted us across a cattle grid. The car's back end slid out, before gripping suddenly on the tarmac of a small side road. Dropping the speed, Paddy rested his chin between his knuckles atop the steering wheel. The stereo was now off and he was gazing up at the sky through the windscreen. Matt had been woken up by the cattle grid and now had his head completely out of the window. All three of us were peering skywards with awe and excitement. We were here at last.

I leant out through my window and breathed deeply. We were kerb-crawling through a straight avenue of the tallest trees I'd ever seen. Rows of huge straight trunks lined either side of the narrow road, their dark bark deeply fissured and corrugated with the rough texture of ancient cork, and their branches holding up the vaulted ceiling of a cathedral of dappled leaves. Light was filtering through in slanted shafts of heaven, almost as solid as the tree trunks themselves. After a few minutes we pulled over onto the side of the road.

The air was heavy with the spicy citrus smell of conifer resin. It was early but the thermals on the surrounding heath were rising, sucking cooler air in from the nearby coast and filling our nostrils with the smell of the sea. High above, invisible in the deep green, I could hear a chorus of goldcrests. The living colonnade we had passed was a double row of tall – very tall – Douglas firs imported from Oregon. These were probably some of the oldest in Britain, judging from their size. A noble species of tree, true aristocrats. But not the trees we were here to visit, apparently. Paddy and Matt had other plans.

Both of them were looking across the road into the timber-dense forest, trying to see something deep inside. Peering in, I caught a glimpse of two giant hulking shadows in the green twilight. Before I could get a better look, Paddy had popped the car boot open with a clunk. I looked down into a tangled nest of old rope, metal buckles and leather straps. Both Paddy and Matt were climbers. But whereas Matt was in his element on rock, Paddy was training to be a tree surgeon and was all about the trees. Matt had his own gear, pretty Gucci-looking rock-climbing kit: a brightly coloured rope, slippery and smooth like an oiled snake, accompanied by a bunch of shiny metal bling.

But the kit Paddy had brought along for us couldn't have been more different: two skeins of ancient hawser climbing rope, two ragged harnesses and a motley bundle of jangling karabiners – some of them clearly homemade. The ropes were stained dark green by algae, tree sap and chainsaw oil, their twisted strands rubbed smooth and shiny by the friction of countless hands. Hand-me-down kit, too old and knackered to be used for work any more.

We were still years away from government legislation design-ed to ensure climbing kit was maintained in good condition. So in 1991 when a tree surgeon retired a climbing rope from service it was generally for very good reasons. Chainsaws and ropes don't mix well and as I ran the loops through my hands I felt the frayed puffs of saw-damaged fibres, an accumulation of nicks and cuts that gave the thing a moth-eaten appearance. But if the ropes were bad, the harnesses were far worse. They each consisted of two wide belts of tattered canvas and leather.

One belt to go round the waist while climbing, the other to slip under the backside like a swing seat. Neither harness had leg loops and both stank of hard work and fear, a heady mixture of stale sweat, oil, petrol and tree sap.

Shouldering the gear, we crossed the road and entered the forest. I hopped over a ditch and breathed deeply, filling my lungs with the peppery spice hanging in the air. My muscles began to relax after the jarring car journey. Paddy and Matt carried on in silence, making a beeline for something further in. I followed and emerged from the shadowy colonnade into an open grassy ride. As the branches cleared, I beheld two of the most astonishingly beautiful, massive trees I'd ever seen. They were unlike any other trees nearby and stood like sentinels on either side of the open ride. Living obelisks at least 160 feet tall, they were a clear hundred feet taller than the oaks in the wood beyond them. The top third of their tapered canopies was bathed in morning sunlight but their enormous flared trunks were still shrouded in shadow. The one on the right appeared to be a little shorter, with a sharper, less weather-blunted top than its companion. But the other tree was a veritable giant. I couldn't help imagine what the view must be like from way up there, perched high on its shoulder. I knew we had come here to climb a tree, but seeing as I'd never climbed one with ropes before I thought this was one hell of an introduction. To attempt to climb one of the biggest giant sequoia's in Britain on my first ever foray was jumping in at the deep end, to say the least. I just hoped they had a good plan for how to do it, because I didn't have the faintest idea.

Paddy and Matt had almost reached its base now. Their silhouettes merged with the shadows at the giant's feet. They looked tiny – like astronauts approaching an Apollo mission launch pad. By the time I joined them, Paddy had uncoiled his rope which lay in open loops at his feet. He was trying to lob an end up and over a branch some thirty feet above his head. Again and again the small bundle of rope slapped against the tree with a hollow sound before falling back to earth at his feet.

I ran the open palm of my left hand across the bark. It was soft and yielding. A thick, fibrous coat that drummed when I tapped it. From about head height to the ground the trunk flared out wildly, disappearing into the bare compacted soil with a circumference at least twice that of the trunk twenty feet up. A few roots broke the surface of the ground in a frozen tangle, but who knew how deep the rest went.

Paddy wasn't having much luck and it was beginning to dawn on me that our adventure might fall at the first hurdle, when Matt delved into his rucksack to produce a pair of ice axes. He waved them with a flourish. It had clearly been his plan to use them all along, but I eyed them suspiciously.

'Are you serious?'

'Got any better ideas?' he said.

I hadn't. But it seemed an insane idea that was likely to end up with him in a crumpled heap at the base of the tree. This wasn't an ice climb; he had no top rope to hold him or any opportunity to screw in anchors as he went. Until he made it up to the first branches he would be on his own, exposed and at the mercy of the unknown strength of the tree's bark. The

machined, aggressive metal spikes seemed in stark contrast
with our soft organic surroundings. It just didn't feel right to
me – not because the spikes, vicious as they were, could damage
the tree in any way. The bark was way too thick and padded
for that. No, for me it was more to do with respect. This tree
was a living entity, an organic being, not some inanimate lump
of geology to stab full of holes. An abstract deference for
the tree mingled with a superstitious desire not to tempt fate,
jumbled with my nervousness at not having climbed before.
But of course I couldn't articulate all these feelings properly.
And even if I could, the others would have just called me a
pillock and pressed on regardless.

Matt clearly had no such misgivings as he whacked both
axes several inches deep into the tree before bending down to
strap on a pair of crampons. He stepped up and dug his toe
spikes in. He was off. 'Thwack', 'whack', step, step. 'Thwack',
'whack', step, step. The tapered trunk rising to the vertical
made his situation look even more precarious as he climbed
higher. He's going to kill himself, I thought. 'If he slips …'

But he didn't. I had to hand it to him – he got a tricky job
done swiftly and with style. It isn't a technique I've ever seen
used by a tree-climber since. Probably because without a flip-
line going round the trunk to stop you falling backwards, it is
verging on suicidal. But a lot of daft things seem like a good
idea when you're sixteen years old.

Matt made it up into the branches. The lowest ones were
all dead so he carried on up into the living canopy before tying
in, kicking off his crampons and lobbing the axes down to

the ground. One of them buried itself up to its handle in the leaf litter.

Paddy was next. He tied the end of his rope to Matt's. Matt hauled it up, passed it over the base of a branch and threaded it back down to him, its sinuous end writhing back down along the fissures in the bark like a hunting snake. Paddy was up there in a flash. Bracing feet against trunk and hauling himself up hand over hand like a monkey. I knew there was no way I was going to measure up to these two on this, my first ever proper tree climb. Paddy pulled my rope up in turn and threw it over a branch ten feet above him. Its end dropped back down to me and I clipped it into the two metal triangles on the front of my harness. I was now attached to a branch fifty feet above me.

'What do I do now?' I called.

'Take that small loop of rope and wrap it twice around the main climbing rope then back through itself. The way I showed you,' he shouted down from his perch. He wiggled the rope and I did as he said. I'd just made a sliding knot known as a prussic.

'Clip the other end into you with a karabiner. No, not there; on the front: here!' he said, hooking his thumb through his own harness rings.

This was the basic, age-old climbing system that Paddy and every other tree surgeon used every day at work. Tree-climbing techniques had not progressed an inch since the 1960s, but it was all still brand new to me. I was still too preoccupied with trying to shake off the fog of a heavy night to think through what I had to do next. Taking a firm grip on the bronze-burnished rope, I used my right hand to slide the frayed knot up a foot or so.

As I transferred my weight from the ground to the rope its elasticity pulled me onto my tiptoes. I stood teetering, trying to find my balance. It was clear that I had to commit fully. So staggering towards the base of the tree, I slid the knot further up the rope until both my feet were planted firmly against the trunk. I was now barely inches above the ground, but the rope had me. Until I reached the first branch I would be relying on this one saw-gnawed thread to support my whole weight. I swivelled my hips from side to side, trying to get comfortable in the harness. Without any leg loops to prevent the belt from sliding up under my arms, I had to lean back fully, almost horizontally, to maintain balance. I took a deep breath and arched my back. Without any other handholds, I was hanging like a clumsy spider on a thread, the rope dangling me wherever it wanted. All I had to do was climb it. Simple. In theory, at least.

After a slow start I got into a rhythm of bracing both feet against the tree trunk while sliding the knot up to capture a few inches of progress. I repeated this procedure again and again, until I was sweating freely despite the morning's coolness. Every time I pulled down on my climbing rope it rubbed over the top of the branch high above to dislodge a fine green dust that floated down through the morning light. It filled the cool air with a soft, earthy aroma.

As I climbed higher, I felt the rope become sticky with sap. This helped me grip and added friction to my top anchor, effectively reducing my weight. I was now above the tapered base and hanging perfectly vertical against the bark. Again I marvelled at how soft and yielding it was. Hard to the touch, but then spongy as I pressed against it. I had a sudden desire to take off my shoes and socks, to feel the tree's skin against my feet and feel its life flowing through me. I'd never live it down, though, so I leant forward to press my cheek against it instead. It was now warm in the sun and the bark felt soft and friendly, like the bristles of a huge prehistoric animal that was allowing me to clamber on to its massive back. I was entering another realm, a place of safety and retreat, and experiencing a kind of baptism – my first immersion in the canopy.

I climbed slowly – not entirely by choice. My technique was halting and lacked the confidence and rhythm that comes with experience. At thirty feet off the ground I reached the first branches, a dead thicket of light-brown, powder-dry snags. They vibrated with a hollow sound when I tapped them. Although they looked fragile, they were surprisingly tough and I found that by placing my feet at their base I could use them as a ladder. Cautiously, I started to climb the tree itself. I transferred my weight from my harness to the branches, relying on my rope to catch me should one of the branches pop.

Paddy and Matt were now only ten feet above me. Matt stood balancing like a gymnast on a branch, his chest pressed against the tree as he peered up its stem to select the best route. With his left arm hooked over a branch, he used his right to throw a bundle of rope higher and was soon off in a flurry of clinking karabiners. Paddy was sitting on a large branch to my left, finishing a crumpled roll-up. Rather than stub it out on the tree, he pinched the cherry between his nails and slid the burnt roach down into his sock. I hauled myself up next to him and looked up at the receding form of Matt scampering like a squirrel from limb to limb above us.

The tree eventually swallowed him from sight. The only sign was an occasional shower of fine dust drifting slowly down through the scattered sunshine, and the constant wriggling of his rope hanging next to me. On the other side, Paddy was in his element. He climbed every day at work, come rain, hail or shine, and usually did it with a chainsaw strapped to his belt. This really was child's play to him. Watching him climb, I became acutely aware of how tightly I was gripping the tree and how tense my muscles were. My hands ached from my rictus grip on the rope, and my neck and shoulders were cramped. I tried to physically relax myself and lower my centre of gravity. I began to feel myself unwind a little, to sink lower down onto the branch. But it took a constant, conscious effort, and the harder I tried the more it seemed to elude me. Every now and then my whole body would spasm with a grab reflex as if I was on the edge of falling asleep. My muscles would ratchet up to clamp the tree with a violent jolt I could not suppress. Paddy broke the silence with a cough:

'Right. Okay – happy?' More of a statement than a question, and I replied that I'd like to hang out there on my own for a while.

'No worries – follow us up whenever, and if not – see you in half an hour or so when we get back down.'

There was no way on earth he was going to let a rock climber beat him to the top of one of England's biggest trees, and he was off in hot pursuit. Paddy and Matt just made it all look so easy.

I was in two minds. At sixty feet up I was currently level with the surrounding oak canopy and could sense that only a few feet above me, just beyond where the sequoia's cone-laden branches were swaying lazily in the breeze, was a world-class view. But I was literally still trying to get to grips with my new environment and pretty nervous about venturing beyond the familiar security of the surrounding oaks. So that's where I stayed. Perched on a branch a third of the way up, feeling the tree's massive bulk sway around me, almost imperceptibly, in the morning breeze.

All around me the lower limbs of this huge giant stretched out and curved down in long graceful arcs. They rose back up at their tips to become almost vertical. Dense clumps of cones nestled within shaggy dark foliage twenty feet out from the trunk. Some were old, brown and cracked where they'd spilled their seed in past years. Others were smooth, shiny and light green, pregnant with promise. I set myself the challenge of trying to reach one. I shuffled out along my perch and as I began to slide down the curve of the branch, it flexed and sagged beneath my weight. The branches were big, but felt surprisingly brittle and I soon reconsidered, inching my way back up towards the trunk. Somehow I needed to keep my weight in the harness rather than on the branch. I needed to re-anchor my rope higher up so that it could support me fully as I tiptoed out away from the trunk.

I'd watched Paddy and Matt bundle their ropes up into small coils before throwing them with easy accuracy over the branch they'd wanted. But even this was a lot harder than it looked. When I finally got the rope over the branch I was aiming for, there wasn't enough weight on its end to come back down to me. I pulled it back and it slunk down to coil around my head and shoulders.

Attaching a spare karabiner from my harness to weight it down, I pulled through a few coils of slack and tried again. This time it went over and came back down nicely, but it also slid down the branch to end up six feet out from the trunk. I put my weight on it, but the branch began to sag. I unclipped and whipped the loop of rope back into the base of the branch next to the tree stem. If I kept some weight on the rope I could hold it in place so it didn't slide down the curved bough.

Very slowly I stood up to balance on my branch. While leaning back in my harness I brought my right foot behind my left and began to walk backwards towards the cones hanging out on the canopy edge. Keeping my feet facing the tree, I twisted my upper body far round to the left to see where I was going. With my right hand tightly gripping the sliding knot, I inched it down the rope. I held my left arm out, fingers grasping in air for the cones still five feet away.

My right leg was beginning to tremble. I was only fifteen feet out from the trunk, but I felt exposed and unbalanced. Forcing myself to let go of the rope completely, I bent my legs into a crouch to lower my centre of gravity. The tremble now moved up to my thighs as I held the posture, but I felt much more in control, much steadier. I was able to cover the remaining few feet and take hold of the end of the branch. The unripe cones were hard to pick off the branch, so I settled for one of the older ones instead, plucking it away from its stem before dropping it down inside the front of my t-shirt. I swivelled back round to face the tree, and headed back up the branch.

Halfway up, my left foot slipped on the smooth, dust-slick surface. I fumbled my grip and found myself swinging, spinning on the end of the rope, back towards the trunk. Before I could think, I hit the tree with a dull thud. The force of the impact was a shock, but the soft bark cushioned it kindly. Looking around, I could see that I'd only fallen a few feet. Rather than undermining my confidence, the soft landing relaxed me and left me trusting the climbing kit all the more.

I braced my legs against the tree, hanging in my harness next to the branch I'd fallen from. The tree was now swaying more noticeably in the breeze, its huge bulk rolling softly from side to side. As I hung limp in my harness, I enjoyed the drag and pull of this gigantic living thing.

Down below me, the tree didn't appear to be moving at all. The bottom third of the trunk was rigid and it seemed I was hanging in a liminal zone between earth and sky, as if the ground was gently relinquishing its iron grip, and the tree was breaking free to become a creature of the air. I closed my eyes to fall into its embrace. All I could hear was the gentle sigh of the breeze through conifer needles and the occasional creak from deep inside the timber.

When I looked up, a bright-blue sky stretched high above me. I had long since lost sight of Paddy and Matt but could hear their voices drifting down to me, occasional laughter bouncing off the surrounding branches. They must have been well above the surrounding oak canopy by now and I could only imagine the view up there in the gods. But at that moment, I knew I wasn't ready to climb higher. I was proud enough of my first branch-walk. I lifted my t-shirt up at the front to pull the cone out for a closer look.

It was dark brown and its crisscrossed cracks held hundreds if not thousands of infinitesimally small seeds. I tapped a dozen or so out into the cup of my hand. Each one no more than a mere flake of paper-thin wood, with a graphite-grey pencil stripe down the middle. I took a deep breath and blew the little pile out through my fingers into the canopy beyond, where they fell like fairy dust. How could something as massive and perfectly formed as this tree have grown from such a minute speck of dormant life? I dropped the cone with its remaining seeds back down inside the front of my t-shirt and relaxed into the silence around me. I felt incredibly peaceful, full of positive energy. Despite spending most of my childhood *with* nature, I'd never been so much *inside* nature as I was right then. As I swayed gently in the arms of the tree, I felt connected to the very earth itself.

A flurry of dust and debris from above brought me back to my senses. A few seconds later I heard the hollow bangs of climbing kit on timber. Matt and Paddy were wild-eyed, pumped up and on top of the world, and I looked up at them with envy. But there was no way I would make it to the top of this tree without getting some more climbs under my belt first.

1994

I leant forward and walked my hands up the tree trunk as I stood up to balance on the branch. Paying out some rope, I bent my legs to jump up and grab the large limb above me. I pulled myself up with both hands, swung my left leg over and pushed up with my forearms to get on top. Draping my left arm around another branch to steady myself, I wrapped a short climbing sling around it and clipped in. Undoing my rope, I let it fall and unravel from the branch below before pulling it up to lob it over a different branch ten feet above. I was making my way quickly up towards the middle of the tree and I smiled to myself as I swiftly passed the highest point I'd reached three years earlier. It was a glorious late afternoon in autumn. The low sun seemed to scatter its light through a prism to set the forest ablaze. I glanced up through the back-lit branches. Night was coming and I needed to be quick.

After our first climb together, Matt, Paddy and I had returned to the real world back on the ground. I never saw Matt again, I moved school and we drifted apart, but even while I was away at sixth form I'd returned to the forest as often as I could to climb trees with Paddy. The New Forest offered almost endless potential for us. You could climb five different trees a day for life and not scratch the surface. Paddy and I were partners in a never-ending quest to find the ultimate climbing tree.

I was now studying photography in London, living in Tooting. I kept my climbing skills up by messing around in the trees on Tooting Bec Common while my mates sat in the sun at the lido. But my heart was always in the New Forest and whenever I had the cash or the time I jumped on a train at Waterloo to head back west. Southampton was the threshold for me: beyond lay the world of trees and home. The further away from London I got, the more charged and focused I became. I loved living in London, it felt like being inside a huge organism that breathed and beat with a rhythm and zest for life that was hard to find elsewhere. But I always felt it took more from me than it ever gave back. And from the moment I returned to my Tooting digs until the moment I could jump bale again and escape to the woods, I felt as if I was running on an auxiliary power source that dwindled all too fast.

I had stepped off the train in Brockenhurst that lunchtime and cut fast through the forest on my own towards 'Goliath'. Paddy and I had named it after our first climb, three years previously, and this was my first time back since. I was a pretty good climber now, but I had been saving up the return to Goliath until I was fully ready. I didn't want anything to stop me exploring those massive branches as I pleased, or prevent me from enjoying the epic view from the top that I'd been imagining for the past three years.

Soon I was eighty feet up, and looking down the trunk I could see the forest floor begin to deepen into shadow. But high above me I could still make out the very tip of the tree still bathed in rich autumnal light. It promised to be a clear night. The distant traffic noise had long since faded and instead I could hear tawny owls, the surrounding firs echoing with their plaintive woodwind hoots. I also caught the occasional guttural groans of rutting fallow deer. If the rain held off, the noises would probably continue through the night.

I was exactly halfway up the tree, at its very centre, where the branches were biggest and where they writhed around each other. The dense canopy of foliage down the outside of the branches hid everything beyond the tree. I was cocooned inside Goliath: the perfect place to rig my hammock. Suitable anchor points were everywhere and I even had a perfect view east over the tops of the surrounding trees where the sun would rise in the morning. I pulled up my trailing rope, the heavy bag on its end bumping and bouncing off branches below. Flipping a short nylon sling around a branch, I clipped my rucksack in and pulled out a lightweight camping hammock made of fishnet nylon. I strung it tight between two huge branches that stretched out from the tree stem into the canopy. It looked pretty flimsy and was obviously designed for use closer to the ground, but there was no reason it shouldn't hold my weight eighty feet up. Still, I'd keep my harness on all night and sleep with the rope clipped into its anchor above, just to be safe.

I was still pretty warm from my climb, but the sun had now set and the sweat was already beginning to chill on the nape of my neck. The wind had dropped and evening shadows were crawling up the tree trunk from below as the branches above began to blur into an impenetrable tangle in the fading light.

Sitting on a branch, I removed my boots and tied the laces together. I hung them over a branch next to the hammock and tucked my trousers into my socks. Under my t-shirt I put on a thermal vest, and over it I pulled a thick sweater. My sleeping bag flopped down like an animal skin when I prised it from my bag, and it smelled as musty and damp as ever. I'd bought it third-hand from an army-surplus store five years earlier, a German Cold War design with a rubberised, waterproof outer skin and warm padding inside. It even had sleeves for my arms, and a double-front zip – perfect for sleeping in a hammock while remaining attached to a climbing rope. I wriggled into it and pulled up the rubberised hood which fit snugly over the top of my woolly hat.

Now came the tricky part: getting into the hammock without capsizing. I pulled open the taut green mesh sides and wedged my bum into the gap. Swinging my legs up and over I tucked my feet down into the net before wriggling my shoulders in, to lie on my back. I clasped my hands behind my head so my elbows could push the sides of the hammock away from my face, and lay there gently swaying. The owls were still hooting. Darkness now filled the canopy, but as I looked out through the black silhouettes of shaggy foliage, the stars began to appear against an ultramarine sky. Cold and distant, they seemed to hang like fairy lights on the tips of the branches curling up into the heavens.

I pushed my fingers through the netting, pulled the sides of the hammock up together, and clipped a spare karabiner through them. I was now completely cocooned, like a long green caterpillar, hanging nearly a hundred feet in the air. For a moment I savoured the wonder of it, but soon my exhaustion overtook me and I fell headlong into a deep sleep.

Around two or three in the morning, I awoke with a start. The ghostly memory of a tawny owl perched on the branch two feet away from my head lingered in my vision. Had I dreamt it? An owl hooted its answer from twenty feet above me, before silently floating out into the moonlit void beyond. The three-quarter moon was riding high in a clear sky. My world of branches was crisscrossed in a fine filigree of silver and black, while the forest beyond seemed draped in white satin. I could hear the distant groans of the rutting deer: the perfect autumnal night. This was it – this was the moment – the whole reason for spending a night up here. I wanted to relish and savour the experience for as long as I could, but before I knew it I had sunk back into deep sleep once again.

The next time I awoke it was morning. The sun had just risen and its warmth was seeping out across the surrounding canopy to burnish the skin of the green seed cones hanging beside me. The tawnies were now silent, but the fallow deer bucks were at it with renewed vigour. They'd had a busy night. The distant nasal whine of a high-powered motorbike broke the spell. I could track its movements along the forest roads by the sound of its gears and acceleration. Rummaging through the bag hanging next to me, I pulled out a fat thermos of tepid baked beans for breakfast.

Swinging out of the hammock, I removed my socks and took a moment to reacquaint myself with where I was. The tip of the tree above was already bathed in light, but looking west, the tops of the surrounding oaks were still in shadow. Barefooted, I began to make my way up towards the top of Goliath and the promise of a fantastic view. The handholds and branches led me in a natural spiral as I wound higher – moving towards the summit, where tree simply stopped and sky began. The branches grew denser as I climbed. It was becoming harder to squeeze my bulk between them. And while the base of this monolithic tree measured several metres in diameter, up here its smooth trunk was now thinner than my waist. Ten feet below the top, I stopped and threaded the rope around the main stem for added strength. The brittle branches were now no thicker than my wrist, and the ground was a very long way down. I deliberately avoided looking at the view and focused on the climb until I was finally right at the top.

Wrapping my right arm around the tree as if it were the top of a ship's mast or the neck of a friend, I pulled my rope tight, leant back in my harness and turned round to face the rising sun.

I shall remember that sight until the end of my days. I was 165 feet aboveground, at the top of the tallest tree anywhere in the forest, with the surrounding blanket of canopy stretching away to the horizon in every direction. To the north-east I could see the spire of a church; to the south the world seemed to end suddenly with an abruptness I realised must be the coast. The Solent, lying beneath a shimmering azure beyond. I could also see the Isle of Wight's tall white cliffs and the chalk stacks known as the Needles rising from the sea.

To the west and a hundred feet below me lay a vast ocean of oak trees glowing gold and orange in the morning sun. Way beyond that – right at the very edge of sight – lay a thin strip of purple haze which must have been open heath lying on the forest's western fringe. Goliath's immense shadow lay across the top of the surrounding trees like a huge black monolith, crushing everything beneath it.

The view was more wonderful and enticing than anything I had imagined. I had made it there at last, and looking out over the trees from my perch, high on Goliath's shoulder, I saw that there was an entire canopy-world out there beyond the borders of this forest, just waiting for me to explore.

Chapter 2

Tumparak – Borneo

1998

Thousands of tiny yellow fruits lay mouldering on the jungle floor around me. The sickly-sweet smell of fermentation hung heavily in the musty air and thick clouds of tiny fruit flies hung over everything in a low mist, swirling like dust in the shafts of early-morning sunlight.

The smell was almost intoxicating. It reminded me of my failed attempts at home-brew bubbling in barrels under the stairs back home. Bending down for a closer look, I realised these must be the wild figs I was looking for. Some were hard, about the size and shape of a marble. Others had clearly been there a while and lay ruptured and rotting. They didn't look very much like figs to me; but this was a wild, tropical rainforest species bearing little resemblance to anything stacked in supermarkets back home.

They didn't look very palatable either, but judging from the amount that had been knocked down by animals foraging in the canopy 200 feet above me, I was in the minority. The ground was absolutely littered. Taking out my knife I cut one open. The skin was tough but the spongy flesh inside yielded to the blade and was filled with dozens of tiny powdery buds. Its centre was hollow, home to a couple of squirming grubs.

So here were the figs, but where was the tree that had produced them? I peered through the thick vegetation around me.

• • •

Everything about the Borneo rainforest was so exciting, alien and wild to me. The sheer diversity of life here was staggering. Everything I saw demanded closer inspection and the deeper I peered, the more complex it became. Like looking through binoculars at the night sky for the first time and seeing rank upon rank of new stars appear in the former emptiness beyond familiar constellations. This was a living world of infinite depth and bewildering beauty. To enter it was to be transported to another time and place, to tumble down the rabbit hole into an ancient world totally dominated by trees. Here more than anywhere else I'd been, the trees were in control. An entire ecosystem moulded around them.

The jungle seemed perfectly balanced and in tune with itself, infinitely subtle and intricate. Yet there was also something wild and dangerous about it. I had no doubt that its beauty and wonder would fade pretty quickly in the event of an accident.

Even a twisted ankle would become a big issue, while getting bitten by a snake didn't bear thinking about. I would have to keep my wits about me and not get distracted. But it was hard as I was still on a massive high from simply being here.

I'd arrived in the Danum Valley Conservation Area a few days ago with John the cameraman, and Gen, the assistant producer. We were a small team, due to spend the next six weeks filming in this 43,000-hectare region of pristine rainforest for a Bristol-based company. My role was to camera assist John, but also to get him safely up into the canopy to film orangutans feeding in a fruiting tree. They were both currently scouting a different part of the forest with Dennis our local Dyak guide, which left me to search the jungle on my own for a suitable fruiting tree to film. I was in heaven. But that's not to say I wasn't finding the rainforest a challenging environment to work in. The few days since I'd arrived had been a steep learning curve.

My first challenge had been acclimatising to the incredible heat and humidity. The jungle was locked in a perpetual cycle of rain, mist and sweltering heat. As soon as the nightly rainfall stopped, humidity levels rocketed and the trees exhaled to fill our river valley with thick mist. The morning sun would rise over the nearby ridge to set the scene ablaze and the swirling fog would lift to evaporate into the sky. By late afternoon the clouds would be building. Towering thunderheads of moisture sucked up from the forest. Bubbling up for thousands of feet to teeter ominously before collapsing in an avalanche of rain that evening.

Walking into the jungle was like entering a steam room. Within minutes my shirt was soaked with sweat that had nowhere to go. The surrounding air was so full of moisture that perspiration couldn't evaporate. Clothes stayed damp and mouldy for days on end. I understood why indigenous tribes still dressed so minimally in the jungle. European clothes become a grungy breeding ground for bacteria and quickly fall apart.

Then there was the challenge of covering long distances on foot through the forest without getting lost. The trees had an uncanny ability to play with your head and confound any innate sense of direction. To walk in a straight line was almost impossible. This was not a linear world and the weaving web of animal trails and tracks seemed to shift constantly. The rainforest was living up to its mysterious and secretive reputation.

This was the world that had waited beyond the New Forest's horizon. What would it be like to climb up into the canopy? How would the animals I met there react? What would it be like to be in a tree so massive that its lowest branch was the full height of Goliath aboveground, and the size of an entire oak tree? I couldn't wait to find out.

Letting the fruit drop through my fingers, I looked around me. Dense foliage was punctuated by the massive vertical trunks of tropical hardwoods, each one the size of a cathedral pillar. Their bases were completely hidden by thick vegetation so that they seemed to float disembodied in the space between understorey and canopy. But these weren't the trees I was looking for this morning – none of them was responsible for the bounty of fruit spoiling at my feet. In many respects the tree I was seeking was the very antithesis of all the others in the forest. It was a social outcast, a pariah of the tree world, with a dark and sinister reputation. I couldn't wait to meet it.

Craning my neck, I could see the branches the fruit had fallen from, but it was impossible to tell to which trunk they belonged. So I followed the trail of fallen fruit off the path into a small glade. The fallen fruit was even thicker here and the vinegar-tang of fermenting sugar was tainted with the earthy smell of pigs that had been here during the night. Fruit, soil and leaf litter were churned into one.

In the centre of this small clearing I found it: a strangler fig. And what a strange, twisted creature it was. A tortured skeleton of a tree, unlike anything I'd ever seen before.

In place of a single trunk it had several intertwined stems that untwisted fifty feet above me, to descend in a thicket of stilts. Dozens of long, thin roots hung down to the ground like tendons. Several of the larger stems were enmeshed within a creeping lattice of sinews. In fact, the whole tree appeared to be entirely trapped within a web of its own making, struggling to break free from the sticky strands threatening to throttle it.

Stepping forward into the space between the stilts I looked up to see a huge section of dead trunk suspended in a tangle of roots ten feet above me. These were the rotting remains of the strangler's victim – its host tree. Its dark-brown surface was pitted with decay and encrusted with fungi. Large holes gaped like a ghoulish mask. It had been there a long time and the fig's roots had pierced it again and again. Once upon a time it had been full of life. A giant tropical-hardwood tree several centuries old, standing 250 feet tall.

Having germinated from a seed dropped by an animal in the giant's canopy, the fig had sent its roots down to girdle its host's enormous trunk. Ever-tightening roots became a living cage that slowly engulfed the trapped tree. Decades later, by the time the strangler was big enough to stand alone, the last vestiges of life had been squeezed from the giant now imprisoned within it.

There was something forlorn about the host's husk hanging there like that. Cocooned and sucked dry like the meal of a giant spider. Soon it would turn to dust and crumble away to leave nothing but a macabre vault of roots.

The trees of Borneo are amongst the tallest growing anywhere on earth, which means the strangler figs here are also some of the tallest of their kind. There was a dark side to the giant killer in front of me, and yet the life it had so brutally stolen had been channelled straight back into the forest via the strangler's fruit. It is the way of things in the jungle: energy seems to cycle through nature so much faster than anywhere else.

The figs were almost ripe and the dislodged fruit all around me on the floor was testament to the fact that for some animals the banquet had already begun. As if to confirm this, there was a splash of leaves from high above followed by the soft patter of falling figs. Something was moving around up there, feeding. Peering up through the dense understorey, I thought I saw branches moving, but it was hard to be sure.

Sliding my rucksack off my shoulders, I unpacked my climbing gear. My plan was to climb the fig and use it as a lookout from which to choose a suitable neighbouring tree for our filming platform. John the cameraman could then use this base to film what was going on in the fig's canopy from a discrete distance. It's no exaggeration to say that all the jungle's fruit-eating animals go crazy for figs. And those that don't eat fruit are lured in to hunt those that do. So the chances of John getting some amazing footage of animals were good – as long as I got a move on.

I intended to climb one of the stilt-like stems, using the latticework of wood as a natural ladder. The tree in front of me was the ultimate climbing frame and although a climbing rope trailed from the back of my harness to be used if necessary, it seemed more fitting and more fun to do it the old-fashioned way – to free-climb up as far as possible.

Besides, this was the first tropical tree I had ever climbed, and I felt the need to earn the experience in the most hands-on way I could.

Before I'd entered the forest that morning, Dennis had told me that figs – especially stranglers – were very special trees in his native Dyak culture. The home of powerful forest spirits, both benign and malevolent. These needed to be appeased and placated by asking their permission to climb the tree before intruding upon them. He had looked into my eyes with such an earnest expression that I didn't question him and vowed to do as he suggested.

'And one more thing,' he'd said as I turned to go: 'Don't urinate anywhere near the fig. You'll annoy the spirits and bring bad luck. This is their forest, just remember that. Respect them and the tree at all times.'

Various Dyak tribes had lived in these forests for thousands of years and I had to assume they knew a thing or two about how to behave. They certainly knew more than an Englishman, so who was I to question the way things were done? I wasn't going to dismiss Dennis's concerns when I was about to climb twenty storeys up into the tropical canopy for the first time.

So, dutifully I leant forward and touched my forehead against the strangler. Who knows? Maybe something inside the fig tree was placated and soothed by my deference. Besides, Dennis's words had resonated deeply within me and it felt like the most natural thing in the world to do.

I began making my way slowly up one of the stems, with hands and feet groping for holds amongst its twisted roots. The bark felt smooth yet rough, like a fine grade of sandpaper, and I was surprised by how strong even the thinnest strands were. It was still early and cool, but within minutes of starting I was drenched with sweat. Reaching the top of the stem, I began climbing the structure above, hand over hand. I was now around fifty feet up and level with the surrounding forest's understorey. A fall from this height would be bad, so I used my rope as a safety to catch me in the event of a slip. It was nice not to have to rely on the rope completely though – there were still plenty of handholds to choose from and I made quick progress.

The trunk was full of holes, sometimes deep enough to swallow my entire arm. Who knew what was living within that musty hollow darkness? Spiders, centipedes, scorpions, even snakes, perhaps. I was having fun, but I reminded myself not to get complacent.

By the time I was 150 feet up I was filthy and in need of a rest. Clipping into the tree, I sat back in my harness to take a look around.

The fruit-laden canopy above was hidden by dense curtains of creepers, but I could see the next twenty feet of trunk well enough and it didn't look encouraging. It was totally smooth and offered no handholds at all. The first large branches were growing directly above this sheer face. If I could lasso one with my rope I should be fine, but it was a long throw from an awkward angle.

Bundling up a short length of rope, I lobbed it up as hard as I could. Five times it fell short, falling back down to land in a tangled heap around my head and shoulders. My right arm felt like I'd wrenched it out of its socket. It was full of lactic acid and heavy. But I kept plugging away until I got the bundle over the branch, then wiggled the rope gently to coax the end back down to me. The branch was much further out from the trunk than I had realised and the rope dangled in space way beyond reach. Using my lanyards to hook it back in, I attached myself to the rope, breathed out slowly then let go of the tree and swung out into space.

Relinquishing life and soul to a thin strand of nylon is something I've never got used to. It's one thing to climb a rope, to feel its tension hold you firmly in position and support your weight while ascending. But it's quite another to let go of a perfectly good handhold and rely on a rope's ability to catch you 150 feet aboveground. There is a sudden drop as the nylon stretches, followed by a rush of air and a tightening in the stomach as you accelerate out into the void. This is followed by a split second of weightlessness at the top of the arc as the effects of gravity reverse and propel you back in towards the tree.

The rope gradually slowed, to leave me spinning gently. After the initial rush, the tension in my muscles subsided and the adrenaline seeped away to leave me feeling calm. I traced the thin line into the branches above, where a flock of tiny electric-green birds flitted between the leaves. Looking down, I watched in amazement as a *Draco* flying lizard glided below me with wings opened flat and thin tail trailing. One hundred and fifty feet seemed pretty high to me, but what must it look like through the eyes of such a tiny, base-jumping reptile? This forest was full of surprises.

Content to hang there for a while, I leant back in my harness and closed my eyes to enjoy the sensation of swinging on the rope. Without the distraction of sight, I tuned into what I could hear.

The song of the rainforest was incredible. Millions of animals and insects; rank upon rank of unseen voices rising up in a wave of sound. The distant call of a gibbon, the ragged rush of air through a hornbill's wings. The constant swirl of singing insects and the high-pitched piping of treefrogs. I was immersed in a natural symphony – the sheer complexity of life here was overwhelming. Opening my eyes, I felt as if I was seeing the rainforest for the first time. It rushed in from every direction, as if a veil had been lifted. The jungle was so much greater than the sum of its parts and I was nothing more than an atom adrift within this overwhelming tide of energy. It was a truly humbling experience and with it came a feeling of acceptance and belonging – not just to the forest, but to nature itself – and as the emotion rolled over me in a wave I burst into tears of joy.

• • •

It's almost impossible to appreciate just how complex a tree is from the ground. You have to get up into it. From 150 feet I could now see what could only be described as the strangler's 'waist', the place where its long stems fused together into a short torso of solid trunk before expanding out again into branches. Another few metres and I would enter its canopy and the surrounding forest would be smothered from view. So I span round to take a look at our filming options.

What I needed was a tall tree growing close by in which I could place John's platform. There were plenty of options. Massive trees rose up all around. Some were draped with dense vines. Others were clean-limbed, naked and beautiful. But all were by far and away the tallest, most impressive trees I had ever seen. Several towered head and shoulders above the strangler, which meant they were approaching 270 feet high.

Many of them were members of the Dipterocarpaceae family, a large group of tropical hardwoods found throughout South East Asia. But it wasn't just the size of these trees that was so impressive, it was their shape. They had a graceful symmetry that belied their bulk: tall, vertical trunks ten feet in diameter, rising 160 feet into the air before spreading their limbs in all directions, like a giant three-dimensional ladder. Many of the branches stretched out horizontally – a feature that immediately spoke of strong timber. The leverage on the tree at the base of those huge limbs would be insane, and I noticed how the trees had distributed and balanced these forces across the scaffold of their canopies with effortless grace. Each tree was a master class in structural engineering, and their enormous canopies of thick foliage seemed to float above the forest like islands. Unexplored worlds brimming with tantalising secrets.

Directly opposite the strangler was one dipterocarp that looked perfect for our filming platform. It was close enough for John to film animals visiting the figs, but far enough away not to disturb them. The place I had in mind for our platform lay fifty feet above the dipterocarp's lowest branch. Around 200 feet up, I reckoned. Although the huge tree looked obvious from here, I knew it would be tricky to find once I was back on the jungle floor. So I used my compass to fix a quick bearing before turning my attention back to the strangler.

Continuing up my rope, I was soon engulfed by thick, dark foliage. The leaves were long and shiny, with a pale-green rib running down the middle. The end of each sprig was crowned with a tiara of bright-yellow fruit. Against this dark background the figs shone out to all passing animals and birds. There were hundreds of kilos of food hanging for the taking all around me. With no other fig trees growing nearby, all eyes would be fixed on this one as its remaining fruit slowly ripened over the next week. It promised to be quite a feast, so I needed to get the platform up as soon as possible.

• • •

The thin twilight of dawn was seeping through the cracks of my cabin walls when I awoke the next morning. It was half past five and I lay listening to the distant calls of gibbons from the top of their tree somewhere deep in the jungle. The thought of them swinging around in those high branches galvanised me. Impatient to get climbing, I wolfed down breakfast, grabbed my gear and headed into the misty forest.

The ghostly shadows of huge trees loomed up through the fog as I moved swiftly along the ridge. Enormous columns of timber, standing like silent sentinels, watching me pass. Some were no more than shifting blurs and shadows, while others closer to the path seemed to step forward to reveal themselves, only to slink back into the gloom and disappear entirely as I passed them.

The first rays of sun were soon piercing the mist in oblique shafts of gold, like a cinema projector, the leaves scattering each beam into a spectrum of smaller ones that gently merged and divided as the sun rose higher. The forest began to give up its moisture to the sun's heat, and vapour twisted in tendrils from the surface of leaves. Airborne droplets of water drifted gently through beams of light.

I was keen to climb the dipterocarp, but had to take time out to appreciate the ephemeral beauty around me. Dropping my rucksack, I sat down in the leaf litter to watch in silence.

For a few glorious moments the air was alive with vibrancy and colour and I was surrounded by a shimmering rainbow of drifting moisture.

Within a few minutes the last of the mist had evaporated through the forest canopy, to reveal a thin veil of blue sky beyond. The coolness of morning wouldn't last for long; it promised to be a very hot day. So I checked my compass and headed further up the ridge to find the tree I was to rig the platform in.

Before long I was standing at its base. Huge buttresses flared out in every direction and long serpentine roots followed the contours of the ground before plunging below the leaf litter in search of whatever grip they could secure in the forest's thin soil. The trunk itself was ten feet in diameter and over sixteen storeys tall. A similar size and shape to Nelson's Column. The canopy it supported above was an immense living dome that rose into the sky, a living vault of leaves braced by enormous beams of timber. The last of the morning's mist drifted through this distant foliage, making it look remote and inaccessible. This was a seriously big tree, and looking up at the faint outlines of its branches I felt the first flutters of nervousness.

Lowering my gaze I ran my hand across its corrugated bark. I felt enormous strength in the timber, the immovable steadfastness of a healthy tropical hardwood in its prime. Long vertical lines ran up the trunk to converge at the edge of sight. The tree's skin was a mottled patchwork of silver and deep tannin browns, a beautiful pillar of living wood that would be a joy to climb.

The immediate issue was how to get a rope up there in the first place. Everything else rested on this. I had come prepared with catapult, fishing line and lead weights, but had never tested my homemade system on a tree this big. Shooting lines into the English canopy was one thing, but this was a different scale entirely. I had no idea if my small catapult was even powerful enough to get that high.

What would I do if Plan A failed? It wasn't as if I could free-climb this monster from the ground as I had the strangler. There were absolutely no handholds for the first 160 feet and the trunk itself was far too wide to wrap arms or lanyards around.

An awful lot rested on the performance of the two thin strips of catapult elastic I'd brought with me from England.

Unpacking my rucksack, I selected a small fishing weight the size and shape of an almond and tied it to a thin cord. Placing it snugly in the pouch of the slingshot I raised my arm to take aim and pulled the elastic back to my ear. The yellow rubber turned white with the strain. Aiming a few metres above the lowest branch, I released and immediately lost sight of the tiny weight as it shot into the canopy. Loops of line whipped up silently and an ant crawling along one of the coils was taken on the ride of its life. Within a few seconds, over a hundred metres of line had been payed out, and since it hadn't fallen back down in loose coils I presumed it had gone over something up there. Whether that something was the branch I wanted was hard to tell.

By gently tugging the line with my left hand while holding my binoculars with my right, I used the twitching movement of leaves high above to locate the weight. As I focused on the tiny dangling silhouette, a small bird darted out from the canopy to give it a jab with its beak, before flitting back to the end of its twig and chattering angrily.

The line wasn't where I wanted it to be, but at least the catapult had the power to get up there. Gently pulling it back down, I set about having another go. It took four attempts, but I eventually got it exactly where I wanted it: right at the base of the lowest enormous branch.

My rope was exactly 330 feet long and by the time I'd hauled it over the branch and pulled it back down there was nothing to spare. I'd guessed about right, the branch was 165 feet aboveground. Exactly the same height as Goliath, almost to the inch. But whereas Goliath had a thick ladder of branches ascending all the way to its top, the monster in front of me had none at all below its main canopy.

The climbing ropes were now anchored around the base of an adjacent tree, and I was ready to go. There was a daunting amount of stretch to be pulled out of the rope, but a few minutes later I was hanging in my harness ten feet off the ground, doing my final safety checks. The mountaineering-style climbing technique I was using was still new to me. I'd been trained how to do it only days before leaving the UK, so the repetitive rhythm of sliding clamps up rope still took a lot of concentration.

Focusing on the branch high above, I started moving up towards it. Whereas the strangler had slowly revealed each section of the climb as I reached it, this tree was completely open and exposed. I could brace my feet against the trunk, but it offered scant security since there were no handholds. Slowing my pace, I made an effort to channel my energy and relax. It was shaping up to be a very hot day indeed, and I was already sweating freely.

Climbing on, I fell into the rhythm and bounce of the rope's stretch. The furrows in the bark began to flatten out and at sixty feet I emerged from the shady underworld to enter the sunlit space between understorey and high canopy.

The sunlight was bright and stark. It'd taken me longer than I'd expected to get the ropes up and it was now late morning. The heat from the sun was unbelievable. I wasn't wearing a helmet so I felt its full force on my scalp. Sweat trickled into my squinting eyes and I dried my face on my sopping t-shirt. Feeling dehydrated and in need of a drink, I realised I'd left my water bottle on the ground. Deciding not to waste time retrieving it, I carried on regardless, but within a few minutes I realised this was a big mistake. Water and salts were being wrung from every pore of my body and even my copious sweating wasn't helping to keep me cool. My core temperature started to rise unchecked.

Halfway up I turned to look for the strangler. The air was simmering with UV and I had to shade my eyes, but the strangler was right there, less than 200 feet away, its drooping canopy looming over the forest with a dark, brooding intensity. Apart from one long, slender branch which dipped down to touch the understorey, its crown was totally isolated. But even from here I could see the bright specks of fruit sprinkled amongst dark leaves, and a low line of turquoise hills running along the horizon beyond. A wide valley swept away to the east but I wouldn't get a proper view until I climbed a bit higher.

Twenty minutes later I arrived at the first branch, soaked with sweat, covered in grime and panting like a dog. The vein on my forehead was about to pop and my eyes were stinging from the sweat streaming down my face. I was struggling to think straight and there were white rings of dried salt on the front of my t-shirt. The air felt thick and claustrophobic and a distant peal of thunder drew my eyes skyward. Heavy grey clouds were already building on the other side of the valley. The shade of the canopy was gently cooling and I searched for a way to get higher.

I was at the very top of my rope. The thin white strand passed over the branch in front of me before plummeting straight back down to its anchor sixteen storeys below. The place I wanted to install the platform was another fifty feet higher and I wouldn't be able to reach it unless I rigged another rope. What I'd originally thought was a convenient ladder of branches turned out to be way too big to free-climb. I'd struggle to even get an arm round these limbs. I'd brought my lanyards with me, so I bundled up a few coils and lobbed them over the highest branch I could reach.

Any view of the surrounding forest was again obscured by thick canopy but the branches gradually got smaller the higher I went. They were still big, but at least I could now hook an arm round them easily and my pace of climbing quickened. I was 200 feet aboveground and making good progress but in desperate need of water. My tongue felt like leather and my head was pounding. I'd already had to stop to massage cramp out of my left forearm and now my calf muscles were beginning to follow suit. This wasn't the irritating cramp of sitting in an awkward position, but a deep stabbing pain that spread through my tissues like fire. Ignoring the warning signals, I carried on climbing.

Arriving level with where I intended to strap the filming platform to the trunk, I took a closer look to ensure it would work. The stem had narrowed to a couple of feet in diameter and I added up the rope lengths to estimate that I was now 210 feet aboveground. The location afforded a cracking view down onto the strangler. Anything feeding on the fruit in its branches would be in plain sight from here, the perfect camera position.

The view beyond the figs was simply stunning. Endless canopy rolling away to merge with the distant hills at the end of the valley some twenty miles away. This undulating sea of foliage was punctuated by thousands of huge emergent trees, their upper crowns standing proudly above everything else. I could see the unmistakable silhouettes of giant shaggy ferns growing in the forks between branches high up in their canopies. Several of them showed signs of weather damage: stumps and cavities where enormous limbs had been torn away by high winds. Raising their heads above the shelter of the crowd was clearly a risky business for any tree here, and it looked like many had either dropped limbs to lighten the load or had them violently ripped off by storms.

As if in answer to my thoughts, another peal of thunder came rolling up the valley towards me. A crescendo of kettle drums culminating in a resounding hollow boom that I felt in my chest. A dark smear of rain was lurking over the trees a few miles away. Long black streaks of watercolour obscured the horizon. A squall was on its way, but the sky directly above me was still clear. With only another fifty feet of tree to go I couldn't resist making a quick dash for the top before the squall arrived. Besides, a bit of rain never hurt anyone, and to get above 250 feet in a tree for the first time would be a big milestone for me.

So grabbing hold of the next branch I braced my foot against the stem and lunged upwards with every bit of strength I could. Pulling myself up to swing my leg over, I kept the momentum going and propelled myself towards the top as fast as possible. I soon found myself completely above the surrounding forest canopy. The view was already mind-blowing and could only get better.

The thinner branches were now the perfect diameter for hands to grasp and my boots found easy grip on the bark. It felt so good to be climbing the tree itself, rather than the rope, and I couldn't stop grinning. I was exhausted but exhilarated. Experiences like this had to be earned to be enjoyed fully. My muscles were still wavering on the edge of cramp, but I felt the deeper strength in my bones and knew I had plenty more to give. I had already climbed past the top of the tree's main stem and was now on a near-vertical branch that led straight to the summit of the crown. This final section of tree stood way above any other on the ridge. The strangler had long since merged into the green background of jungle far below, and I realised that by fluke I had stumbled across one of the forest's biggest trees, growing in one of the most prominent positions. The forest flowed away to the horizon in every direction and I couldn't wait to reach the top and revel in the epic view. I threw myself into the remaining thirty feet with every ounce of energy I had.

A few moments later I was stopped in my tracks by an explosive cannonade of thunder. It came from nowhere to tear the heavens apart right above me. Caught totally unawares, I instinctively threw my arms around the tree's stem and cowered against the bark; everything was muffled and my ears were ringing as my head spun. At that same moment, my left forearm cramped up again, but this time it was accompanied by a sharp stabbing pain that made me wince and groan out loud. The minerals I'd sweated out had caused the nerves in my muscles to lock up and without any fluids or electrolytes it was slowly getting worse. I'd totally underestimated the effects of chronic dehydration and a few seconds later the same thing happened to my right arm. Feeling the panic rise within me, I watched in horror as my hands were twisted into useless claws by tendons that threatened to snap. Telling myself to calm down, I tried to prise my hands open by pushing them against the tree, but my fingers were locked in painful spasm. Cursing myself for ignoring the warning signs, I realised that it was now too late, the damage was done. There was no way I could carry on climbing, and as the reality of my predicament crashed in on me the storm hit with brutal ferocity.

First of all came the wind, a fast-moving wall of solid air driven ahead of the rain to hammer the forest around me. The top section of my tree heeled to the gusts, and sprigs of leaves were snapped off and hurled spinning into space. Wrapping my useless arms around a branch, I hunkered down to ride it out, but the wind's intensity increased and soon the whole canopy was twisting violently around the tree's main stem. Huge branches lower down were tugging the tree from side to side in a series of gut-wrenching lurches. Hugging tighter, I pressed my face hard against the bark and gritted my teeth.

The sky was dark and the tree was lashing around like a ship anchored in a storm. Wind howled through its branches like a banshee and ominous bangs and thuds echoed up from deep inside the timber. Massive branches thudded into each other and I fully expected to hear the terrifying sound of ripping timber any second. Time and time again the tree was hit on the recoil by a fresh gust of wind, the whole canopy locking up and shuddering to a halt as hundreds of tonnes of timber were stopped in their tracks and forced back in the other direction.

I was still tied into my rope, but this wouldn't be much consolation if the whole top section of the tree snapped off. The thought of being attached to a five-tonne lump of wood as it plummeted 250 feet to the forest floor was enough to make me screw up my eyes and grind my teeth as the storm continued to shake and throw the tree around like a rat in the jaws of a terrier.

Just when I thought things couldn't get any worse I saw the flicker of lightning scudding towards me beneath the black rolling clouds. A blinding flash and a jagged vein of electricity hit the forest half a mile away with an explosion that made my ears ring. The top of an emergent tree standing on a ridge was not a clever place to get stranded in an electrical storm, and I thought my adrenaline glands were going to pop as strike after strike of forked lightning stalked on long legs towards me.

To stay where I was would be almost suicidal, but without the use of my arms I didn't really have a choice. My dehydrated brain was floundering in indecision and still the lightning grew closer. Resigned to fate, I took a deep breath, loosened my grip on the bark and sat back in my harness with feet braced against the trunk to ride it out. The thunder was now a continuous rolling broadside that made me dizzy. I had never felt so helpless in all my life but there was nowhere to hide. Had I really travelled to the other side of the world only to get struck by lightning in the top of a tree? But just as I was about to take my chances and attempt a descent as best I could, there was one final explosion and the storm front rolled over the ridge to crash down into the next valley like a tsunami.

The gusts of wind died as suddenly as they'd begun. Air pressure dropped like a stone and steel-grey sheets of rain lashed in from the east. Water trickled down the bark's furrows around me. I lapped it up straight from the tree, desperate to get fluid back into my cramped muscles as quickly as I could. Thimbles of water soon collected in the funnelled leaves of a small plant growing on the branch next to me, so with crooked hands I bent it forward into my mouth. Water, ants and dirt all went down together. Each time it refilled, I drained it until I felt the painful tension in my arms begin to yield.

Within a few minutes I was able to unbend my fingers and open my hands. Before long the excruciating fire in my muscles was subsiding. I opened my mouth to the sky to drink more. It was the freshest, most invigorating water I'd ever tasted, and my mind slowly unclenched as blood flowed freely through its capillaries once more.

Despite the rain the forest was already steaming. Electricity still flickered over the next valley, but the forest around me had fallen eerily silent in the aftermath of the storm.

By now I was more than ready to get out of the tree, so feeding my rope down through the branches I clipped in and began to abseil. My rope wouldn't reach the ground from here, but all I needed was a way back down to the original rope I'd used to get up onto that first branch. A few minutes later I was hanging next to it and clipped back on ready for the final stage of descent to the ground 160 feet below. Glancing back at the other rope I'd just left behind, I saw its end dangling in space no more than a foot below where I'd stopped abseiling. There wasn't a knot in it. I stared in disbelief. There had been nothing at all to prevent me slipping straight off its end. By blind luck I'd stopped barely a foot away from a sixteen-storey plummet. A fresh spike of adrenaline passed through me and my hands began to tremble. Forgetting to tie a knot in the end of my rope was the second basic error of the day to almost cost me my life.

I'd had more than enough near-misses for one day and with a feeling of extreme relief I got the hell out of there.

. . .

Dennis walked back into camp. It was late afternoon, the light was fading and he had just returned from checking the strangler:

'There are plenty of ripe figs on the ground and a troop of macaques has been up there eating all day.' This was a very good sign. The banquet had begun.

'But that's not all. A big male orang has nested nearby. Looks like he's on his way to the figs, and there's a chance he'll be up there first thing tomorrow.'

It was now a week since I'd been caught in the storm. When I'd recounted the story to Dennis he'd smiled and named the tree 'Tumparak'. Thunder. It was a good name and it stuck.

I'd been back to rig the filming platform in Tumparak's canopy without any issues. Since then we had checked the figs every day, waiting for them to come into full ripeness. Dennis's news was very encouraging. We could expect the feast to last a week or so. Assuming the orangutan had been drawn to the area by our tree, there was more than enough fruit to keep him hanging around for several days. So getting up at half past two the following morning I headed into the darkness to climb Tumparak before it grew light. If the orangutan put in an appearance, John would come with me the day after to start filming.

It was a spectral walk through the forest. The mist was thicker than I'd ever seen it and visibility was barely ten feet in any direction. Tumparak's stem loomed bigger than ever in the darkness and the entire trunk was swallowed by fog twenty feet up. Clipping onto the rope, I turned my headlamp off to let my eyes adjust before climbing. The sweat on my body chilled in the clammy air as I inch-wormed my way up into the canopy through the dark. I couldn't see my hand in front of my face but figured all I had to do was keep climbing until I reached the top of the rope. I'd then turn on my lamp to help me do the changeover onto the other (now safely knotted) rope, which would finally deliver me up to the platform.

By half-four in the morning I was sitting 200 feet above-ground with my back to the trunk. Fireflies floated through the canopy in misty bubbles of neon green and the air was thick with the calls of treefrogs and insects. The greyness of dawn was still an hour away, so I closed my eyes and drifted in and out of a relaxed doze. By 5am I heard the first gibbon calling. A descending arpeggio repeated over and over, followed by a slow crescendo that escalated into a series of high-pitched warbles. Each cadence grew faster and faster until the call bubbled over into a joyous tremolo as he swung through the canopy. Before long he was joined by the female in duet and the burnt-orange sky was filled with their heart-lifting song. Orange turned to gold and I heard the telltale rustle of a large animal moving through the understorey far below. Definitely a primate, but the sound wasn't the leaf splashes of monkeys leaping through foliage. It was a continuous hiss of vegetation as branches were methodically bent within reach of each other.

The orangutan's deep-red hair blended surprisingly well with the green foliage but I caught tantalising glimpses of a large intelligent face looking up at the strangler as he climbed towards it with purpose.

As far as I could see, the strangler's trunk was the only possible route up for such a large animal. I presumed he would use this to gain access to the canopy as I had. Yet he was moving with purposeful grace towards that single slender limb that hung down from the rest of the fig's branches to touch the understorey far below. Arriving beneath it, he raised a long arm to grasp the drooping end of the long, thin branch, his strong fingers gripping it tight to give a gentle pull. The foliage in the canopy high above slowly sagged under his weight. The branch was no more than four inches wide at its base, and I expected it to tear free. But it held. Having tested its strength, he raised a foot past his hand and brought the other arm up to haul himself completely out of the understorey. His long red hair hung down in matted dreadlocks as he sat motionless for a few minutes, deep in thought on the end of the swaying branch.

Then very slowly he unfolded his long arms and began to ascend. Foot followed hand past foot, as he climbed smoothly, taking great care not to shock-load the thin branch. Moving with graceful intent, he pulled himself up the eighty feet into the canopy in one continuous fluid movement.

Here was a master at work. It was a remarkable piece of climbing, and with the whole tree to himself he settled comfortably on a fruit-covered limb and with infinite care began selecting the ripest figs to eat.

By now the sun had risen to flood the valley with light. Golden mist was lifting free of the trees and the air was alive with birdsong. The storm was nothing more than a distant memory and I took a sip from my water bottle before settling back to watch the orangutan show me how to *really* climb.

• • •

The rest of our time in Danum went well. John got the shots he needed of the orangutans, plus great footage of gibbons doing their thing high up in the branches of the tallest trees. Theirs was a joyful, dynamic style of climbing that involved huge leaps and acrobatic swings. I'd been in the canopy the first time I'd seen them – a family of three moving through the branches at blistering speeds of up to forty miles per hour. Their sheer poise, speed and unpredictability of movement was jaw-dropping, and it was obvious that the three of them were chasing each other. They were playing games for the sake of being able to do pretty much anything they wanted, in any direction and at any speed. To watch a gibbon land on a branch, run four steps, launch themselves into space at full pelt, plummet seventy feet before catching a passing vine to swing across onto the next tree – *and then go round to do it all over again purely for fun* – was to be rewarded with one of the most breathtaking spectacles in the whole of the natural world.

Certainly from a tree-climber's point of view, it didn't get much better. But then, to me, this summed up my whole Borneo experience. I couldn't imagine anything better than this. But then it was my first visit to any jungle, and at that time I had no idea what other wonders lay just round the corner in other rainforests around the world.

Chapter 3

Apollo – Congo

1999

The plane's controls seemed to move erratically, with a life of their own, as we bumped through the turbulence. Noise from the tiny aircraft's single propeller made conversation difficult, so leaving the pilot beside me alone to concentrate I stared out of the window at the clouds towering above us. We'd taken off from Libreville, Gabon and headed east for an hour before crossing the border into the République du Congo. A line of rocky escarpments marked the edge of the Congo Basin and from 10,000 feet up the forest stretched unbroken to a flat horizon in every direction. The canopy far below was a subtle blend of a thousand different greens. Endless rivers flowed through the forest like veins in a leaf, and apart from the occasional village set on their banks I hadn't seen any other sign of human habitation. We'd crossed a frontier to enter a place beyond the modern world. Down there, it seemed, lay endless secrets and mysteries just waiting to be discovered.

A week later I was deep inside the forest, in a region of pristine jungle called the Goualougo Triangle that had recently come to the attention of scientists for its large population of chimpanzees. Hundreds of them had been found living here, insulated and protected from the outside world by the vast wilderness surrounding them. But what made the Goualougo chimps so special was that, unlike any other population, they'd had no contact with people, so displayed no fear. If anything, they seemed just as interested in us as we were in them, their natural curiosity drawing them in to take a closer look at us. Such encounters could last several hours and allowed Dave, the resident primatologist, to document new natural behaviour. Surrounded by a dozen chimps sitting only feet away, staring at us intently, I was often left to wonder who was studying who.

• • •

National Geographic magazine was running a series of articles on the region, and their staff photographer, Nick, was very keen to get up into the canopy to record the chimps in their own world. I'd bumped into Nick while working on a different project earlier that year. He'd walked into camp unannounced one afternoon, introducing himself in a soft Alabama accent. We'd talked for an hour or so about working in the canopy before he offered me a job as his camera assistant, telling me to finalise details with the *NG* offices back in Washington. He'd then strolled back into the trees to leave me wondering whether the whole encounter had really just happened or not. It had been a mysterious but fortuitous meeting, and I was excited at the prospect of working with such an esteemed photographer.

Nick had sent me on ahead to the Goualougo with instructions to install a platform in the canopy opposite a suitable fruiting tree. It had taken Dave and me the best part of a week to find it, but the moment we'd seen the huge fruiting fig tree we knew it was special. Its enormous branches groped out through the surrounding canopy like tentacles. Unlike the stand-alone giants of Borneo, the canopy here was one continuous highway of tangled branches and it was often impossible to tell where one tree stopped and the next began. Branches became entwined with those of their neighbours to form one vast interconnected web. This African fig seemed to ramble on through the surrounding canopy for hundreds of feet in every direction, huge limbs twisting and kinking their way through the branches of neighbouring trees until they merged into one.

At 150 feet, it wasn't nearly as tall as the towering strangler-fig trees of Borneo, but what it lacked in height was more than made up for in character and sheer presence. Its gnarled appearance seemed to epitomise the mysterious, brooding nature of this dark forest.

It carried by far the most fruit I'd ever seen on any tree, and all the figs were massive, the size of tangerines. Each one hung from its own short stalk sprouting directly out from the tree's bark. I'd assumed fruit always grew delicately from the tips of twigs, but the massive trunk and branches of this tree were absolutely smothered in a haphazard jumble.

Presumably the tree produced a crop like this every year, which was an incredible thought in itself, given the amount of energy required. How could so much fruit be eaten before it spoiled and fell rotting to the forest floor? Any animal browsing along the branches was sure to dislodge and waste just as much as it ate. But this, of course, was the point. The tree had some pretty big stomachs to fill, both in the canopy and below. A clan of thirty chimps would go through these branches like a dose of salts, as would a family of gorillas. And then there were all the smaller primates, not to mention the fruit bats and the birds. Far below, the ground crew would hoover up any spoils. Elephants, pigs, buffalo, antelope … the list was endless. They would come from miles around to visit the tree. Long-lived, intelligent animals with excellent memories had learned from their parents where this tree stood and what time of year it fruited. It was an important landmark and the junction of ancient game trails at its base was testament to this.

Wasting no time, I rigged a canopy platform as quickly as I could. I'd found a good view of the tree's laden branches from eighty feet up in a smaller adjacent tree, and once the platform was in position I installed a canvas hide to sit in. There was a week or so until Nick could join us, so I decided to spend some time up there before he arrived. Nothing happened at all on the first couple of days. By midday on the third I was beginning to despair, when I suddenly noticed a tall, slender tree next to me starting to shake and sway.

Something big was climbing up from the ground eighty feet below. Whatever it was climbed quickly with great strength, stopping every now and then, presumably to peer up through the foliage. It must have seen my platform from the ground and come in for a closer look.

The narrow window of my camera hide prevented me from seeing anything other than what lay directly ahead. So I sat there patiently waiting for my visitor to reveal itself. Honeybees buzzed loudly in my ears. Dozens of them were crawling over my sweat-soaked shirt to lick the salt. I was wearing a head-net, which covered my face, but every now and then one squirmed up through the tiny gap at my collar to sting me on the cheek or ear. To open the net and let it out was to invite the other hundred in. So I sat there as stoically as I could, waiting to see what the next few minutes would bring.

The thin tree stopped swaying long enough for me to think the mystery climber had gone back down. But a few minutes later there was an ear-splitting scream that cut through the noise of bees and I realised I'd been rumbled. Curiosity had drawn a chimpanzee up into the canopy and it didn't like what it had found. I regretted not camouflaging my hide a little better. But then, how do you conceal yourself effectively from an ape that has grown up in this forest and knows every tree individually? I was clearly an intrusion that wouldn't be tolerated and I worried the game was up.

But five minutes later there hadn't been any other sound and I realised it must still be there in the tree looking at me. Crouching inside my sweatbox, trying not to move or flinch as I got stung yet again, I held my breath as the chimp decided what to do next. The thin tree eventually began to sway again and an adult female climbed into view twenty feet away. Muscular, with a broad, dark face and grizzled grey hair, she could now see me clearly through the hide's open canvas flap. Without taking her eyes from mine, she climbed onto a branch and sat down to stare intently across the open space between us.

My heart was racing and I did my best to keep still as I returned her gaze. She didn't seem scared; in fact, with an elbow resting on her knee she looked surprisingly relaxed as she slowly scratched her chin with the back of her hand. There was great intelligence behind those beautiful hazel eyes. This could easily be the first time she'd ever encountered a human being, and there was little doubt I was the first she'd ever met in the canopy.

A minute or so later she was joined by a second, much smaller chimp – her son, a three-year-old with a pale face and enormous ears. There was a wonderful air of mischief about him. All elbows and knees, he clambered over mum to hang staring while swinging from one arm. After exchanging a few soft hoots of reassurance with him, the female leant gently back against the tree and closed her eyes. They flicked open again a few seconds later as if to check I hadn't moved, and then closing them again she went to sleep. Her son quickly lost interest in me and took full advantage of this uninterrupted playtime by climbing and leaping around the branches like a lunatic. I couldn't stop myself from laughing as he jumped and swung around the canopy with a freedom that I could only dream of. Eventually mum, waking, stretched out a hand and grabbed him firmly by the ankle, but he wrestled free again so she gave up and went back to sleep. An hour later, tired from his antics, he climbed onto his mother's tummy and fell asleep in her arms.

Brushing the bees off my binoculars I focused through my head-net to take a closer look at the pair while they slept. The youngster's face was hidden but I could see his mum's clearly: her soft, black skin crisscrossed with fine lines and wrinkles. Wisps of white hair grew on her chin and there was a small scar beneath her nose. A heavy brow shielded her eyes and I could see pale patches of skin on her eyelids. But what amazed me most was the way in which those eyelids were twitching. Her eyeballs were moving from side to side beneath them and I suddenly realised she must be dreaming. I stared in amazement and couldn't help wondering where she had gone to in her sleep. What images were flashing across her mind's eye right at this moment? Was she swinging through the familiar canopy of her own jungle world, or had she slipped its borders to enter a realm far beyond anything I could ever imagine?

The afternoon slid by slowly as I watched them sleeping. Occasionally one stirred and opened its eyes to look at me, but for the most part I was ignored. By five o'clock the shadows were rising and it was obvious the chimps intended to sleep the night there. Not wanting to disturb them, I climbed out the back of my hide as quietly as possible and hung on my rope ready to abseil. The chimps remained asleep and it felt good to be out in the open canopy alongside them. The bees had disappeared, returning to their hive for the night. They'd be back in the morning, but for now I removed my stifling head-net and breathed the cool, fragrant air deep into my lungs. It was wonderful to be free of the sickly smell of bee venom and the incessant buzzing. It was also good to see the forest clearly for the first time in twelve hours, rather than through a dark blur of nylon mesh.

For a few more minutes I hung there watching the mother and child sleeping in the branches twenty feet away. The ground below was now in darkness, but the canopy was still bathed in the soft apricot glow of the setting African sun. The female must have felt me watching her and stirred. Sitting up, she glanced across before bending several branches in towards the trunk to make her nest for the night. She then lay down on her side to face me. Her son had awoken too, and was on his back next to her, playing with his feet while casually looking at me with innocent eyes that sparkled in the evening light. Why, of all the trees here, had they chosen to spend the night in one so close to me? I'll never know, but it was a scene of profound beauty. A fleeting glimpse of how things must have been millions of years ago before animals learned to fear us. An echo of Eden.

I could have stayed there for hours just watching them. I wanted to experience the forest at night the way they did –

rocked gently to sleep in the top of their tree. But I couldn't. It was getting dark and time for me to go. Leaning back in my harness, I edged down the trunk until I was below the understorey, then abseiled the final fifty feet to the forest floor. Stashing my harness at the base of the tree, I stood in the gloom to allow my eyes to adjust. The forests of the Congo are no place for a person to be caught walking around after nightfall. Big things move through the shadows and blundering into an elephant in the dark could be a fatal error.

It was a forty-minute walk back to camp and turning on my torch I made my way silently and warily down the trail. Huge, complicated networks of elephant paths wind through these forests. These endless corridors provide an easy way for all sorts of animals to get around. But extreme caution is required. For such enormous creatures, elephants can be surprisingly quiet, especially when moving along these soft, sandy trails. A point-blank encounter with one can be a terrifying experience, especially if it decides to charge. As the figs came into ripeness, this whole area would become busier and it wouldn't be safe for me to wander around on my own like this for much longer.

So the following morning Dave asked Djokin, one of the Bayaka pygmy trackers who worked with him, to accompany me back to the tree for safety. I had developed a great respect for Djokin. A quiet, bashful man with sad, knowing eyes and an almost supernatural understanding of the forest. I have never met anyone else so in tune with their environment. His intuitive understanding of the jungle was uncanny and his ability to detect animals from a great distance before they could be seen or heard had helped us avoid many dangerous confrontations in the past. Others from his village had told me of Djokin's alleged ability to shapeshift; to move through the forest in the guise of an animal, gathering knowledge for the tribe. The Congo can be a mysterious place, so who knows? I liked to think it was true.

Djokin and I stepped onto the trail just as it was getting light. My plan was to get back up onto the platform as early as possible. I was curious to see whether the mother and infant chimps would be tempted by the fruit, despite the fact that it still looked green and unpalatable. Nick was arriving in three days and I wanted to be able to brief him as to how long he'd have to wait to get shots of animals feeding. We walked through the green twilight in silence, Djokin carrying his machete in the crook of his arm while I walked a few steps behind.

After a while he came to an abrupt halt, stopping me with the flat of his machete. He stood perfectly still, staring down the path with wide eyes. '*Nzoku*,' he whispered, before thrusting his jaw forward with pursed lips to point in the direction of an approaching elephant. I peered through the gloom, but there was nothing there.

For several minutes there was absolute silence and no sign of movement. Then, just as I was beginning to think he was mistaken, I heard the faint hiss of dry leaves on leathery skin and an enormous bull elephant strode out of the dense undergrowth onto the path less than fifty feet ahead of us. Djokin was gripping my arm tightly, as if to say 'Don't even breathe'. The bull was colossal, weighing around five tonnes and standing well over nine feet tall. A thin black stripe of hormone dribbled down from a gland behind his eye to show he was in musth, a state of heightened testosterone that makes bulls particularly aggressive and unpredictable. He held his enormous head high and his long, straight tusks almost touched the ground, their ivory stained deep ochre by the tannins of the forest. A tidemark of orange mud showed where he had been wallowing and the tassels of hair on the end of his tail were matted with clay.

He was an unbelievably impressive and intimidating animal. But what struck me most was the effortless, almost delicate grace with which he moved. Within two strides he had crossed the path and disappeared back into the thick foliage on the other side. A few seconds later he had vanished completely – swallowed whole by the forest, to leave no more than a faint musky smell in the air and a few footprints the size of steering wheels in the dry earth.

Djokin's face relaxed into a gentle grin and I knew the danger had passed. I realised I'd been holding my breath and now the blood surged through my veins as I exhaled with relief. How on earth had Djokin realised it was there so long before it revealed itself? I asked him: he just shrugged and looked away. We waited several more minutes to let the bull put some distance between us before we moved off down the path and got out of there as quickly and quietly as we could.

I had been charged by a forest elephant before and will never forget the gut-wrenching terror of it. The helpless panic of having nowhere to run, of becoming ensnared within a tangle of vines, and the ear-splitting screams of the enraged animal as it ploughed through the forest after me like a tank. I'd been lucky that day. The elephant had passed me by in the chaos and I'd managed to double back and escape. But it had taught me a valuable lesson. These magnificent beasts are the architects of the forest, establishing and maintaining its shifting trails and clearings, and were to be given a wide berth at all times.

By the time we arrived at the base of the fig tree the sun was up and the sleeping chimps were gone. Climbing up past their empty nest I opened the back of my camera hide, checked for snakes then squeezed in to begin my twelve-hour vigil. Within an hour the honeybees had returned, accompanied by clouds of a smaller stingless variety known as sweat bees. These tiny black insects turn irritation into an art form and soon become insufferable as they crawl into eyes, ears and nose in search of salt. Insect repellent is useless, so once again I pulled on my head-net.

The next two days slurred past in a smear of languid heat and claustrophobia. Nothing entered the tree to feed on its fruit and I was left to broil and sweat in solitary confinement. The forest simmered like a pressure cooker, with nothing to mark the passing of time except the mind-grating buzzing of bees and the lethargic, monotonous calls of cicadas. When the heat got too bad and the air too oppressive I would become lightheaded and pass out into a short, troubled sleep, only to wake a few minutes later with a jolt as I threw my hands out to grab hold of my safety rope in panic of falling.

Then, the day before Nick arrived, the chimps returned. The first I heard was a soft mewing coming from the branches directly behind my hide. Peeking out through a small tear in the canvas I saw the mother and infant thirty feet away, peering at me through the leaves of a neighbouring tree. They knew I was in there and had come back for another look. Half-expecting them to settle and make a nest again, I was surprised to suddenly hear a loud scream from a third chimp hidden in the canopy somewhere above. The female shot an anxious look up into the branches before grabbing her infant and climbing away quickly with him on her back.

A moment later my tree shook as the unseen chimp swung across into it. Leafy debris fell onto the roof of my hide and I felt the unmistakable vibrations and trembles of the animal moving around in the branches above me. There was a sharp intake of breath and the air was filled with noise as the chimp screamed at the top of its lungs before setting the whole tree asway by thrashing its branches. It was a threat display, so this chimp had to be male probably a high-ranking adult from the female's own clan. She must know him well and had clearly read his body language before making herself scarce. He was now really going for it and my tree lurched erratically as he leapt between the branches. I still couldn't see him but my ears were ringing and I fully expected him to crash down through the roof of my hide any second. Then after one final crescendo I heard a hollow bang of branches colliding as he climbed across into the fig tree's canopy and I was left alone.

Leaning forward to look out of my hide, I watched him walk down one of the fig tree's enormous fruit-covered limbs. A big adult male in his prime, slightly grizzled but immensely strong and powerful. With hair still bristling from his display, he paused and leant forward to smell one of the figs. Then to my amazement he tenderly squeezed the fruit in his hand without picking it. He was checking its ripeness and seemed to know that to pluck it from the tree prematurely would be to waste a future meal. Continuing along the branch on all fours, occasionally stopping to smell and squeeze other figs, he eventually resigned himself to the fact that nothing was ready. Then as a light rain began to fall he sat down in the fork of a branch and stretched out a leg to groom himself.

So that was it: undeniable proof that the tree wasn't quite ready to receive its guests. As the rain fell in pearly sheets, I looked across at the ape sitting with hunched shoulders and an expression of miserable resignation on his craggy face. The grizzled grey of his coat was bejewelled with droplets of water as he sat there motionless, dwarfed by those massive branches. The rain leached colour from the scene and his dark, muscular silhouette blended into a background of muted greens and greys. That image seemed to encapsulate the Congo more than any other.

• • •

Three months had passed and I was now in another region of the Congo – a national park called Odzala, containing 8,000 square miles of virgin jungle, unexplored rivers and impenetrable swamp. Apart from the occasional poacher or scientist, hardly anyone ventured here and for the most part it was left well alone, its thick, tangled forests home to some of the highest densities of elephants and gorillas anywhere in Central Africa. I was working again with Nick for *National Geographic* magazine.

My first job was to find him a decent tree overlooking one of the forest's marshy clearings. The plan was to install a canopy platform from which he could photograph animals emerging from the forest to feed in the open below. There were many such clearings, known as 'bais', dotted through the forest, and some attracted more animals than others. So I'd spent the last few days scouting for options.

Everything had been going well, but today things had taken a turn for the worse and we'd been lost in the jungle for well over seven hours.

Jacques, our local guide, crouched at the base of a tree, keeping watch for elephants, while I tried to come up with a plan for finding our way back to camp. I liked Jacques a lot, but I couldn't believe the mess we were in. We'd left camp at six that morning to visit a bai known to be good for gorillas. Jacques led the way, but by late morning we still hadn't arrived and it was obvious something was wrong. His anxiety was easy to read as he darted furtive looks around him. He'd covered his face with his hands and muttered 'I don't know' when asked if we were still heading in the right direction. I'd stared at him in disbelief as it dawned on me he knew as much as I did and we were completely lost. We'd been walking for hours and any chance we might have had of backtracking to pick up the correct trail was long gone. To keep walking aimlessly around the jungle like this was to invite disaster. The park was the size of Northern Ireland and still only represented one tiny corner of a mighty forest stretching almost unbroken across the entire African continent. The chances of being able to survive more than a few nights without a machete, food, first-aid kit or torch were pretty slim. We didn't even have a compass with us. To be lost in an urban environment is a temporary inconvenience. To be lost in the world's second largest rainforest is cause for serious concern. We were teetering on the edge of a dangerous situation and I tried to keep calm and come up with a solution, but it wasn't looking good and the panic was becoming hard to suppress. To be caught out here at nightfall would be an adventure both of us could do without. The forest was crawling with elephants and buffalo. Most of the trees around us had been used as rubbing posts and were smeared with dark-grey mud. It was obvious this was an area of extremely intense animal activity.

Scanning the trees around us I looked in vain for clues to help orientate ourselves, but the jungle was just too dense. We were lost in a labyrinth. So out of sheer desperation I decided to free-climb into the canopy without a rope or harness to try and regain our bearings. The chances of my seeing our camp itself were zero, but I might just get lucky and catch a glimpse of a distant wisp of smoke rising up through the trees, or even a river. Any landmark, however tenuous, would be a huge help in our current situation. I needed to get up high and I needed to do it quickly.

The *moabi* tree in front of me was the biggest in the area, a monolith rising from the soil in a vertical column of dark-brown timber ten feet wide, its perfectly straight trunk spreading into a broad canopy 150 feet above us. Squinting up into the light, I could see it standing clear above the surrounding forest. The view would be unparalleled if only I could get up there, but without ropes or a harness there was no obvious way. The first branch was way up and its massive trunk was a living wall of wood without any handholds.

There was, however, a thick woody vine, a liana, dangling all the way down to the ground from its branches. It wasn't part of the tree itself, but might just offer a way up. I took a closer look. It was rooted in the soil and emerged to lie flat on the leaf litter like an engorged python before rising up into the moabi's canopy where it eventually threw a giant coil over a branch high above us. It was strong – as thick as my thigh – but unstable, swaying like a huge tentacle as I gave it a shake. It would be a tricky climb for sure, but it might just work.

Removing my clumsy wet boots I placed a bare foot on the liana. Its surface was twisted into a spiral like an enormous ship's cable and moss grew between the woody strands. My toes found easy grip amongst its coarse ridges, but my skin was tender from too many years in shoes and it would be slow going. I looked up and felt the acid rise in my stomach. Was I foolish to even try this? Probably, but I was sure it could be done just as long as I took it slowly and thought about each move. Looking back down to the ground, I saw Jacques sitting with his back against a nearby tree, still keeping watch.

The first fifty feet were really tough. The liana dangled in open space away from the tree trunk, like a rope in a school gymnasium. Not a problem when you are twelve years old, but my strength-to-weight ratio wasn't what it was, and I was too used to climbing with the aid of ropes and clamps to be very proficient at climbing a free-hanging vine. A chimp would have run up it in the blink of an eye but I was already tiring and a voice inside my head warned me not to get complacent. There was no safety rope and I still had a long way to go before I could hope to get any view over the surrounding forest.

Despite the risk, though, I was enjoying the freedom of climbing without equipment. It felt great to strip everything back to basics, to channel the energy of my muscles into every move and immerse myself completely in the moment. By wrapping my legs around the liana I was able to grip with my feet while sliding my hands further up to gain height. I could then pull myself up with my arms and clamp the liana again between my legs. It was awkward, but seemed to work. The vine was alive with movement as it swayed and rippled in response to my shifting weight. It took every ounce of my strength and concentration to avoid falling. But the liana's rough texture was easy to grip and the great strength I felt within its twisted fibres gave me the confidence to climb swiftly.

At fifty feet aboveground the vine met the moabi tree and divided in two. One fork looped precariously out into space, while the other continued to rise vertically alongside the tree's sheer trunk. Taking the latter route, I pushed on, bracing my feet against the moabi while hauling myself up. The liana wobbled and knocked heavily against the trunk showering me constantly with soil and debris. My skin was crawling with ants, but I couldn't risk letting go to brush them away. One of them bit my lower-left eyelid and remained latched there with tiny legs waving in front of my eyeball until I brushed it away with my bicep. Its body came free, leaving the head behind, and I could feel its sharp mandibles every time I blinked.

Eventually, covered in dirt and shaking from the exertion, I made it up to the enormous branch from which the vine hung. This was the tricky bit and it took a huge amount of strength and balance to edge my leg up and over. I had free-climbed to around 120 feet and reached as far as I could go. The vine now slumped over the branch to sag down into an enormous loop on the other side. The next branch was way out of reach in the canopy above. This was the end of the line, but was I high enough to see anything? With great disappointment I realised I wasn't. After all that effort and risk I was still within the forest's dense canopy. The outside world existed as mere glimpses through a tangled curtain of creepers hanging thirty feet away.

The adrenaline was leaving my bones and I felt tired. It was great to be up here, above the cramped claustrophobia of the forest floor, but it was pointless to stay any longer. We had to find our way back to camp somehow. So while I still had the strength, I lifted my leg over the branch in front of me and twisted my body round to slide back down onto the vine.

Just then I heard a distant flurry of wings, like a flock of waders taking sudden flight along the seashore. Craning my neck round I caught a flash of crimson through one of the narrow gaps in the canopy. A huge flock of African grey parrots was wheeling over the trees a mile away. I'd only ever seen them flying in pairs, chuntering and whistling to each other on their way to roost in the evening. So to see a thousand swirling in flight together was a sight to lift the soul. I took it as a sign that things would be okay, and as the flock dropped back down below the level of the trees I realised with a flash of hope there was probably open ground beneath them. I'd only ever seen them congregate like that at bais, where they landed on the ground to lick minerals from clay. That was it: the clue I'd been looking for. The parrots had shown me which direction we should go.

Yelling down to Jacques, I pointed so that he could remember which direction we should walk in. Wrapping my legs around the rough vine, I slid as fast as I could down past the fork and to the ground. I was drained. My muscles were trembling like jelly and I was covered in dirt, but things were looking up. Even if the bai wasn't the one we had set out to find that morning, Jacques might recognise it and it might lead us to another clue. It had to be worth a go.

Snapping the branches of thin saplings to mark our passage, we set off quickly through the forest. I realised it would take an hour to cover the mile, plenty of time to get lost again. So we stopped regularly to squint back along our trail of broken foliage to ensure we were heading in a straight line.

We soon found ourselves standing in the shadowy eaves of trees, peering out into a sun-blasted space beyond. The air shimmered and clouds of yellow butterflies danced in the mid-afternoon heat. There was no sign of the parrots, but a small herd of elephants grazed on the far side of the clearing. A very young calf suckled from its mother's breast, nuzzled up into the gap beneath her front legs. When it wasn't drinking milk, it was twirling its tiny trunk round and round like a propeller. No more than a few months old, it seemed fascinated by the floppy thing attached to its face.

But what really interested us was the large group of gorillas in the centre of the clearing. Sixteen were moving slowly through the grass towards us. They were scattered over a large area, engrossed in eating the roots they pulled up. Several of them were chest deep in the swamp and I watched an infant climb up onto a clump of grass and spin round for fun until it got dizzy and fell over. Two adult females were obviously pregnant and I could see the hulking shape of the silverback on his own off to one side. It was an idyllic scene, but we had to move on if we were to find camp before nightfall.

Water was draining into a series of marshy pools and brooks at the far end of the bai, so we skirted round through the forest until we found the stream they emptied into. From here we headed downstream in the hope of reaching the Mambili River, the major water course that we had travelled up to get into the park. Even if we emerged onto its banks miles downstream from camp, at least it would lead us home eventually. As luck would have it, we stumbled across a trail just as it was getting dark. It could have been one of a thousand anonymous game paths winding through the forest, but hanging from a vine was a freshly caught electric catfish. Its pallid body was strung up at head height and I would have walked straight into it if it hadn't jerked with an audible pulse of electricity as we approached. Another of our team must have caught it in the nearby river and left it there to collect later. Luckily for us he'd forgotten it. Knowing for sure that we were on the right track at last, we unstrung the fish and carried it home for supper.

• • •

The Congo is a place of great beauty and wonder, but it can also be extremely tough. A place of extreme highs and terrible lows, and now – several weeks later – I was feeling ground down by a sinister rash that had recently appeared all over my body.

Nick had headed further up the Mambili River to scout a new photography location and I'd remained behind on my own to try and sort myself out. It had been raining for two days now and I'd been stuck in my tent going slowly mad as the rash became welts that ripened into angry red boils. I was covered in them, ninety in total: all over my legs, crotch and torso. There were also several on my head. All of them were extremely tender and growing bigger by the hour.

My wet climbing harness hung from the ridge pole above me, going mouldy in the rank humidity of my tent. I had intended to rig one more canopy platform for Nick before I left next week, but I could now barely walk, let alone climb a tree. It soon became too painful even to wear clothes, so I spent all day in my underpants, crawling out to lie on my back in the rain whenever the tent's confines grew too sweaty and claustrophobic. I was entering a downward spiral and knew that I had to get downriver in search of medical attention. But without a canoe, let alone a paddle, I was, so to speak, up shit creek. Lying around feeling sorry for myself wasn't going to solve anything, though, so on day three I decided to dig out whatever was hiding in me beneath the mysterious welts.

Selecting a particularly large boil on my thigh I reached for a sterile syringe and slowly slid its long needle into my flesh. The pain was excruciating, but I was determined to find out what was going on inside the angry welt. I pushed deeper. I'd expected the boil to burst open as I probed, assuming it was some kind of infection that could be cleaned out and treated with antiseptic. But there didn't seem to be anything inside. I was still no closer to knowing what was happening to me, and now – several hours later – the whole area was inflamed with a creeping red infection. I'd made things worse. So dosing up on heavy antibiotics, I decided to wait until the boils were ripe enough to squeeze properly. Something had to come out of them eventually, even if it was only puss.

The rain continued and I lay there listening to it on the tent's flysheet as it grew dark. A few hours later I was woken by something moving beneath the skin of my scalp. At first I thought I'd dreamt it. But a little while later I felt it again: a soft grating on the bone of my skull. There was something squirming around in there. By daybreak I could feel dozens more – whatever they were – wriggling around within the rest of the boils, and the pain was growing unbearable. I had to do something to sort this crazy situation out, but right now

I had a more immediate issue to deal with. I'd just squeezed two large spine-covered maggots out of my left testicle. So that was it: botflies. But these two maggots were merely the tip of the iceberg. There were at least ninety more of the little bastards still inside me, growing bigger by the hour. I was not in a happy place.

Thinking back over the past few days, I began to understand what must have happened.

Nick and I had spent the previous week photographing gorillas in a forest clearing. We'd pitched our tents close by, which meant we couldn't light a fire for fear of scaring the animals away. The forest understorey was dark and humid, and without a campfire to dry things out, what got wet stayed wet. I'd been caught in a storm while climbing a tree and stayed soaked and covered in mud for three days. A blizzard of large black flies with bulbous red eyes had found me in the canopy and buzzed around aggressively as I sat on my platform trying to swat them. I now realised they hadn't been trying to bite me at all. They'd been laying eggs that must have hatched on my warm, wet clothes, releasing tiny maggots that burrowed unseen into my skin. The grubs were now developing inside me, growing fat on my flesh. Life is nature's way of keeping meat fresh, and like any other animal I was nothing more than a convenient sack of protein ready to be exploited by anything able to pierce my skin.

So after another dose of antibiotics I took a swig of whisky and opened the first-aid kit. I'd had enough of the incessant pain as the maggots chewed their way through me, and now that I knew what they were I'd be damned if I was going to let them grow any fatter at my expense. Determined to bring things to a head I readied myself to dig them out one by one.

A few hours later I had forty of them pickled in whisky next to me. I'd swapped the needle for a pair of forceps that I sterilised in the flame of a candle. Some maggots had popped straight out; others had to be dragged out of me piece by piece as I winced with pain and clenched my jaw. There were dozens more across my back and buttocks that I couldn't reach. Since I was on my own, I'd have to wait until they chewed their way out of me. The pain of them squirming around was now so bad that I couldn't sleep. The last of my whisky was gone – probably for the best – and all I could do was sit cross-legged in the rain, staring at the river in the hope that someone would paddle past before too long.

That afternoon I heard an outboard coming upstream. A canoe carrying four guys with Kalashnikovs appeared round the corner and I ducked down in the grass until I was certain they were park rangers rather than ivory poachers. I had a shouted conversation with them from the riverbank as they passed. They didn't stop and who could blame them? It must have been a desperate sight: a naked white bloke covered in sores, standing in the rain, yelling at them in appalling French. They'd looked understandably alarmed, but I was relieved when one of them said they'd send help.

As I sat on the riverbank the following morning, feeling miserable after another sleepless night, a Bayaka pygmy man walked out of the forest towards me. He wore yellow swim-shorts and green jelly shoes. At first I thought I was hallucinating, finally losing the plot for good. But without a word he smiled and motioned for me to stand while he opened a small plastic tub of palm oil. He then dabbed the orange fluid over each of my remaining welts. Several had now developed tiny air holes and I realised he was covering these up to suffocate the maggot inside. Once finished, he motioned for me to wait a while. We sat cross-legged next to each other, looking out over the river in silence for ages before he began squeezing the remaining boils on my back. I heard the satisfying pops as maggot after maggot came out, but I was in too much pain to be happy about it. Stars danced in front of my eyes as I flinched again and again. An hour or so later he had finished and apart from a few left in my backside, I was now pretty much maggot-free.

The relief was incredible. I was still extremely tender and every movement hurt, but the worst of it was over and guessing he'd been sent by the park rangers I thanked him over and over again. He smiled broadly before giving me the tub of oil and walking away. In five seconds he'd disappeared completely, without a word, and melted back into the jungle. I never saw him again but I will be eternally grateful for his help.

Ten days later I was back in England lying in the Bristol Royal Infirmary with cerebral malaria. It seemed the Congo had saved the best for last. My brain boiled in a fever of 42 degrees as I lay hallucinating in starched white sheets. As far as I was concerned that was it: nothing on earth could drag me back out to Central Africa. Or so I thought.

• • •

It was now October. Six months had passed since I'd recovered from malaria and vowed never to return to the Congo. But the lure of the jungle is strong and there was no way I could turn down the opportunity to film gorillas in the canopy. I'd been invited to join a small team from Scorer, a Bristol company shooting a documentary for the BBC. I joined the team alongside producer Brian, principle cameraman Gavin, and fellow assistant Ralph. A great crew. I was back in the rainforest and loving every minute.

The glow from my watch told me it was just after three in the morning. I was doing my best to choke down a bowl of mucsli. We'd run out of powdered milk the previous week, so I poured water over the cereal, gave it a stir and tucked in. It was far too early, my stomach wasn't ready for this, but I needed the calories if I was going to get up into the canopy before daybreak. The tree was an hour's walk away through dense forest and my filming platform was seventy feet up in its branches. I'd rigged it opposite a huge fruiting tree that we hoped would attract the troop of gorillas we'd been filming. Nineteen of them had nested beneath it the previous evening, so there was a good chance of catching them that morning. I needed to be in the canopy with a camera by 5am, before it got light.

My head torch cast a pool of weak light onto the table of rough wooden planks in front of me. The shadow of my hand rose and fell mechanically as I shovelled the tasteless cereal down my throat as fast as I could. Turning off my torch to save batteries while I ate, I looked out into the night. The camp lay bathed in soft moonlight. Trees cast long, crisp shadows over the silver ground, and the jungle was alive with the soft murmur of insects. Someone snored gently in a hut nearby and the world seemed at peace. The hours before dawn have always been my favourite and I sat still for a few moments to enjoy the serenity.

Raising my rucksack onto my back I stepped into the moonlight and was just crossing the clearing to enter the forest when I was stopped in my tracks by the deep, rasping call of a leopard. Spinning round to pinpoint the sound, I realised the animal was hidden in the trees on the other side of camp, no more than 200 feet away. The deep growl echoed through the forest like the rapid strokes of a saw ripping through timber. Feeling exposed and vulnerable in the moonlight, I instinctively edged into the darkness beneath the nearest tree. The leopard must have known I was there, must have heard me moving around camp and seen the flash of my torch as I walked through the moonlight towards the shadowy wall of trees. I was pretty sure there was nothing to fear, but I have always had a pretty vivid imagination. I'd read enough tales about man-eating big cats to know full well what a leopard could do. They regularly took full-grown chimps and a 350-pound adult male gorilla had been killed and eaten by one here not long ago. Trackers had found its eviscerated carcass butchered in the middle of a blood-splattered area of flattened vegetation.

The last roar echoed through the clearing and everything was silent again apart from the soft chirring of insects. I stood still, trying to wrestle my imagination under control while deciding what to do. Was it foolish to walk into the forest while a leopard was prowling around or was I just being paranoid?

It was because of the leopards that most sensible primates slept high in the trees. Everything about leopards is designed for hunting under the velvet cover of night. As a fellow primate I was just as hardwired as a chimp or a gorilla to fear the darkness, and I felt a strong urge to get up into the safety of the trees as quickly as possible.

This was the first leopard I'd heard, let alone seen. But that didn't mean they weren't around us all the time, moving through the trees like ghosts. These forests have one of the highest densities of leopards anywhere in Africa and I'd had plenty of near-encounters in the past. Seen their scats and smelled the acrid scent of their urine. Found saliva fizzing on the half-digested grass they'd coughed up on the trail barely seconds before I'd arrived. But all these incidents had occurred during the day, never at night. No wonder the mother chimp I'd watched all those months ago in the Goualougo had chosen a tall, slender tree for her and her son to spend the night in. The leopard called again, this time from further away in the opposite direction to where I was headed. It was moving off, but I'd feel a lot more relaxed once I was up in the canopy.

The darkness beneath the trees was absolute. Dense vegetation pressed in from either side to close in above, and all traces of moonlight disappeared. I turned on my head torch and followed its bubble of light down the black tunnel ahead of me. The forest here had the thickest, most impenetrable understorey I had ever encountered. Huge trees towered above, but down below was a dense monoculture of big-leaved 'prayer plants'. Gorillas love the stuff (they eat the shoots), but it's a nightmare to get through and with visibility no more than ten feet in any direction it would be all too easy to blunder straight into a family group. Such point-blank encounters can be extremely explosive, especially if it elicits a charge from the group's silverback. But none of the gorillas were sleeping so close to camp that night, so I knew it was safe to hurry along – I had to get up that tree before daybreak.

The tangled foliage seemed to writhe in the shadows around me as I passed down the tunnel behind my bubble of light. I was looking forward to getting safely up the tree and wanted to complete the walk as quickly as possible. Thankfully it was a well-maintained path and there was little chance of getting lost, but I made a point of stopping at every junction to triple-check I was still on track.

It was while standing at one such fork in the trail that I heard the leopard again. This time from less than fifty feet ahead of me. I froze, rooted to the spot, straining my eyes to penetrate the inky blackness beyond the torchlight. I'd been walking for half an hour and was over a mile from camp in the opposite direction from where I'd last heard the animal. Was it the same leopard? It was impossible to tell, but either way somewhere close, on the trail in front of me, was a big cat and I knew it could see me standing in my pool of light. The hairs on my neck stood up and my heart beat loudly in the silence of the seconds that followed.

I glanced at my watch: 4am. I had an hour left before daybreak to get up into the tree, ready to film. My instinct was to turn the torch off, to slink away and hide in the shadows. But what good would that do? Leopards can see through the darkest night. In a desperate display of defence I opened the blade of my pocket knife, but it isn't a leopard's style to make an exposed frontal attack. There would be no warning. I thought of the chimp sleeping safely aboveground with her infant.

After a few tense minutes I again heard it calling from further away, this time from within the dense foliage to my right. It was skirting around – unless I had blundered between two different animals, of course. Either way, I made a supreme effort to calm my nerves and started moving slowly forward again.

Another fifteen minutes passed and I had the platform tree in my sights. I took my head torch off and muffled its beam with my fingers. Nineteen gorillas were asleep in their nests somewhere close by and I didn't want to wake them. But neither did I want to blunder into Apollo, the group's 400-pound silverback, in the dark. So allowing a faint sliver of torchlight to escape between my fingers, I inched my way down the last hundred feet of track. The air was thick with the sweet, musky smell of gorillas – they were very close and I took my time to avoid stepping on twigs as I crept along.

Arriving at the tree, I reached out for the white rope hanging in front of me. Suddenly all the hairs on my neck stood up and my skin crawled. Spinning round, I saw a low black shadow slink away into my peripheral vision. My body tensed and I strained my eyes to see what it was. But it had gone – melting away like oil into the darkness beyond. My heart was beating in my throat and my nerves felt tight enough to snap. Had I really just seen it? Had the leopard really followed me here?

My need to keep watch for the cat overruled any desire to hide from gorillas, so I uncovered my head torch and, keeping my back to the tree, shone the light down the trail while I hurriedly pulled on my harness. Fear was making me fumble and my foot got caught in the leg loops, nearly tripping me over. The karabiners jangled noisily as I wrestled the harness up onto my waist. My heart was thumping and my imagination was running wild. Reluctantly turning round to face the tree, I clipped into the ropes and started to climb as quickly as I could.

I felt hopelessly vulnerable with my back to the darkness, but the feeling of safety I got from being in the tree was immediate. Once above twenty feet, I began to relax and collect my scattered nerves. Turning off my head torch, I sat back in my harness and took a deep breath.

The forest looked astonishingly beautiful from up here, a shadowland of misty blues and pale greens. The three-quarter moon was low in the west and its light slanted in through the canopy to dapple the scene with silver. I looked down into the darkness, to where the trunk disappeared into the shadows of the thick understorey. It was a relief to be free from its creeping claustrophobia, to be beyond any threat. I was pretty sure the leopard had followed me out of nothing more sinister than curiosity. I can't imagine it had ever seen a human wandering around the forest at night before and I don't suppose it ever intended to attack. But millions of years of instinct are hard to suppress. Every one of us alive today is only here because one of our ancestors listened to their instincts when it mattered most. Evolution hammered that intangible sixth sense into us for very good reason.

Looking up the trunk, I could see the square silhouette of the platform high above. It was almost 5am and the moon was setting. Arriving at the platform, I squeezed into my hide and hauled up the rucksack containing the camera.

By 5.15 I was settled and looking out through the front of my canvas tent towards the fruiting tree. Its massive trunk lay in dense shadow beneath the wide spreading canopy above. A few minutes later I heard the faint snapping of foliage and could see the dense understorey below me sway as something moved through it unseen. A soft squeal from an infant, followed by the deep grunt of an adult told me the gorillas had arrived. Nineteen of them were on the move, passing right beneath my platform. But all I could see was a moving ripple of foliage as they headed towards the fruiting tree.

Mist began to rise up through the canopy and the early rays of sun brought colour to the scene. The first gorilla to emerge from the undergrowth was a female. She climbed a vine to enter the fruiting tree where it forked into three at the top of its trunk. Moving higher into the canopy, she was immediately followed by two more who took exactly the same route. These were then followed by another female with her tiny newborn baby on her front. Then came Apollo the silverback.

He was at least twice the size of the females and his broad back shone in the early-morning sunlight. Grasping the vine with huge hands and feet, he climbed slowly with great deliberation. The muscles in his back flexed like corrugated iron as his enormous black arms hauled him up with effortless ease. He was more than twice the weight of an adult male orangutan and to see an animal of such size and bulk climb with such dexterity was incredible.

By now the females were much higher up in the misty canopy, sitting to warm their bones in the sun's horizontal rays as they foraged for fruit. Apollo was followed by a couple of youngsters, more interested in playing on the vines than feeding. About half the group was now up in the tree and I noticed how respectful they were to each other while climbing. Each individual was given space to go where they wanted and females were constantly shifting to allow others to pass by safely. Compared to the mass hysteria displayed by chimps, the gorillas seemed incredibly polite and organised in their approach to foraging.

Apollo was too big and heavy to access the outer reaches of the canopy, so stayed within the centre of the crown, where he snapped off branches to bring fruit within easy reach. Resting the branch on his enormous belly, he'd sit there picking only the ripest morsels before dropping the branch out of the tree and reaching for another. The tree was full of gorillas foraging peacefully for their breakfast. The only noise I heard was a short scream from one of the females that made Apollo stand up on all fours and posture with a tense expression of tight-lipped annoyance. But a few seconds later he sat back down to resume breakfast and all was again quiet apart from a soft chorus of satisfied belches and the constant smacking of lips.

After half an hour or so, Apollo began to climb down. Once again I was amazed by how civilised they all were to each other as the rest of the group followed him down from the higher branches in a peaceful, organised manner. Cogs whirred softly in my right ear as film raced smoothly through the camera's shutter. The film ran out just as the two youngsters dropped back down into the dense understorey. The tree still had plenty of fruit left in its branches, but for now the gorillas had moved off in search of other food. They clearly enjoyed a very balanced diet. I remained on the platform all day, but never saw them again.

• • •

Apollo's group had been habituated to human presence by Magdalena Bermejo, a Spanish primatologist and world authority on western lowland gorillas. No one had ever managed to habituate lowland gorillas before. Two years later an outbreak of Ebola ripped through the heart of the area, killing 130 of the 143 known gorillas in just four months. Apollo and his entire family – including a newborn baby named James – succumbed, and it is with great fondness that I recall those special moments spent alongside them in the canopy. It had taken Magdalena and her husband seven years of relentless hard work and determination to get to know the gorillas and I can only imagine what they must have gone through during those horrendous four months.

With the coming of the virus, something amazing had been lost to the world forever. I have no idea what species the enormous, beautiful tree in which I watched them feed was. But it seems fitting that it should be remembered here as Apollo.

Chapter 4

Tree Of Life – Costa Rica

2001

The canopy around me was one huge shaggy mass of ferns, bromeliads and orchids all growing on top of each other like a treetop coral reef. The tree's branches were literally dripping with life – one huge hanging garden rising in tiers like a living tenement. Every spare inch was occupied: insects, spiders, lizards, snakes and a million other creatures living out their lives fifteen storeys aboveground. And despite the incessant rain, I was loving every second of being here.

Getting soaked, covered in mud, bitten by ants, stung by wasps and all the rest of it is a price well worth paying to hang on a rope 150 feet aboveground, surrounded by dozens of glittering hummingbirds while they sip nectar from flowers and hover inches from your face to peer into your eyes. To see the whole canopy reflected in the dark glistening eye of an iridescent bird no bigger than your thumb was the best twenty-sixth-birthday present I could have wished for.

• • •

It was mid April in the Caribbean lowland rainforests of Costa Rica and it had been raining heavily for the past week, an incessant deluge that stopped for a few hours around midnight, only to start again at dawn each day. The jungle was utterly saturated, the ground was leaking like a sponge, as if hidden springs were welling up through the thick leaf litter. Steady sheets of silver beads hit the leaves with such force they atomised, filling the canopy with a persistent grey mist.

This was my first visit to a Central American jungle and the canopy around me was by far and away the lushest and most verdant I'd seen anywhere. It was also my first time working with Sir David Attenborough – on his *The Life of Mammals* series for the BBC – and I was pretty nervous at the prospect of getting him safely up into the canopy.

Three of us had travelled out to La Selva Biological Station to spend ten days rigging trees ahead of the main crew's arrival. Phil was rigging another tree half a mile away and Sean the assistant producer was helping him haul the cables and platforms up into position.

Phil had been instrumental in helping me into the industry. After my year in London I'd gone on to study in Derby and again took to the urban canopy to get my fix. I was learning about the structure and strength of so many different species:

invaluable climbing experience that taught me to read a tree's body language at a glance. But I had grown tired of seeing nothing but Victorian terraces from the top branches, and of being shouted at by council officials in hi-vis jackets. Tired of getting my ropes covered in dog shit, and tired of having to step over plastic bags full of glue dumped by sniffers at the base of trees in our local park. There were certainly some beautiful moments, but they were few and far between. I was missing the wild trees of the New Forest. The thing I longed for most was the unique sensation of climbing a tree in a forest. To smell nothing but earth and hear nothing but birds, the low creak of timber and wind in the leaves. To see nothing but other trees all around me and feel completely immersed within their world.

The year before I left Derby forever I attended a talk on the making of David Attenborough's *The Private Life of Plants* at the BBC Natural History Unit in Bristol. Part of this talk included a shot of Attenborough climbing in Borneo, his blue shirt soaked with sweat as he dangled on a rope 200 feet above the jungle floor. I was introduced to Phil, the tree-climber turned BBC producer who'd rigged the ropes for that shoot.

Phil invited me down to have lunch in the Beeb canteen. It was amazing to be there, sitting in the very heart of wildlife TV, talking with him about his jungle adventures. People like Phil are rare indeed. His knowledge of tropical wildlife and the rainforest canopy is second to none. He had a deep, heartfelt love for it and had worked with David on many occasions. This had a massive influence on me, and just when I thought the day couldn't get any better I heard a familiar voice call out

Phil's name and before I knew it Attenborough himself had sat down at our table. I was impressed to see he had a lunchtime beer on the go and before long he and Phil were earnestly discussing the behavioural traits of the New Caledonian crow between mouthfuls of cheese-and-pickle sandwich. My head was reeling as I sat there listening in silent wonder.

Phil and I kept in touch and a couple of years later he called me out of the blue:

'How would you like to go to Borneo for six weeks to help a film crew get into the canopy?' he asked.

Once I'd found my voice I thanked him over and over again.

'That's alright, mate. You'll just owe me for the rest of your life,' was his laughing reply. And never was there a truer word spoken. That phone call changed everything for me; made anything possible.

We met at Phil's Bristol flat to chat about the job. Bows and arrows from New Guinea hung above the fireplace and beautiful pictures of tropical birds covered his walls.

'You can't use normal rope techniques to climb those jungle giants,' he said. 'Most of the trees you'll see will be 250 feet tall and many won't have branches for at least the first 150. You can't simply lob a rope up and haul yourself into the canopy hand over hand like you've been doing – you'll kill yourself. Get some proper training under your belt before you go, because you're going to need to use stuff like this,' he said, handing me a high-powered crossbow.

He pulled a red rucksack out from under the stairs and tipped it up to disgorge a tangle of climbing clamps and karabiners. Everything looked different to what I was used to, suspiciously like rock-climbing gear. Even the harness was strange, and it was the first time I'd ever even seen a climbing helmet. This was going to take some getting used to – I was about to take a very big leap into the unknown. But Phil was there to help me on my way and over the years he became a good friend and mentor.

I'd spent three years climbing in the rainforest since then, but I still had a lot to learn and it felt great to be working alongside Phil now in Costa Rica. It was also comforting to know that responsibility for David's safety wouldn't rest entirely on my shoulders.

But things weren't going very well so far. This was the eighth tree I'd climbed in the hacking rain over the last seven days and I was beginning to get desperate in my search for a suitable tree in which to film David. Both Phil and I had been faced with an embarrassment of riches when we first arrived. Every huge tree had appeared perfect from the ground and we'd assumed we'd struck lucky and the rig would be a doddle. But as the rain had set in, and we found ourselves going up and down trees like a fiddler's elbow, we saw our options dwindle one by one. We just couldn't seem to find the right tree, or more accurately, we just couldn't seem to find the right *four* trees, since we each needed to connect two adjacent trees with horizontal canopy-level traverses.

Phil had the task of rigging the ropes along which David was to travel while talking about the animals and plants he encountered in the canopy. I had to rig a long cable-cam between the crowns of two emergent trees, from which David would be filmed perched on a branch.

Both of these were big, ambitious rigs – which is why there were two of us here to install them. Poor Sean had spent most of his time running around on the ground below us, carrying ropes from tree to tree, trying to hear what we were shouting above the noise of the rain. We'd have been stumped without him, but as the three of us headed over to the research-station canteen for lunch each day he had to put up with quite a few exasperated grumbles from Phil and me. It was turning into a proper scrabble to get things done before the rest of the crew, including David, arrived and I knew that the rain would be no excuse if we failed to deliver. In fact it would probably stop entirely the moment the crew arrived, and no one would be any the wiser about the ten days we'd spent snorkelling around the treetops.

The latest candidate I'd found – my ninth tree – was growing on the banks of a narrow, fast-moving river. The rain pummelled the murky water mercilessly and at this rate it wouldn't be long before the river burst its banks to flood the whole area. Tensioning the climbing rope with my weight had wrung the water from it so that a muddy dribble ran down my shirt sleeve every time I pushed my climbing clamps higher. It was impossible to look upwards as I pushed through the understorey towards the canopy, like trying to peer up through a waterfall, and I wasn't able to stop blinking long enough to see anything clearly. Swimming goggles would have been ideal, but funnily enough, they weren't the first thing I thought to pack for a month in the jungle.

The glistening foliage danced and bounced continuously under the onslaught, and hummingbirds dodged this way and that to avoid the worst of it as they made their way from flower to flower. Continuous water ran from the ends of long tapered leaves like water from a tap, so all I had to do was open my mouth beneath them to drink my fill. I'd never seen anything like it, not even in Borneo. But this rain wasn't the result of a sporadic storm; it was just the way things were. Business as usual in the lowland coastal jungles of Central America. I'd been told the region experiences an incredible thirteen feet of rain every year, but had presumed most of this would fall during a defined wet season. In retrospect I now realised the guidebook had described the seasons as alternating between 'rainy' and 'rainiest'. Nice for frogs – tricky for climbers. Anyhow, we were here now and there was nothing to be done about it. I was obsessing over the weather in a way that only an Englishman can, so I tried to put it from my mind and crack on regardless. If nothing else, the rain kept me cool   not to mention hydrated.

Despite the name, rainforests aren't usually continuously wet. Some have long wet seasons followed by big intense dries. Others have shorter seasons that alternate regularly. Some forests dry out completely between rain events, while others spend months on end trying to keep their heads above water. Some occasionally struggle to get enough; others struggle to dump the excess. The forest I was now in was clearly of the latter kind. Yes, it made for tricky climbing conditions, but the benefits of so much water were clear for all to see in the abundance of life. Bromeliads grew in profusion. These trumpet-like plants collect rain in their centre, little tanks of water that are often home to a veritable soup of aquatic larvae and insects – sometimes even tadpoles and frogs.

It was also the most colourful canopy I'd ever entered. A thousand shades of dappled green were decorated with random splashes of tropical reds and yellows. Even the animals and birds seemed more vibrant here. The hornbills of Africa and Asia had been replaced by large scarlet macaws that patrolled the sky in pairs, and I'd just seen my first morpho: a large, iridescent blue butterfly that glided like royalty through the understorey below me. Its neon-blue wings flashed like Morse code as they opened and closed in lazy beats.

Turning my attention back to the rope, I carried on climbing up towards the huge, plant-covered branch I was hanging from. I had a good feeling about this tree and was starting to believe I might have found what we needed for the cable-cam. I was now around 150 feet aboveground and the canopy was opening up around me to reveal a spectacular view, and most importantly of all – there was another monster tree rising above the canopy opposite me. A twin-stemmed colossus about 300 feet away standing around 170 feet tall. Its enormous branches carried plenty of bromeliads, but it was less smothered than my tree and offered several good positions for David to perch in while the camera travelled towards him down its cable.

Just as things were beginning to look good, I was knocked off balance by a very loud noise coming from a few feet behind me. Spinning quickly round on my rope I found two male howler monkeys no more than ten feet away. They were jet-black and each about the size and weight of a Highland terrier. Both of them were leaning forward to scream into my face. They must have seen me from a distance, and quietly sneaked in behind my back to take a closer look while I was distracted by the view. Their open red mouths contrasted strongly with their jet-black faces. As I watched, three more climbed onto the branch to join the fracas. I was now faced with five extremely angry monkeys shouting at me to get out of their tree.

The noise was deafening. Howlers can be heard from several miles away when they engage in these territorial choruses. In fact they are the loudest land animal on the planet and my head was reeling. It was like standing in front of a speaker at a heavy-metal gig and I could feel my ears fizz with the distortion. I slid off the branch to dangle on my rope in preparation for bailing out. As I did this, they moved forward together to claim lost ground and soon there were eight of them lined up side by side on a branch less than five feet away, howling at me with ear-splitting defiance.

My last image as I dropped away into the understorey was of scowling black faces and, bizarrely, eight pairs of white testicles quivering with rage as the monkeys leant forward to hurl abuse at me. Jet-black with a bright-white scrotum is quite a strong look. I was out of there before they decided to urinate on me.

Splashing down into the water at the base of the tree, I squinted back up to catch one last glimpse of the monkeys strutting along the branch in triumph high above.

Irate monkeys aside, however, I was happy to have found my canopy location and was looking forward to getting back up there after lunch to start rigging the cable-cam. Providing the local male-voice choir had moved on, of course.

• • •

The fern-covered howler tree and the other giant I'd spied from its branches were growing 300 feet apart, like two enormous bookends. They stood proudly facing each other, but between them lay a solid canopy of smaller trees and thick vegetation – an unbroken sea of foliage over the top of which I had to tension a six-millimetre-thick steel cable for the camera to move along. It would be impossible to hoist it up through the understorey from the ground, so I had another plan.

The crossbow dangled on its strap from the back of my harness as I climbed back up after lunch. It was a powerful bow: it would need to be to propel a weighted bolt towing a fishing line at least 400 feet. I'm not a huge fan of crossbows, but they are ideal for this kind of work since it's almost impossible to use a standard bow or even a catapult while dangling and twisting on a rope in free space.

Arriving in the upper canopy, I was glad to see that the monkeys had cleared off, and I set about preparing myself to take the shot. I was back in the same place I'd been before, about 150 feet aboveground, but this time I noticed something strange. The tree's stem was exposed here and its hard, smooth bark was deeply gouged with long claw marks that I didn't recall seeing earlier on. They'd been made recently by a large animal as it climbed up into the canopy, but I was at a loss as to what kind of creature might be responsible. Monkeys don't have claws like that and tend to enter trees from an adjacent canopy anyway. Coatis wouldn't be able to find enough grip on such a smooth surface and tended to climb vines rather than enormous tree trunks. Costa Rica has no bears and nor could I believe that they had been left by any kind of cat. Costa Rica does have cats that climb – the margay spends a great deal of time hunting prey in the canopy; but again, they just didn't seem to fit the bill. It was a real mystery, but in the absence of any time to investigate further I turned my attention back to the job in hand.

Unslinging the crossbow, I took a closer look at the tree opposite me – the one I hoped David would be happy in. It was a real beauty. Standing exposed against a backdrop of verdant green, its tall, slender, grey trunk divided into two dominant stems about eighty feet aboveground. These two stems, mirror versions of each other, then rose for another hundred feet or so, throwing out large horizontal branches either side as they went. These limbs were festooned with plants and long tendrils of leafy creepers that hung down from the upper crown to touch the understorey far below. It was a magnificent tree that was sure to become a character in its own right as David perched high in its arms, below the other end of the steel cable, to deliver his piece to camera.

Having chosen a suitable branch to aim for, I placed the bow over my knee and cocked the string. The thin fishing line was already tied to the bolt, which I slid home into the breach. Keeping my fingers well away from the fishing reel mounted below the fore-grip, I raised the bow to my shoulder, released the safety and waited for my rope to gently spin me round in the right direction before squeezing the trigger. The stock thumped into my shoulder and I held the bow in place as the bolt flew clean over the canopy, trailing its thin blue line. It came to rest dangling just below the third branch up on the right-hand side of David's tree. It was a good shot, or maybe just a lucky one, and had put the line exactly where I wanted it. Releasing the clutch on the reel I let the bolt drag its line down to the base of the tree, hidden from sight in the forest fifteen storeys below. Sean was down there somewhere and a few minutes later I felt the pull as he reached up to retrieve the bolt. Another few minutes passed, then three sharp tugs told me the thicker cord was tied on. Winding it in through the canopy until it reached me, I weighted its end with a karabiner and lowered it spinning down through the foliage to the base of my tree far below. The twin canopies of these two huge trees were now connected via a high traverse of cord. Things were at last beginning to take shape, and as the rain set in again after an all-too-brief respite, I started my abseil back down to the ground. It had been a good day and everything else could wait till the following morning. It made a nice change to leave things on a high note.

About halfway down I caught a fleeting glimpse of something hopping beneath the drooping leaf of a vine. Breaking off another leaf, I rolled it up like a newspaper and used it to carefully lift up the foliage for a closer look. There, underneath the dripping leaves, making its way slowly up the root of an orchid, was the tiniest, most beautiful frog I'd ever seen. It was a bright, almost metallic minty-green colour, covered in large black spots. I'd never seen a poison-dart frog before, but it was unmistakable, just exquisite, like a tiny living gem, and it held me captivated. The rain was now coming down in rods and the forest was growing dim as the afternoon rolled into evening, but I couldn't take my eyes off this miniscule creature as it made its way slowly up towards the canopy – and what an epic journey that was for such a tiny creature. What I didn't realise at the time was that if I had peered closer I might have been lucky enough to see a tiny tadpole on its back. Poison-dart frogs often piggy-back their tadpoles high up into the canopy to deposit them within water-filled bromeliads where they complete the rest of their development. Sometimes it hopped, sometimes it climbed, but it seemed unstoppable. Like a tiny robot programmed to make this journey or fail utterly in the process.

As I stashed my harness in my kitbag at the base of the tree, I took one final look up into the lush gardens hanging high above. I was reminded of the words of Don Perry, the father of all modern-day canopy exploration, who had based his pioneering treetop research in this very same forest at La Selva. There had been various unsuccessful attempts to use ropes to access the tropical canopy earlier in the twentieth century, but Perry was the first person to really make it work. In the late 1970s he designed and built what he called his 'canopy web', an interconnected system of ropes traversing the treetops, from which he could access not only the tips of branches, but also the space between canopies. In a very real way he opened up this dynamic realm to the rest of us, proving it was possible to use rope-based climbing systems to gain safe access to a completely unexplored high frontier.

Perry recognised the tropical canopy as being 'the most botanically diverse ecosystem on the planet'. He'd called it 'the floating kingdom of life' and I went to sleep that night dreaming of an existence in which I'd never need to come down from the trees.

• • •

The following morning we were back in the forest shortly after daybreak. It was a subdued, dour day of particularly heavy rain and little visibility. The jungle seemed to sag beneath the weight of the weather, as if it had given up any hope of ever seeing the sunshine again. Phil and Sean were putting the final touches to the other canopy rig, so I left them at a junction in the trail and headed towards my own tree. Apart from the high-pitched piping of treefrogs rejoicing in the wet, there was no sign of animal life anywhere. No birds flying, no lizards scuttling, no insects – just rain, mud and dripping leaves.

The only creature I saw on my way through the forest was an agouti, a medium-sized brown rodent, rather like a long-legged guinea pig. It had found shelter beneath a large leaf, where it trembled under a swarm of large mosquitoes. There were hundreds of them on the poor creature's skin. On its eyelids, in its ears: everywhere, covering its whole body in a macabre shimmering cloak. The agouti seemed incapable of moving, rooted to the spot as if in shock as they drank their fill.

It hobbled out into the rain towards another bush further away and stared at me with wide, terrified eyes as I approached. I made an attempt to catch it, to scare away the insects. But it jinked back to its original shelter and I realised there was no way it would ever let me get close enough to help, so I reluctantly left it to its torment. It was a depressing, pitiful sight and I was reminded of my time in the Congo, where the jungle had reduced me to nothing more than a convenient source of protein. Life: nature's way of keeping meat fresh. Unable to do anything else for the trembling animal, I trudged on through the mud towards the base of David's tree.

The steel cable lay on its reel where Sean had left it the day before. I tied its end to the cord hanging down from the canopy above, then used my machete to fashion a crude axle for the reel so that it would rotate freely when pulled. Once I was happy that all was set, I headed over to the base of the howler tree.

Pulling the rain cover from my kitbag, which I'd stashed in the buttress roots, I opened up the top. Reaching inside for my helmet, I pulled it out only to drop it again with a shock. There was a snake coiled up inside it. A hognosed pit viper had somehow managed to slither in through the bag's drawstrings during the night. It seemed I wasn't the only one fed up with the rain. Thankfully it was still sluggish and lethargic, or I would've been bitten before I knew it. My hand had been millimetres away from its snout. My red helmet lay where I'd dropped it, and I could see the snake's coils wrapped tightly around the chinstrap. It clearly had no intention of vacating its dry home, so I used a stick to gently evict it. Once in the leaf litter it suddenly came alive and made a lightning strike towards my boot before lunging away towards the darkness beneath a rotten log.

Wet weather brings out frogs, and where there are frogs there are snakes hunting them. I have plenty of debilitating fears, but thankfully snakes aren't one of them. But neither am I suicidal, so I made a mental note to open my kitbag more carefully next time, and to avoid using the log the snake had vanished under as a seat!

The near miss with the viper was a clear warning to take things carefully. I was knackered, soaked to the skin and at a low ebb, which is exactly when accidents happen and things start to go wrong in the jungle. So I made a special point of checking my ropes thoroughly before climbing, paying particular attention to the part lying over the branch at the top anchor – a metre-long section of nylon normally hidden from the ground. On past trips this section had been chewed through by animals during the night, so I pulled the ropes round in a loop and checked every inch. This took quite a while, but the confidence it gave me was worth every minute.

Carefully pulling my harness out of the bag, I saddled up then clipped onto the rope and pulled the slack through. Stepping up off the ground, I began my ascent into the branches. I wanted to pull the cable through from up there, to help navigate it through the tangled curtains of hanging plants. Everything appeared as I'd left it the day before, but as I approached the first branch around 100 feet up, I again noticed a mysterious series of deep claw marks on an exposed section of trunk next to me. They appeared fresh, just like the others I'd found higher up, and again I was at a loss as to what could have made them. I carried on climbing.

Hauling the heavy cable up on my own was a serious mission, and by the time I'd threaded it back down to the ground at my end, I was exhausted and covered in dirt. It felt good to have broken the back of the job, though, and from here on it should be relatively simple to finish. However, my climbing ropes were now hanging in the way of the cable, so I headed further up into the canopy to reposition the top anchor.

I hadn't been this high in the tree before, and at around 170 feet I noticed a subtle movement on a branch, behind a thick, hanging curtain of vines. Pulling them to one side, I came face-to-face with the biggest iguana lizard I'd seen in my life. A huge male, well over six feet long, stretched out full-length on a luxurious bed of bromeliads and orchids. Just what he was doing up here, seventeen storeys aboveground, was anyone's guess and he looked just as surprised to see me as I was to see him. We stared at each other for what seemed like an eternity. He was massive, like some sort of arboreal dragon, casually lounging there in resplendent grandeur. The scratch marks on the tree trunk were a mystery no more – here was the culprit. One look at his long, curved claws and strong, sinewy legs explained everything.

His emerald skin was encrusted with gem-like scales and a long ridge of tall spines flowed down his back to the base of a long striped tail. After a minute or so his dark-yellow eye narrowed and he slowly raised his head to unfurl a huge dewlap from beneath his chin. Bobbing his head twice, he posed with head held high and dewlap fanned out, eyeballing me in defiance as beads of rain ran over his scales. He was dazzlingly handsome, just magnificent. I'd expected to encounter primates and birds this high in the canopy, but never a six-foot-long lizard. Gently closing the curtain of vines behind me, I continued upwards, all the better for having met one of the canopy's most glorious visitors.

The next branch up was home to a second iguana, equally big and impressive. He stayed motionless, only his yellow eye swivelling to follow me as I climbed past him. It was remarkable to encounter these animals draped so casually over their branches so high up. They seemed completely at home in their penthouse suites and once again I was left to marvel at the sheer abundance and variety of life in this incredible tree.

But I couldn't hang around looking at them for too long. I had one day left to finish the rig and there was still plenty to do.

• • •

Three days later and I was lying on my bed in our lodge trying to get back to sleep after being rudely awoken at 2am by a cockroach. I'd felt its long antennae on my face as it leant in to drink saliva from my open mouth. I'd flown out of bed to turn on the light, almost knocking myself out on the bathroom door in the process. It sat there on my pillow looking at me while nonchalantly running a long spiky foreleg through its mandibles, presumably to lick the last traces of my saliva from it. Kneeling down I shone my torch beneath the bed to see a dozen of them hanging around, just waiting for me to turn the light off and start dribbling again. I'm not a huge fan of cockroaches, not in my mouth anyway. So for the first time since I was twelve, I went to bed with the light on. Honestly, sometimes you're better off in a tent.

Now that I was awake, though, it was proving impossible to get back to sleep. David and the rest of the crew had arrived the day before and we were halfway through filming the canopy sequences. The rain had stopped just in time and we'd completed Phil's sequence earlier that day. David had looked and sounded great as he talked to the camera about canopy diversity and the sorts of animal you might expect to find a hundred feet above the rainforest floor, such as sloths, coatis and monkeys. Behind those effortless images lay ten days of hard graft from Phil, a spirited head for heights from David, and an experienced hand on the camera from camerawoman Justine.

Now it was my turn and I was feeling pretty nervous about it. Today was the day we hoisted David 150 feet up into the canopy and sent a twenty-kilo camera down a 300-foot-long cable towards him at thirty miles per hour. However many safety components there are in the system – and I'd made sure there were plenty – it was still a nerve-wracking prospect. Sleep was slipping further away from me as I lay there watching cockroaches scuttle across the floor. This was

David Attenborough, after all, and my sister's characteristically helpful words, given to me just before I left the UK, came back to haunt me: *For God's sake, don't drop him.*

• • •

Water droplets hung from the steel cable, glistening in the early-morning sun like a long strand of pearls. I gave the cable a tap and watched the droplets fall away in a shimmering curtain towards the canopy below. The rain had stopped a short while ago and the pressure was now on to get the shot before it set in again. Looking across the void towards the other tree, I could see a familiar figure in a blue short-sleeved shirt hanging in the canopy beneath the other end of the cable. I was acutely aware that David had now been up there for half an hour, waiting patiently for us to ready the shot.

Suspended from the cable next to me was the camera on its dolly, ready to go. The dolly was a basic two-wheeled contraption beneath which hung the camera as the whole thing free-rolled down the cable under the effects of gravity. The only thing preventing it from crashing straight into the anchor at the other end was a long tether of stout cord carefully flaked into an open bag hanging from my climbing harness. I'd measured this line out meticulously to ensure the camera would stop twenty feet short of piling into the tree. A simple but effective system that I'd used many times before, although, it has to be said, without the added pressure of having anyone perched beneath it at the far end.

Signalling for David to get ready, my heartbeat went up a gear as the film whirred quietly past the camera's shutter and I released the dolly. It slid silently away from me down the cable. Slowly at first, then faster and faster. Soon it was hurtling along beneath a mist of fine spray from its wheels. The yellow safety cord was whipping up out of my bag in a blur and the whole cable was vibrating with a high-pitched whine as the camera flew along high above the canopy, straight towards Sir David Attenborough. Counting down in my head, I began to tighten my grip around the cord in order to gradually slow the camera on its approach. Three, two, one – stop. The camera hung there in space, twenty feet from David. I suppose I could have let it get a bit closer than that. The safety cord would have prevented anyone from getting hurt, but in all honesty I didn't have the nerve to cut it that fine. It was close enough and had worked well, and just like that it was all over. Ten days' work for a twenty-second shot. And as David prepared to head back down to the forest floor, I hauled the camera back towards me with shaking hands.

• • •

After Phil had lowered David down and the camera was safely back on solid ground, I was again left on my own in the canopy. There was still a lot to do. The de-rig would take several hours. But all that could wait until tomorrow. For now I was making the most of simply being up here. All filming pressures were gone and most of the crew had returned to the lodge ahead of the impending rain. A huge weight had been lifted from my shoulders and I was enjoying the feeling of just being in my harness, hanging in the canopy. Dusk was approaching, bringing with it a subtle change in the forest's

125

atmosphere – as much felt as heard – as the day shift prepared to hand over to the creatures of the night. The ghostly roar of distant howler monkeys came and went in waves on the edge of hearing, and as the first few drops of rain began to fall I heard the high-pitched notes of a treefrog calling from its hiding place somewhere in the canopy nearby.

I'd be sad to leave this tree. In a few days' time I was due to fly home, then on to Ecuador. There would be amazing trees to climb out there as well, but the tree I love the most is the one I'm in at any given moment, and this Costa Rican giant – this tree of life, or *árbol de la vida* – was nothing short of perfect. The monkeys, the iguanas, the hummingbirds and all the rest of the incredible creatures that called its canopy home, were living proof that trees like this stand at the very centre of life in the rainforest. They are elegant reminders of the interconnectedness of all things, and in a very real way climbing one is nothing short of a pilgrimage for anyone passionate about the natural world. In David's own words: 'it's up in the canopy, a hundred or more feet aboveground, that the real richness of the forest lies'.

That tree in La Selva seemed to embody everything that had lured me up into the canopy in the first place. A 'floating kingdom' like no other.

Chapter 5

Castaña – Peru

2003

Sliding my climbing clamps up the rope as far as they'd go, I sat back in my harness to take stock of the situation. I'd reached the top of my line, which meant I was now around 150 feet aboveground in the canopy of the greatest rainforest on earth. This was a big moment for me. It was my first time in the Amazon and everything about the place was overwhelming. I was struggling to get my head around the sheer scale of it. I was also struggling to get a clear view of the jungle. The canopy I was in was so dense I'd have to climb a bit higher to find a gap in the branches. Transferring onto a shorter rope, I disconnected from the main access line and began making my way up from branch to branch towards the top of the tree, where I hoped to be rewarded with my first canopy-level view of this incredible forest.

The Amazon really is the ultimate rainforest. It represents half of all remaining tropical jungle on our planet, sprawling across nine different countries to cover more than 2.1 million square miles. An area twice the size of the Congo, which could swallow the island of Borneo seven times over, and Britain twenty-six times. The huge tree I was now climbing was one of an estimated 400 billion in the Amazon. That's around fifty trees for every person alive today, or to put it another way: four times as many trees as the total number of humans *that have ever lived.*

Ten per cent of all species on earth call the Amazon home, including twenty per cent of all known bird and fish species. An estimated 2.5 million species of insect live alongside 427 species of mammal, 378 species of reptile and more than 400 species of amphibian. All of which is enough to make your head spin.

But animals aside, it is of course the plants that dominate any jungle, and the Amazon has around 40,000 species. To put this in perspective, Borneo has 15,000, while the Congo has 10,000. Of these 40,000 plants 16,000 are native species of tree. By stark comparison, Britain has around forty-five. And that's on a good day.

The sheer biodiversity of the Amazon is unparalleled, and given that the vast majority of these organisms are to be found living up in the trees, its canopy can be a truly humbling place to explore. But in order to see the big picture it's sometimes best to start small.

The wonder of any rainforest, let alone the most intricate and diverse on earth, can only be truly appreciated by taking a closer look at some of the relationships between its organisms. Which is exactly why I was here, climbing up through these branches. I was in search of some very special flowers. I'd caught a glimpse of one from down on the ground – a creamy- yellow cluster of blooms, held erect like the flowers of a horse chestnut back home. Indeed, the local Spanish name for the species of tree I was climbing was *castaña*, or 'chestnut', although this had more to do with its world-famous fruit, known to the rest of us as the Brazil nut.

Brazil-nut trees rely completely upon just one type of bee for pollination and it was this delicate relationship between flower and insect that I was here, as part of a film crew, to try and document. It was a fascinating story that had the potential to throw light on some of the ecological complexities that have helped shape the Amazon.

But first I had to find the flowers and now I was up here I was struggling to see any. They seemed to be growing on the very tips of branches, beyond the dense canopy of leaves that hung down around me like a huge shaggy umbrella. I'd have to get a bit higher and walk out along one of the tree's limbs to get a closer look.

Throwing a bundle of rope over an enormous branch stretching right across the tree above me, I clipped in and swung out to hang in the empty space beneath it. The view out over the forest was still hidden, but I'd just caught a tantalising glimpse of some yellow petals, so I pressed on.

Sunlight dancing on the smaller branches above hinted at a gap. I climbed towards it.

Turning round into the light, I looked out through a window in the leaves. The tree I was climbing stood on the edge of a plateau and the view over the rainforest that now greeted me was immense, just awesome, in the true sense of the word. It wasn't just the scale of the forest, or the sight of infinite trees marching to the horizon, that was so breathtaking – it was the sheer diversity of their shape, size, form and colour. My eyes were instantly drawn to a huge emergent in full bloom, half a mile away. Its entire canopy was full of bright-pink blossom, so that the whole tree shone like a beacon across the otherwise green forest. Way off to my left were two more, just the same. In fact, there were quite a few of the same species dotted through the forest, and it amazed me to think that all these trees were tied together by invisible threads as insects and birds transferred genetic material between them.

Here and there, tall, domed emergents like the tree I was now in rose above all others to bask in the undiluted tropical sunshine. Others were fruiting and had dropped their leaves to reveal thousands of seedpods dangling from bare branches. I recognised these as kapok trees – true New World giants, their enormous spreading limbs reaching up into the sky as if in prayer. Kapoks are favourite nesting sites for harpy eagles, the world's most secretive and powerful raptor, although my optimistic hope of spotting one in the trees' open canopies was in vain.

Some tribes use the fluffy 'silk cotton' from kapok seeds as wadding for their blowpipe darts, and I was struck by the thought that the forest I was now looking over was also reputed to be home to an unknown number of uncontacted indigenous groups. More than any other, it is this fact about the Amazon that continues to astonish me most and goes some way towards indicating what a vast tract of impenetrable wilderness it truly is. I wondered whether right now, somewhere deep within this landscape, there might be a group of people living wild and free as they had done for thousands of years.

To cap it all, floating way beyond everything else like another world, was a long line of snow-clad mountains on the horizon: the high Andes. The mere sight of those crystalline peaks was enough to dispel any last memory of the suffocating humidity lurking on the jungle floor 170 feet below me.

I was enjoying a harpy's view of the Amazon in all its glory. For a tree-climber, it didn't get much better. But just as excitingly, barely ten feet away in front of me, was one of the flowers I had come all this way from England to find. It was one of several on the outside of the tree's canopy, where it was sunniest.

• • •

The first thing to know about Brazil nut, or castaña trees is that they are staggeringly beautiful; often standing as forest emergents, head and shoulders above the Amazon's other trees. They can grow to be 200 feet tall and in my mind are one of only a few New World tropical trees to rival the natural grace and form of the dipterocarps in Borneo. Their trunks

131

are tall and straight, their timber strong and their canopies broad and spreading. In fact, they are pretty much the perfect tree from a climber's point of view, and the one I was in was a classic example of how lovely they could become with age. This tree could easily be six or seven centuries old: pre-Columbian, in fact.

The forest below me was sweltering in thirty-five-degree heat, but up here I was sheltered from the sun by the castaña's canopy of long green leaves. Hidden amongst this dense foliage were dozens of large round seedpods, each containing up to thirty of the tree's familiar nuts. Each pod was the size of a grapefruit, rock-hard, and weighed around two kilos. They hung like enormous cannonball baubles, swaying in the breeze from the ends of last season's flower spikes. They were still a couple of months away from being ripe enough to fall, but even so, I was glad to be wearing my climbing helmet. Although how much help it would be in the event of a direct hit was a moot point. Despite this latent threat, it was still a huge pleasure to be here, up in the branches of one of the world's most impressive rainforest trees.

But in many respects it was the castaña's pale waxy flowers that held the most intrigue. For if ever there was an apt metaphor to illustrate the exquisite ecology of rainforests, it is the extraordinary story of their relationship with a bee, an orchid and a large ground-dwelling rodent. But to tell this story properly, we first had to film the bee pollinating a flower.

Despite the clear afternoon sky, a hollow peal of thunder warned of rain on its way. The flowers weren't going anywhere, and in the absence of any foraging insects I decided to come back early the following morning to try and catch a glimpse of pollination in progress. It felt good to have finally found the flowers. So taking one last look at them and the alluring view beyond, I dropped back down into the stifling gloom of the forest understorey and headed back to camp to share the good news with the rest of the team.

• • •

Seeing those mountains had reminded me what an incredible journey it had been to get here. We had flown east across the Andes from Lima, touching down for a while in Cusco, where the air was so thin I felt my heart race. My first view of the Peruvian Amazon had been from the plane's window as we dropped down over the foothills. Even from 20,000 feet up, the forest had stretched away to the horizon in every direction. The next time we landed was in the sweltering heat of the tropical lowlands at the jungle river port of Puerto Maldonado, where the air was so thick it felt like oxygen soup. From Puerto Maldonado we had travelled by boat up the Madre de Dios River for five hours before finally arriving here at Los Amigos Biological Station. Around the station lay 360,000 acres of protected, old-growth Amazonian forest, which in turn was but part of a 20-million-acre block of jungle that had been protected in this remote corner of south-east Peru.

It was October, the end of the dry season, and despite the fact that this was meant to be the height of the flowering period, the castaña tree I'd just climbed was the first we'd found in bloom. Mirko, a local biologist, and I had been wandering through the jungle in search of a suitable candidate for the past week. Castañas grow in groves and we must have looked at well over a hundred trees in mounting frustration. Some had green unopened buds, while others had clearly finished flowering many days before. The plan was for me to rig a system of ropes to hoist cameraman Kevin up into position alongside David, an ecologist from the Smithsonian Tropical Research Institute, who would help interpret the biology for the viewer at home.

We thought we'd found a suitable tree a few days ago. A huge thing, larger even than the one I'd just climbed. It had looked perfect from the ground, its upper canopy dripping with flowers. So I had fired my line up into its immense branches and begun my ascent only to encounter a hidden bee nest halfway up the trunk. Thankfully they weren't honey bees, only a local stingless variety, but they had powerful pincer-like jaws and my initial relief at not getting stung turned to panic as a couple of thousand swarmed all over to bite me relentlessly.

They latched painfully onto my lips, nose and eyelids, and squirmed around, secreting a strange sticky resin all over my skin. I was swamped as they wriggled down my back, into my ears and through my hair. By the time I felt them buzzing up my legs I'd had enough and quickly abseiled back down to the ground. They followed me down to smother Mirko as well, and the air turned blue with earthy Spanish curses.

Less of a laughing matter had been the inch-and-a-half-long bullet ant that crawled down my face while I was halfway up another castaña. It had stung me twice on the left cheek while I dangled a hundred feet aboveground. The pain had been immediate and extremely intense, like a cigar stubbed out on my skin, turning the whole left-hand side of my face numb and making my lips tingle. The headache that followed could have felled a rhino and I was left with a black eye for two days. Bullet ants carry the most potent toxin of any insect, ranked top of the Schmidt Sting Pain Index. Even stronger than the mind-numbing sting delivered by tarantula hawk wasps – which I can personally vouch for, having been stung on the forehead by one in Sumatra. Bullet ants look like menacing black hornets without wings, and the one that got me then ran down the front of my shirt before I managed to flick it off, again towards Mirko, who hurled abuse at me and threatened to cut my rope.

To rub salt into the wounds, what I had originally thought were fresh flowers up in the tree had turned out to be old and wilted – we'd missed them by a few days.

And therein lay the issue: castaña flowers are so short-lived, it makes finding one in full bloom very tricky. Several times we encountered large areas of leaf litter smothered in their fallen petals. We'd knelt down to watch steady streams of leaf-cutter ants carry the confetti off to their nest. Nothing was wasted in the rainforest, but as fascinating as this was, it wasn't the story we were after, so the search continued.

Then the day before yesterday we'd finally stumbled across our tree. Having climbed up to check the flowers and marvel at the view, I'd just arrived back at camp when the peals of thunder delivered on their promise, and the heavens opened. The sky had turned black and the pounding rain settled in for the night. My last thought as I fell asleep that evening was whether such delicate flowers could possibly survive such an onslaught.

For two solid days that storm thumped and flashed away in the clouds directly above Los Amigos. We were coming out of the dry season, and this was the first big rain to hit the area in weeks. It seemed to be making up for lost time, and as each violent squall swept in to hammer the forest even harder than the last, my hope of finding any flowers still intact up in the castaña dwindled more and more. At this rate, we'd be lucky if there were any left to film in the entire forest.

• • •

The rain eventually stopped at 3am two days later. By 4.30 I was heading out of camp with my climbing gear. I was on my own and wanted to take full advantage of the ceasefire to get up into the tree for a proper look at what remained of the flowers. I was soon sweating through the humid darkness of the forest and had to hold my head torch in my hand to avoid the clouds of tiny biting flies attracted to its light. At one point I noticed an orange glow weaving along the path towards me. I stood still and watched entranced as a beetle flew past my face with what I can only describe as green headlights on its thorax and red tail lights behind on its abdomen. I'd never seen anything like it before – like a tiny spacecraft.

Arriving at the bottom of the castaña, I hauled the climbing ropes I had left there round in a loop, examining them to make sure they hadn't been nibbled by rodents or ants, then pulled on my harness. The sky was growing light, but it was still half an hour or so until sunrise, by which time I hoped to be up in position, keeping an eye open for insects visiting the flowers. David had described what to look out for – a species of orchid bee – and providing I saw them buzzing around, I could rig the ropes to get him and Kevin up here to film pollination tomorrow. Mind you, at this stage I was more concerned with whether I'd find any flowers left at all. There were an alarming number of bruised petals strewn across the leaf litter at the foot of the tree.

Thankfully the flowers in the tree were largely intact. It was nothing short of a miracle that so many had survived; although quite a few looked worse for wear and there were plenty of empty pedicles where entire flower spikes had been ripped off by the wind. Carrying on towards the first flower I'd seen, near the top of the tree, I arrived in the upper canopy just in time to watch the sunrise over the Amazon.

The Madre de Dios River lay far below and as the thick mist lifted to reveal the jungle everything seemed to sparkle in air washed clean by the storm. Several pairs of blue and yellow macaws flew past, squawking to each other, and down in the forest below I heard the squirrel-like chattering of a group of saki monkeys as they moved through the canopy in search of breakfast.

It wasn't long before a small metallic-green bee arrived on the scene and landed on the yellow petals of a flower a few feet away. It was clearly an orchid bee, although it didn't look like the species David had described. It was certainly in search of nectar, though, so I watched closely as it tried to squirm its way in through the flower's petals. The flower wasn't about to give up its precious cargo to any old bee, however, and unable to shoulder its way through into the nectary, it eventually gave up and flew off to try its luck elsewhere. No rare insight to the workings of the Amazon just yet, then. Still, since bees are a million times more sensitive to scent than we are, I hoped it wouldn't be long before the rightful pollinator arrived. So I made myself comfy on my branch and took another long look out over the jungle. Far away the snowy slopes of the Andes glowed soft pink in the first rays of the new day.

Half an hour later my attention was drawn back to the same flower as a large-bodied yellow bee I hadn't seen before came in to land. It was twice the size of the previous metallic-green one and seemed to fit the description given by David perfectly. It certainly knew exactly what to do, and quickly set about gaining access to the flower's hidden treasure. There was no messing around as it forced its head and thorax through a tiny gap, shoving the encircling petals aside. Its strong hind legs, laden with sacks of orange pollen, scrabbled and pushed to drive the insect deep inside. The petals rolled back to close behind the bee and hide it from view, although I still heard it buzzing inside. It re-emerged a few seconds later, covered in the castaña's precious pollen and all the better for an energy-rich drink of nectar. It paused just long enough to run its forelegs over its antennae, before powering away across the canopy in search of another meal. I'd just witnessed one of the jungle's most unassuming yet profound interactions. High time for breakfast, so abseiling back down to the ground I headed back to camp, where I would collect the rest of my rigging gear with a view to getting Kevin and David up there to film the following morning.

Over the next two days we successfully filmed Dave hanging in the castaña's canopy next to the bees. It was a good start, but what about the orchid and the rodent, the other two organisms involved in the castaña's life cycle?

Well, the orchid bees pollinating the flowers were one of only a few species strong enough to get through the flower's defences. Even the males of these species are too puny to gain entry, so all castaña pollination has to be done by females. But the male orchid bee still has a role to play, since in order to attract females to mate, it has to cover itself in perfume from a special orchid growing elsewhere in the canopy. What does this have to do with the castaña? Well, no orchids, no mating. No mating, no female bees to pollinate the tree, so no Brazil nuts. Ultimately, in order to reproduce, the castaña relies entirely upon the female orchid bee's choice of perfume, as does an international trade in harvested Brazil nuts worth nearly £10 million a year.

So where does the rodent come in? To tell this second half of the story, we would need to come back to Peru in a couple of months' time, when the castaña's cannonball pods were ripe enough to drop to the jungle floor.

2004

Arriving back in Puerto Maldonado was a shock to the system. I thought it was oppressive last time, but it was now January, the height of the wet season, with humidity averaging 90 per cent and temperatures simmering around thrity-two degrees centigrade. Nice if you're on a beach, but tough if you're climbing trees. We'd left England in a blizzard and the memory of watching a car spin slowly off the M4, narrowly missing an articulated truck in the middle of a whiteout, seemed like a distant dream as I lay sweating on my hotel bed, cursing the ceiling fan for turning so slowly. Outside, the streets were steaming. The rain had just stopped and water was evaporating in the heat of the sun. My room began to shake, and poking my head out through the bars of my first-storey window, I watched an enormous logging truck lurch up the street below in a cloud of diesel fumes. Fat sections of freshly felled old-growth mahogany lay chained to its trailer, while long strips of bark trailed in the mud behind the enormous wheels. A sobering reminder of the environmental pressures this part of the world was under.

Puerto Maldonado is – or was – the archetypal jungle frontier town. Founded during the heady days of the rubber boom, it was a melting pot of ranchers, miners, loggers, drug-traffickers and prostitutes. Nowadays the area around it is practically logged out, but illegal gold-mining is still a major issue, nothing short of an environmental disaster, as gallons of liquid mercury are poured into the Madre de Dios every day. Ironically, eco-tourism is big business today. But thirteen years ago you could still pay for a drink with gold dust, and watch tankers pour neat oil onto the dirt streets to keep the dust down. I couldn't wait to get out of town and back into the trees.

Kevin was heading back to film at Los Amigos with producer Rupert, while Mirko and I travelled up the Madre de
Dios in the opposite direction. Our destination: Lago Valencia,
an oxbow lake on the Bolivian border. Mirko had assured me
there were hundreds of castaña trees in the pristine forest
surrounding the lake, so I planned to rig a cable-cam in the
canopy of the biggest we could find and film the seedpods
hanging there waiting to drop.

Our boat's twelve-horsepower engine barely propelled us
faster than the river current, and Mirko and I broiled in the
heat as we slid slowly past the floating shanties of gold miners
anchored mid channel. Each makeshift hut had its own diesel-
driven conveyor belt spewing sludge and mercury back into
the Madre de Dios once the precious dust had been sifted out.

Five hours later, the pilot turned the prow into a small side
channel and we left the main river behind. The jungle closed in
above us and I watched the reflections ripple on the underside
of leaves as we crept slowly forward up the creek. Kingfishers
played leapfrog with our boat, flying ahead only to double
back through the forest as we passed. We eventually arrived
at a ramshackle police checkpoint. A small cement hut in a
swamp, with three shirtless coppers sweating on the porch:
the Bolivian border patrol. They waved us on casually and
a few minutes later we emerged into the open lake beyond.
The swirls and currents of the main river were now replaced
with textured stippling, like fingerprints on the water, giving
the lake a haunting serenity. Fifty families lived on its shores
in the eaves of the forest. For half the year they fished for

arapaima, huge air-breathing fish weighing up to 200 kilos, and for the other half they worked as *castañeros*, harvesting wild Brazil nuts. Looking at the forest, I could already see the characteristic high-domed canopies of tall castaña trees, and I couldn't wait to get a closer look at them.

Our first day was spent trekking through the thick jungle visiting as many different groves as we could. Huge piles of empty pods lay rotting at the base of many of the trees, the spoils of last year's harvest. Each one had been chopped open by machete and the discarded husks had now filled with water to form hundreds of little pools perfect for mosquito larvae.

Although we visited dozens of trees we didn't find anything suitable for filming. Six hours walking, a 25-kilo rucksack, sweat-bees, murderous mosquitoes and a climb into the canopy all combined to leave me wrung out and fried. By the time we arrived back at camp on the lake shore I was exhausted. Thankfully we were greeted with a huge jug of fruit juice by Ketty, the daughter of the fishing family we were staying with. It really hit the spot, but I still went to bed with blurred vision, the candle by my bed wobbling in a double halo of yellow and green.

I was exhausted and fell into a feverish sleep, my head full of turbulent dreams. Early the following morning I sat by a tree on the lakeside with a cup of coffee, watching thin wisps of mist rise from the mirrored water. Mirko strolled down to join me and mentioned he'd heard me turning in my sleep all night long. I described my nightmares and it turned out he and Ketty had both had similar ones involving desperate chases through tangled forest. He then told me about a double murder committed right here forty-five years ago. Two people had been robbed and killed for their gold. He also told me how Lago Valencia got its name. Twenty-five years ago a man called Valencia killed his wife with a machete in Puerto Maldonado, and making his escape up the Madre de Dios, stumbled across this hidden oxbow lake, where he hid until his wife's family found him and killed him. According to Mirko, the area had a bad reputation for haunting nightmares and was infamous for its heavy atmosphere. It certainly had a dark history, but then most places do if you look back far enough.

The rest of that day went downhill from there really. I just couldn't understand it. There were so many castaña trees, we should have been spoiled for choice. But most of them had already dropped their pods and by mid morning I'd had enough of traipsing aimlessly around, so I rigged and climbed another tree in search of a decent view out over the canopy. Reaching the top, I could see at least a dozen or so other castañas around me, and although some of them still had a few ripe pods dangling high up in their crowns, for the most part they looked pretty barren. What we really needed was a canopy full of them, or the camera wouldn't pick them out from a distance. I took a compass bearing on what looked to be the best option, a massive tree with a smattering of pods a quarter of a mile away, then abseiled back down to the ground to go look for it.

Mirko and I bushwhacked our way towards where it should have been, according to my bearing, but two hours later we realised we'd missed it. The forest was so dense and tangled it was barely possible to see fifty feet in any direction, so even an error of a few degrees would take us right past a 200-foot-tall tree without even knowing it. It was all getting ridiculous, and more than a little exasperating. So by the time we stumbled across a narrow trail winding through the trees I was ready for a rest, and dropped my rucksack to lie down. Mirko leant up against the base of a tree nearby, lost deep in thought while idly flicking at a twig with his machete.

A few minutes later I heard the sound of a man coming towards us at great speed, carrying a heavy load. Mirko stood up to face down the path and a moment later a *castañero*, one of the local nut-harvesters, appeared round the bend. His red shirt was soaked with sweat and on his back was an enormous black sack of Brazil nuts. A woven belt was wrapped around the load and strapped across his forehead, and his hands were clasped behind his neck to provide extra support. He leant forward as he half-walked, half-ran, along the trail, ducking and dodging vines and roots at great speed. That bag must have weighed as much as me. This was back-breaking work and I got to my feet out of sheer respect for the man. Looking up at us, he slowed to a halt and slid the sack down to the ground with a thump. Mirko and he knew each other, and sitting down on top of his hefty load the *castañero* lit a cigarette and smiled at us both through a mouth full of gold teeth. He was in his forties, I'd guess. Hard as nails, but as friendly as they came.

They chatted away in Spanish for a while before the man unpicked a corner of the bag and drew out a couple of freshly harvested nuts, handing one to Mirko and the other to me. I drew my knife, only to be told to use my teeth. There's a reason why Brazil nuts are the last to be eaten at Christmas, and the thought of trying to break into one with nothing but my molars didn't really appeal. But when I gave it a go I was astonished by how soft its shell was. It came away like orange peel and the nut inside bore no resemblance whatsoever to the concrete-hard imports we buy in shops back home. It had the milky texture of fresh coconut, breaking easily into soft flakes that tasted divine. Easily the best Brazil nut I'd ever tasted. Turns out that in order to comply with international trade regulations, all Brazil nuts are dried out thoroughly before leaving the country, to eliminate the risk of mould. Sounds sensible, but it's a shame nonetheless, because the nut I'd just eaten was simply delicious and I wish more people back home had the chance to try them in their natural state, full of sunshine.

Before moving on, the *castañero* suggested we check out the grove further down the trail. He'd spent the day there, but there were still plenty more pods swinging in the breeze twenty storeys up, ready to come down. We thanked him and helped him lift his heavy load. Taking a deep breath, he slid the strap down over his forehead, leant forward and took off down the path towards the shores of the lake at a steady trot. We'd run out of time to visit his grove that afternoon, but decided to head there immediately after sunrise the following morning.

• • •

The pod hanging in front of me was the size of a large grape-fruit, chocolate brown and weighing at least two kilos. It swayed gently on its stalk as I gave it a tap with my knuckle – hard as iron. I gave it a tentative pull and was happy to feel it still firmly attached to the branch. For such large pods – or cocos, as they were called locally – they had been surprisingly hard to spot from the ground. I'd caught sight of a few, but the canopy of a castaña is so dense, its dark-green leaves so large and shaggy, I'd had to climb the 170 feet up into the top of this giant just to be sure we'd found our tree at last. And in the same way as I'd struggled to get a clear view of flowers back in Los Amigos last year, I'd spent the last hour clambering around these enormous branches trying to get a handle on how many cocos were hanging here for us to film. Since the seedpods develop from pollinated flowers and those flowers only grow on the branches' extremities, it followed that this was where the vast majority of the cocos would be found. Looking around me now, I saw the silhouettes of dozens more dangling against the bright-white sky. Hundreds more were nestling in the thick foliage of other trees nearby. For some reason, this grove of giants was a couple of weeks behind the other trees closer to the lake shore. There were even a few wilted flower spikes still hanging on up here. These trees never stopped amazing me. The pods around me now had taken at least a year to grow and ripen. That's a big investment of time and energy for any tree. And to think that this tree accomplished such a feat year in, year out, was nothing short of remarkable.

It felt great to be back up in the canopy after so many days trudging around, searching on the forest floor. Mirko and I had left camp just after dawn that morning, barely saying a word to each other about our hopes for what we might find, just in case we jinxed it. But arriving at the *castañero's* grove an hour later, we'd both grinned with relief, dumped the rucksacks and set about peering up through the dense understorey to get a handle on which of the colossal trees we should attempt to climb first. Two huge piles of freshly opened pods showed where our friend had spent yesterday, extracting the nuts, which were arranged in the pod like the segments of an orange. *Castañeros* don't climb up to pick the pods, they simply collect those that have fallen already. And since it was a still day with barely a breeze ruffling the leaves high above us, I figured it would be safe enough to climb up beneath the others that were up there. Even so, I'd make sure to keep close to the trunk, away from the edge of the canopy where the pods were hanging. People are killed by them every year – with or without helmets. Rock-hard pods weighing two kilos, falling 150 feet, take no prisoners.

So having struck castaña gold, Mirko and I set about rigging the cable-cam for a tracking shot through the grove at canopy level. These days a camera shot like this would be done via remote-controlled drone, but back then – in the days of film – we didn't have drones and the camera alone weighed five kilos, so things were a little different. By late afternoon, I was drenched with sweat and knackered. But both trees at either end of the cable run had been rigged, and the steel cable had been hoisted up into position 150 feet above the ground between them.

Just as I was putting the finishing touches to the rigging, a weather front swept in. The sky had been growing increasingly dark to the east, and as I prepared to head down a strong wind blew through the grove. Nothing too violent, just a cushion of air displaced by the heavy rain on its heels. But it was enough to start dislodging pods. The first one came down with a dull thud that echoed through the trees, followed by a yell of warning from Mirko. It had missed him by several metres, but he ran in towards the shelter of the castaña's trunk below me and shouted for me to hurry up and get down – we had to get out of there quickly. The thuds grew more regular as the wind stiffened and a pod come down to hit a branch ten feet away before ricocheting out through the side of the canopy towards the ground a hundred feet below. I yelled a warning to Mirko and dropped faster down the rope.

By the time I reached the floor, the canopy above us was swaying all over the place and we could hear rain coming. I got in as close to the tree trunk as I could, but as I bent over my rucksack to flake the rope in for the night, there was a rush of air and a pod the size and weight of a cannonball hit the ground barely three feet away. It came down with so much force it actually blew leaves aside before embedding itself in the soil so that only its top half was visible. That was enough for both of us, and still in my harness I legged it down the trail behind Mirko as fast as I could, cringing to the sound of more pods smashing into the ground behind us.

• • •

The rain set in for the night, but stopped just after dawn. The sun came out and the jungle began to steam. On our way back to film at the grove, we almost stepped on a beautiful feather lying softly on top of the leaf litter in the middle of the trail. Mirko stooped down to pick it up before presenting it to me with a smile: 'For you: *pluma de águila arpía*.' A feather from the breast of a harpy eagle. What a gift. It was beautiful. Ivory fading to grey, with charcoal bands. 'She has been here this morning,' he said, looking around as if expecting to see her on a branch right above us, 'probably hunting agouti.'

Agoutis were the missing link in our castaña story. Gentle, timid rodents, a little like large brown guinea pigs. The best view of one I'd had was the poor unfortunate creature covered in mosquitoes in Costa Rica. But this humble creature is one of only a few mammals in the entire Amazon with teeth sharp enough to chisel through the coco's shell and extract the Brazil nuts. What's more, being rodents hardwired to squirrel things away for a rainy day, they carry off and bury any nuts they don't eat. And in good rodent fashion, they often forget exactly where they've stashed them (or indeed get nailed by a harpy) before they can return to dig them up. Either way the next generation of castaña trees germinates and round we go.

As if to prove the point, Mirko found a freshly opened coco at the base of our tree. One of the pods that had fallen the previous day. It was now nothing more than a hollow shell with a freshly chiselled hole in its side through which the agouti had extracted each individual nut. The animal had clearly had a busy evening, and somewhere nearby a couple of dozen nuts were buried in the leaf litter, destined to be either eaten at a later date, or abandoned and allowed to germinate. The last amazing fact about the castaña tree is that once a nut *does* germinate, it can remain as a seedling for years, if not decades, just waiting for an all-important light gap to appear in the canopy above. In this way, a foot-tall castaña sapling could easily be thirty years old. Just biding its time for a place in the sun.

Our last day of filming went well. Mirko and I got the shots we needed, and combined with the bulk of the sequence shot by Kevin and Rupert, the castaña's fascinating story had been told. And what a story it is: the jungle giant that relies for its very survival on a bee's taste in orchid perfume, and a rodent's forgetful memory. For me, everything about these magnificent trees seems to embody the very heart and soul of the Amazon, the greatest, most complex rainforest on earth.

Chapter 6

Roaring Meg – Australia

2008

It was a warm autumn day in the temperate rainforests of the Hume Plateau, south-east Australia. The air was thick with the tangy aroma of eucalyptus oil evaporating from leaves in the afternoon's heat. This vapour created a light-blue haze that drifted gently through the trees, the breath of the forest made visible. Leaning against an enormous fallen tree trunk, I inhaled deeply to allow as much of the aromatic air to enter my lungs as possible. My heart slowed as I exhaled. I was feeling calm and relaxed and it felt good to stretch my legs after the long-haul flight from England to Melbourne.

What a journey that had been. Stuck at the back of a 747 for almost twenty-four hours, surrounded by drunk gap-year kids. But I was here now, and there was no time to lose. We had only three days to shoot a half-hour film about climbing and sleeping the night aloft in one of the tallest trees in the southern hemisphere. This was just about manageable so long as everything went to plan. But on top of this, our presenter, Guy, had never climbed a tree before. Talk about in at the deep end. He'd have to learn the ropes pretty quickly, that's for sure. I wasn't too worried about it, though: he looked pretty handy and was up for the challenge. We could give him some training when he joined us tomorrow. In the meantime, before anything else could happen, we had to find a suitable tree, and as usual this was proving easier said than done.

Thankfully, my companions on this adventure included two of Australia's best big-tree experts. Between them, Tom and Brett had discovered, climbed and measured most of the country's champion trees, and the fallen trunk next to me was testament to the fact that Australia is home to some very tall trees indeed.

Eucalyptus regnans, known locally as mountain ash, is the second tallest species of tree on earth, rivalled in height only by the coast redwoods of California. The tallest mountain ash so far discovered is a 327-foot-tall living skyscraper called Centurion growing in Tasmania. Nipping at its heels is the Douglas fir of Oregon (another conifer like the coast redwood). In fact, the fourth and fifth tallest species of tree are also both conifers native to the Pacific North West. So Australia's mountain ash really is an exceptional tree. By far and away the tallest angiosperm – flowering plant – on the planet and certainly the tallest living thing in the southern hemisphere.

In fact, many people – not just Aussies – consider mountain ash to be the one-time tallest species of tree on earth. Legends of 430-foot-tall giants loom out of the mists of the nineteenth century. But such issues are for the botanically pedantic. The bottom line is that at around 300 feet tall, the trees I'd caught tantalising glimpses of from the back seat of the 4 × 4 on our way north from Melbourne were by far the tallest living things I had ever seen.

I'd been desperate to visit these hallowed forests for as long as I could remember. For a tree lover they were the stuff of legend. The dead hulk next to me simply whetted my appetite all the more and I was keen to get up close and personal with a living mountain ash as soon as possible.

Tom and Brett had forged on through the forest ahead of me, a ragged curtain of fern fronds swaying in their wake as the dense undergrowth swallowed them from view. I'd catch them up in minute, but there was something about this fallen tree that bothered me. I clambered up onto its bulk and looked down its length towards the jagged silhouette of its stump 200 feet away at the other end. The whole tree had snapped off just above the ground. I turned round to look up the fallen stem in the other direction in an attempt to estimate how tall it must have been in life, but the enormous column disappeared into a ruin of broken branches and tangled undergrowth twenty feet away. This made the tree's trunk alone about 220 feet long and on top of this would have been its canopy, so the tree could easily have been approaching thirty storeys before it fell. Beneath my feet, long strips of twisted bark had unravelled to expose hard grey timber fractured into jagged cracks by the trunk's impact with the ground. It must've come down with a real wallop. The stump itself looked solid from here, but appearances can be deceptive and on closer inspection it proved to be almost hollow, with a rotten heart. I knew nothing about mountain ash. I'd never seen one of these trees before, let alone climbed one, and its condition begged the question: how would you know if the tree you were climbing was rotten or not?

Jumping back down, I set off to follow Tom and Brett further into the forest. Pushing through the ferns, I felt their serrated edges rasp against my face. Their fronds had appeared soft and delicate at first glance – a tactile reminder that all was not what it seemed, and that plants needed to be tough and resilient to survive here.

Beyond lay an open understorey of thin, moss-covered trunks belonging to young silver wattle and blackwood. Small trees that spread their branches into parasols of delicate leaves twenty or thirty feet above me. Between these stood yet more tree ferns, their dark, scaly stems supporting long, drooping foliage that glowed emerald green in the late-afternoon sun. Their presence gave the forest an ancient atmosphere. Prehistoric survivors from a time long before eucalyptus trees evolved.

The forest floor was a tangled mat of shredded bark. Long, thin strips strewn in a thick carpet, like giant pencil shavings.

I bent down to pick up a piece: tinder-dry and brittle. I crushed it in my hand and rolled the dust between my fingers. It smelled spicy and bitter, the same aroma that filled the warm air. The occasional large sheet of bark lay on top of the rest of the litter. These enormous twisted rolls of parchment had come from the mountain ash towering high above everything else.

Just as I was wondering which way to go, there was a distant 'whoop!' answered by another off to my left. I caught up with Brett at the flared base of a colossal tree. He was squinting up at its summit through an inclinometer, trying to gauge an approximate height – checking and rechecking his calculations. My first impression of the tree was that it was way too thin for its extreme height. It seemed out of proportion. Most other tree species of this height were substantially bigger in volume, more chunky and imposing, but what this tree lacked in mass it more than made up for in grace and beauty.

The base of its trunk flared out in a fluted star shape and the patches of thin, dry moss that covered it turned to powder as I moved my hand across them. Beneath the moss the bark was smooth, with a slightly crinkled surface of mottled brown and ivory. It felt hard and unyielding, like bone.

At a height of fifty feet, long thin strips of bark were flaking away to hang in streamers, as if the tree was shedding its skin like a huge reptile or insect. Above this, its newly emerged bark was silver and looked smooth and fresh, like it had just emerged from a chrysalis. This stem continued on its way upwards, ramrod straight with no branches, for around 200 feet. The lowest branches were no more than amputated rotten stumps jutting out twenty storeys above our heads. The first living branches of any size or strength were another thirty or forty feet higher. For a tree of this size the branches were pretty small. Some were straight, others twisted and gnarled, but I could see from their open unions with the main stem that this was a strong, clean timber. *'Except for where it's riddled with hidden rot and cavities,'* I said to myself in warning, remembering the snapped-off trunk I'd seen.

Brett let the eyeglass of the inclinometer drop back around his neck and set about busily stabbing the keyboard of an anti-quated calculator in a frantic finger burst of algebraic mania. Smart bloke, Brett. He was the mathematical brains behind our endeavour and was charged with finding us a new champ-ion tree to climb for the film. Tom would be Guy's climbing guide, while I would hang on the ropes next to them, filming their ascent and the night they spent in the canopy. All of us would then continue up to the very tip-top the following morning to film Tom and Brett measuring the tree. Brett's initial survey from the ground would give us a ballpark figure, but even in this age of satellites and lasers the only way to be completely sure of a tree's height is to drop a tape measure. There's something reassuringly old-school and lo-tech about this that I love.

Brett was still lost in trigonometry and his expression wasn't revealing anything, so I squinted back up into the dazzling light to take a closer look at the tree's canopy. The branches supported an open crown of feathery leaves, but the canopy was surprisingly small. There just didn't seem to be enough greenery up there to provide energy for such a huge tree. I had noticed this before in places like Borneo, where some of the largest trees appeared to get by with surprisingly sparse foliage. I presumed this was a survival technique evolved by tall trees growing in areas regularly buffeted by strong winds. Open canopies present less wind resistance and minimise sail effect. My hunch that this forest had to contend with some serious weather was further confirmed by the fallen debris strewn across the forest floor and the large amount of dead wood still hanging precariously in the canopy hundreds of feet above us. These loose snags of dead timber seemed to teeter, ready to come down with the next breath of wind. To climb directly beneath one would be tempting fate. Even on a still day, it's all too easy to dislodge loose material with your climbing rope. The last thing a climber wants is a fifty-kilo timber javelin sliding down their line at sixty miles per hour towards them.

On the plus side, these trees were so open that it should be easy to spot the hanging deadwood and avoid climbing beneath it. Unfortunately this same openness would also make for an intimidating and exposed climb. We were going to have to deal with some extreme height and the first 250 feet of branchless trunk were going to be pretty intense.

Most of the world's really tall trees are conifers. In a red-wood, fir or spruce, a climber finds themselves cocooned within a comforting web of branches and foliage. The physical horizon contracts to give a false sense of security and it's easy to forget how high you are until you reach the top. The tallest known tree on earth is a coast redwood growing in California, called Hyperion. It measures a staggering 380 feet tall, and has a dense, welcoming canopy that swaddles a climber like a fur coat. Thirty-eight storeys is still a long way – a full five seconds of terrifying freefall – but the point is that climbing a tree like Hyperion, one that shields you from the precarious nature of your situation, can be a much more relaxing and enjoyable experience than climbing one that keeps your heart in your mouth and has you looking over your shoulder every other second.

The tree I was looking at now was sporting the canopy equivalent of a string vest rather than a fur coat. It was stark and uncompromising. I mentally projected myself 200 feet up. What would it feel like to be dangling there, having not even reached the first branch? I smiled to myself – it wouldn't be long now until I found out. My heart picked up a pace and I felt the familiar tingle of noradrenaline seep into my muscles.

There was another fallen trunk lying in the undergrowth nearby. Tom appeared, walking down its length towards us. He cupped his hands around his eyes to peer up into the canopy before jumping down next to Brett.

'What do you reckon?' he asked.

'Could be a 300-footer; might be a bit less,' answered Brett.

Any tree above 285 feet tall would be a champion: one of the tallest on mainland Australia. We wouldn't know for certain exactly how tall it was though, until we got up there and dropped the tape. First impressions were rarely to be trusted. Experienced hands that they were, Tom and Brett knew this well. So in addition to Brett's trigonometry, they wanted to complete one other final check before committing us to climbing this particular tree …

It had previously occurred to me that in a forest like this, where all the mature trees appeared so similar, it must be tricky to single out the one individual that stood marginally taller than the others. There may be only inches between them and it is notoriously difficult to get a clear line of sight from the ground to a tree's topmost twig. Canopies tend to have domed profiles and often present a series of what mountaineers call 'false summits' to anyone peering up from far below. So who was to say that the tree growing just to our right wasn't six inches taller than the one in front of us? We didn't have time to hedge our bets by climbing several different candidates, so I presumed Tom and Brett had a method for solving this conundrum. I asked Tom and was told to watch and wait.

'All will be revealed,' he said.

The day was getting on and shadows were creeping up the silver trunks like fingers. The three of us made ourselves comfortable on the fallen log, and as dusk condensed I asked Brett why the ash trees around us were so similar in size. Surely younger trees must be growing up through the understorey all the time.

'This is a fire-climax ecosystem,' he replied. 'Every couple of centuries a bushfire of sufficient ferocity sweeps through the forest, wiping out everything in its path. But even as the trees are dying in the flames, the heat from the fire dries their seedpods, which crack open to deposit millions of seeds onto a thick bed of fertile ash below after the fire has passed. And so the next generation is sown, rising like a phoenix from the flames.'

'So these giants aren't as old as they look?' I asked.

'This one here,' Brett said, gesturing towards our current favourite, 'is probably only about 300 years old. This whole stand of regnans is thought to have germinated after a fire in the early 1700s. It's due a burn. It *wants* to burn, that's the terrifying thing.

'These are fast-growing trees,' he went on. 'They invest a lot in speed and leave little energy to deal with the rot and cavities that can eventually bring them down … like this one.' He gave the log we were on a pat. 'These guys around us now are nearing the end of their natural lives. They're already falling apart. If they die from old age before the next fire comes through, before they get the chance to drop viable seed, the mountain ash might disappear from here.'

'Sooner or later it is inevitable, a fire will go through here,' added Tom. 'It'll be a searingly hot day and the whole thing will go up massively, and in the space of an hour or two it'll all be over. That'll be that. It'll be gone.'

I looked around me at the forest, which seemed so ancient and permanent. Three centuries was young compared with the long lives of many other trees, and I found it hard to reconcile the short-lived nature of this ephemeral ecosystem with the sheer scale of the eucalyptus looming above. Taking a closer look, it was easy to see what a volatile environment this really was. The ground, the air, everything around me was bone dry. There was no sign of water and the hot air was full of highly flammable eucalyptus oil. Even the long tapers of oil-soaked bark hanging like wicks from the trees began to take on a sinister appearance. These monumental trees would go up like Molotov cocktails, and all it would take would be one lightning strike or a carelessly thrown cigarette. This was an elemental land, completely at the mercy of the precarious relationship between earth, fire, air and water. A giant tinderbox ready to go.

The evening was getting on and many of the trees were now completely obscured by shadow. But a few of the taller ones, including ours, still had their topmost foliage bathed in beautiful light. Each tree was eventually eclipsed by the rising shadows, snuffed out like candles one by one until only the individual Brett had chosen remained illuminated by the very last rays of the setting sun. It was clearly at least a foot or two taller than its neighbours. So that settled it, we'd found our climb.

• • •

The following morning we were joined by Mel and Guy, director and presenter. The previous day had been time well spent and we headed straight to our chosen tree. Hefting one of our many kitbags onto my back, I bent down and picked up the camera. Jetlag was catching up with me and I'd been wide awake since midnight. It was now just after six and I was already three coffees down. It was going to be a long couple of days. My plan was to allow caffeine to segue into adrenaline once we started the climb.

The walk to the tree was beautiful, the forest was sparkling. The low morning sun seemed to highlight texture in everything it touched. Tiny hairs on the fiddleheads of newly opened ferns shone like halos and fine dust swirled gently through slices of light. The tall silver trunks of trees were slashed with tiger stripes of gold, while high above us the canopy shimmered in the breeze. An exquisitely beautiful forest, but Brett's words came back to haunt me. It was a forest living on borrowed time.

The plan was for Tom to head up first and secure a couple of ropes for myself and Guy around one of the higher branches. I would climb up alongside Guy, concentrating on filming his ascent. I'd also be responsible for his safety: he'd stay permanently attached to two different ropes and I'd remain close to him at all times, so I could easily sort him out if he got in a jam. Mel would remain on the ground, filming us from below. She'd stay in contact with us via radio.

I leant back against the huge fallen tree trunk and slid the heavy rucksack off my shoulders. It hadn't been opened since our arrival and the rope inside still felt cool from the twenty-four hours it had spent at 35,000 feet. I ran every inch of it through my hands as I flaked it neatly onto the ground beside me. The rope was in good condition, practically brand new, so it didn't need checking, but I find the act of running a rope through my hands before use an important part of preparing myself for a big climb.

The taut thump of a high-powered crossbow made me look up. Tom was standing fifty feet away with the bow still raised to his shoulder. I tracked the bolt's progress until it disappeared into the turquoise haze high above. Fishing line whisked off a reel with a high-pitched hiss, tugged airborne in a neon spiral. There was a pause as the bolt reached its zenith and hung there in a moment of apparent indecision, followed by an accelerating whine as gravity won the day and it came barrelling back down. Tom let it run like a fish, winding the slack in gently to keep it snag-free. Squinting up through the ragged propellers of tree ferns, I traced the line's route, but lost it in the bright haze twenty-five storeys up. The sun was now high and the sky burned with a cool intensity. A stark, almost metallic blue that seemed to fizz with ultraviolet. Pulses of reflected light raced up and down the fishing line as it billowed gently in the breeze. The crossbow bolt was now hanging five feet aboveground on the other side of the tree, spinning slowly on its thread. A gentle breeze blew through the canopy high above and the bolt rose a few inches before dropping back down to continue spinning.

'Can you see which branch it's over?' I asked Tom.

'Not sure. Hoping it's the top right-hand fork,' he replied.

The branch Tom referred to was the right-hand prong of a pair of limbs that crowned the top of the tree like antlers. The line could be pulled back over a couple of smaller snags and dropped into a snug position between the antlers a few feet below. But to my surprise Tom started attaching his climbing rope to the line straightaway. No adjustments necessary – he was happy with its position and eager to get on with the climb. A thin red climbing rope snaked up on its thread like an Indian rope trick, as Tom turned the handle of the fishing reel. Taking hold of the line with gloved hands when the rope reached the top branch, Tom hauled it over, back down to the forest floor. The climbing rope was eight millimetres in diameter. Made of low-stretch, high-tensile Kevlar, it had the load capacity of a much thicker standard nylon line, but was so thin it looked like bootlace. I normally climb on ten-millimetre, and believe me – those extra two millimetres go a long way towards helping you relax at height.

Tom wrapped the rope end around the fallen trunk next to us and pulled himself up off the ground to test the strength of the branch high above. I could see the antler flexing, dipping like a fishing rod in response. It held and nothing gave, so he repeated the process with the combined weight of him and Brett. The branch bent further but continued to hold. If it could support two people's weight at five feet aboveground, it could hold Tom's weight at 300 feet. The logic was sound, but it still made my teeth itch to trace that thin rope up and over its wrist-thick branch high above. Because the rope passed over the branch from our side and Tom would be climbing from the other, if the branch did break, the rope would be caught by the fork at the base of the antler ten feet below. He'd be spared a 300-foot plummet, but even a ten-foot drop would be quite a ride on a single rope with no elasticity to absorb the shock.

There's no way on earth I would have climbed such a thin rope supported by such a slender and isolated branch. But I knew Tom well enough to realise that he operated on

a much higher courage level than I did. I had never seen him
rattled under pressure and still remember with vivid clarity the
first time I'd watched him climb a few years earlier in 2005
on a trip to Borneo. We'd both been members of a National
Geographic Society expedition in search of the world's tallest
tropical hardwood tree. I'd played a minor supporting role.
But as the teams lead climber, it had been Tom that first found
a way up to the very top of what turned out to be a new world
record. He has an extremely quick and fluid climbing style,
often running along branches to leap out into the void before
landing again with perfect poise like a gymnast on another
branch thirty feet away. I had long since learned to let go of
any misplaced anxiety I might feel while watching him, and
now reminded myself to simply enjoy the experience of
climbing alongside one of the world's best.

Tom was ready to go, so I grabbed the camera. He put
on his helmet, tucked his trousers into his socks and clipped
his chest and hand clamps to the thin red rope. He sat back
in his harness, raised his knees and began to climb, inch-
worming rapidly up through space. All eyes were on him as he
emerged from the understorey into the openness above. He
was hanging fifteen feet away from the trunk, gently spinning
as he climbed. Above him the rope was taut, while below him
it danced in a crazy helix of red energy.

The clink of karabiners and the soft rub of rope drifted
down to us through an unnatural silence. The forest was
watchful, quiet and still – a pensive silence within which the
slightest sound echoed.

While Brett watched Tom's ascent with a smile, Guy stood with arms folded, looking on in silence. His eyes were wide and I knew what he was thinking. Tom's presence gave the scene a sense of scale and he was dwarfed by the monumental size of the tree. I understood Guy's trepidation, but also knew that the only way to nip it in the bud was to get on with the climb.

The low stretch in the Kevlar rope allowed Tom to move swiftly skywards and he was soon arriving in the tree's upper crown. The distant sound of a karabiner banging against hollow timber was immediately answered by the strident call of a kookaburra.

Tom lowered a thin throw line and hauled up our climbing ropes. Anchoring these off around a branch, he sat back to admire the view and waited for us to climb up and join him. After an all-too-brief practice climb, Guy was now waiting for me twenty feet aboveground. I slung the camera over my shoulder and clambered up onto the fallen log next to the tree and slotted the rope into my climbing clamps, which snapped shut with a satisfying click. The rope had me now and I was tied to the giant tree. Everything felt taut and ready to go, so stepping off the log I swung in to begin my ascent. My pulse quickened as I slid the clamps up the rope as far as I could reach. I was off and for the next twenty-four hours this forest giant would be my home.

Guy and I were still below the understorey, but looking around I could see that once we broke through the shelter of the tree ferns and entered the space above we should be able to see for hundreds of feet in every direction. We pressed on, side by side, stopping every now and then to film Guy's reactions to the climb.

We were now level with the lower tips of several enormous shreds of bark peeling off the tree above. Pulling one out towards me, I was surprised by how heavy it felt. I let it go and it thumped solidly back against the trunk to release a small shower of dust and debris that fell down to the ground. Looking up, I could see that it was attached to the tree thirty feet above our heads. The whole trunk was girdled with similar strips hanging down, like a giant half-peeled banana. The dead bark was thick and tough like sun-dried leather, more animal than tree.

I hadn't realised just how much of this heavy material there was hanging on by threads right above our heads. Reaching round the side of the tree with my left hand I gave one of them a gentle tug – solid. So I gave it a proper yank, expecting it to unzip and roll down the tree like wet wallpaper, but it didn't budge. This made me happier about spending the next thirty feet dangling beneath them, but I decided to push on up as fast as we could anyway.

Continuing our climb, I made sure to nudge the strips to one side before placing my feet between them on the solid trunk beneath. While doing this I disturbed a large flat spider that skeeted over my boot to instantly disappear back into the shadows. There must have been an entire hidden ecosystem living beneath the hanging bark. I really wanted to know more about what was going on in there, but had no intention of poking my nose in where it wasn't wanted. I'd wondered why Tom tucked his trousers into his socks before climbing – now

I knew. I followed suit. The insect life beneath the bark also explained Tom's gloves, but there was no way I could operate the camera while wearing mine, so they remained hanging unused on the back of my harness.

A few minutes later I reached the top of the bark strips, the place from where they bent double to hang down in long pennants. This was the place at which the tree seemed to shed its old skin to emerge all bright, shiny and new. But what had appeared uniform silver from a distance was actually a subtle montage of many hues and felt more like human skin than tree bark when my fingers brushed lightly across its surface.

My desire to get above the hanging bark as quickly as possible had been a distraction and the view that now greeted me for the first time as I twisted round on my rope took my breath away. I was above the understorey, hanging in open space above the tree ferns and wattle trees, but still far below the upper canopy. Huge silver trunks marched away from us into the hazy-blue distance on all sides, appearing to glimmer like shafts of light through deep water. The combined effect of those regularly spaced columns was sublime, almost Zen-like in its ethereal beauty. I had never seen such a graceful forest.

Dragging my eyes away from the view I realised that we still had a lot to do and time was passing quickly. It was gone midday and I needed to get on with filming Guy's climb. We also had a canopy camp to build before nightfall, but Guy was hanging spellbound, staring at the view. I hadn't the heart to disturb him, so waited until he was ready before suggesting we press on to join Tom as quickly as we could.

At a hundred feet aboveground we were now about halfway up the trunk, an open transitional zone where the only choice was to continue climbing. Bouncing out from the stem on my rope, I craned my neck to take a look at the canopy still high above. Our ropes seemed to go up forever, to converge on a single point somewhere unseen in the sky. From here I could see hundreds of bright-green tree ferns in the foliage far below. Tom was waiting for us on a huge branch when we finally arrived in the canopy. We were still a good thirty or forty feet below the top of the tree, but these lower branches were perfect for rigging our hammocks in. We'd sleep here. Guy edged back to gently transfer his weight onto the limb next to him. Throwing the end of a short, adjustable rope over a fork ten feet above, I transferred my weight off the long rope connecting me to the forest floor 250 feet below. The shorter rope I now hung from offered the flexibility to move quickly between branches and get shots of Tom and Guy chatting. But it also enabled me to take a closer look at the tree's structure itself. We would be spending the next twenty hours up here so I might as well take a moment to get to know my new home a little better.

There were fewer loose strips of bark up here and the exposed timber was smooth, with the fine grain of ivory. The thin canopy foliage left the entire architecture of the tree fully exposed. Its bones were laid bare, and I found this honesty of structure a refreshing change from the filthy, debris-smothered limbs of jungle hardwoods. I could run the palm of my hand along a branch and feel the flow and grain of timber. Feel the way it swirled around the cracks and cavities of the main stem. I noticed subtle details such as the corrugations at the base of a branch, like ripples in sand, and began to understand how Tom, with his decades of experience in these forests, must see these trees. How he must be able to read the strength in the timber at a glance. His anchor point still high above us on the right-hand fork of the antler was no thicker than my arm, but his decision to trust his life to it had been based on countless hours climbing these trees, rooted in an innate understanding of how they grew.

The main stem was several feet thick even at this height. Looking out into the void below, I reckoned we were about 260 feet up, a full 100 feet higher than Goliath. There were several cavities in the trunk. Some were completely open, and once again I had to suppress my instinct to stick my hand in for a feel. A spider bite twenty-six storeys up in a tree would never do. Other holes were plugged with twisted and cracked spirals of old dead wood, the remains of rotten branches. The whole tree was riddled with nooks and crannies, a fantastic habitat undoubtedly supporting a whole variety of life. I wondered what was going to crawl out of the woodwork after dark.

The main access lines below me began to stretch and I knew Brett was on his way up to join us. It was mid afternoon and high time to rig our camp for the night. Finding enough anchor points to position multiple hammocks side by side in a tree can be a tricky business. Each one requires a fore and aft attachment, and the whole thing can snarl up into a tangle of nylon straps and webbing if you aren't careful. Tom set about rigging his and Brett's, while I sorted mine and Guy's. I was keen to film Guy on our infrared camera during the night from the comfort of my own hammock, so had an interest in rigging them fairly close together. Tom quickly got stuck in, whirling around the canopy like a dervish, and I got a few shots of Guy watching him do his stuff. By the time we were set it was late afternoon and the ground far below was already in shadow. I made sure Guy remained attached to his abseil device, so if we had to bail out of the tree in the middle of the night he could get down to the ground with as little drama as possible. All he'd have to do would be to roll out of his hammock and press the lever.

With the filming finished for a few hours, I unrolled my sleeping bag, dropped down into the hammock and stretched out. The blood in my legs flowed back up into my body and I loosened my harness leg loops a little to get comfy. The others were chatting quietly as I propped myself on an elbow to look out over the forest.

At 260 feet above the forest floor this was the highest I had ever slept in a tree. Peering over the edge, straight down the long tapering trunk to the carpet far below, it suddenly felt absurd to be perched so high up – to deliberately choose to sleep on a bed of canvas hanging twenty-five storeys aboveground. A sharp sweat pin-pricked my forehead and I felt momentarily off balance. I immersed myself in this feeling until it passed, revelling in the cathartic sensation of falling, safe in the knowledge that I was securely attached and wasn't going anywhere unless the whole tree went down. There was no danger of that on such a still, peaceful evening.

The colour gradually seeped out of the scene until all became a watercolour wash of blue and purple. The silver columns of other trees were the last things to dissolve into the night, melting away one by one like ghosts. All was now dark and silent. I rolled onto my back and looked up into the branches. The exertion of the climb took its toll and I fell asleep.

• • •

When I awoke a few hours later, the air was thick, still and inky black. I instinctively groped for my rope, giving it a tug to confirm I was still attached. I'd been jolted awake by something, but what? Lying in the dark, I waited for an answer. There was a pensive atmosphere and as a breeze began to blow I heard the ominous sounds of timber creaking in the darkness around us. The wind grew stronger and was soon accompanied by distant thuds and hollow bangs echoing through the forest as heavy strips of bark swung around like enormous wind chimes. Something was brewing, and I lay there feeling sudden updraughts of air sway my hammock from side to side.

The storm hit us around two in the morning. A wall of warm air came out of the darkness, dislodging deadwood that rained down from the trees to hit the ground with resounding booms. Timber groaned under the strain and the whole tree started to heave like the mainmast on a square-rigger. I felt the pull of my rope as the branches moved up and down in the darkness above me. Turning on my head torch, I peered over the edge of my hammock only to duck back quickly as a blizzard of spinning leaves blew out of the night into my face. The darkness was impenetrable, so I turned my torch off and focused on what I could hear instead. My world was now a blind confusion of swirling sound, and our tall slender tree was swaying all over the place. I found myself wondering how much worse this was going to get – should we bale out? The image of the rotten fallen tree came back to haunt me, and I wondered whether ours was also filled with cavities quietly undermining its strength.

Leaving my head torch off, I viewed the scene through the infrared mode of the camera I'd brought. Guy was moving around inside his sleeping bag, but I couldn't tell if he was awake or not. Tom and Brett's hammocks were on the other side of the trunk from me, and in an effort to see if they were still asleep I made the mistake of standing up in my hammock just at the moment a gust hit the tree. I was knocked off balance and blown out to spin through the darkness on my rope. Pulling myself back in, I leant into the wind and braced my feet flat against the enormous trunk. A spilt second later everything seemed to lean away from me as a powerful gust swept through the canopy like a train, catching my empty hammock like a sail to fling my sleeping bag and kip mat out into the void.

Guy was now awake, staring into the darkness with his right hand grasping the rope above him, but neither Tom nor Brett had moved a muscle. They lay cocooned in their sleeping bags as if nothing was happening. There was no way on earth they could be sleeping through it, so I took confidence from the fact they hadn't bailed out. Relaxing a little, I relinquished myself to the sensation of being blown about on my rope like a conker on a string. Hanging there in the swirling air felt like skydiving.

The violent gusts eventually smoothed out and calmed down a little, so I stepped back into my hammock and lay listening to the distant booms and rattles of other trees dancing in the dark around us. The wind died completely just before dawn. I woke up covered in twigs and leaves and peered down into the forest, but my sleeping bag was nowhere to be seen. The air was still and the storm had passed like a phantom in the night.

The sun hadn't yet risen. There was dust in the air and the predawn twilight had a slightly sickly, yellow cast to it. Tom stood up and swung across, Tarzan-style, to land on the branch next to Guy, who greeted him with: 'Just tea or coffee, thanks, Tom; no need for the full cooked breakfast.' He'd done well, considering this was the first tree he'd ever slept in. It had been a rough night.

We derigged the hammocks and sent them down with Brett. There was still plenty of tree left above us to climb and Tom led the way up this final pitch. The trunk was tapering quickly and now measured two feet in diameter – it also appeared to be completely hollow. I peered into a cavity to see daylight streaming in from the other side. This time I couldn't resist the temptation to put my arm clean through the entire stem. We were climbing a hollow tube and there was still another twenty feet of tree above us.

When I glanced up at Tom, he answered my silent query with a broad grin: 'Don't worry, this is strong stuff. It can survive fine without heartwood.'

Could the combined weight of three climbers in its upper branches tip the balance, though, and cause a catastrophic stem failure? Possibly, but we were here now, so I blanked these thoughts from my mind and pressed on regardless. Tom was now at the top of the main stem, sitting in a large fork where two branches shot up at opposite angles. These were the antlers we'd seen from below. We'd made it to within a few feet of the very top of the tree. As we joined him, he made a quick assessment as to which prong was the highest and threw a bundle of rope over a slender branch before scampering up with the large measuring reel swinging from the back of his harness. We were now about 280 feet aboveground and the branch Tom was shinning up was no thicker than my forearm. It looked extremely precarious, but I had to trust that he knew what he was doing.

The wind was picking up again, hitting the tree in sporadic waves. Every gust put the branches that supported our weight under increased strain. Timber is well designed to cope with dynamic forces, but these were not big branches. As Tom, buffeted by the wind on the right-hand antler, lowered the tape measure it billowed out into a huge white arc. The reel span with a high-pitched squeal as its weighted end accelerated down through space. After what seemed an eternity we heard the distant echo of a thud and Tom's radio crackled into life. Brett had retrieved the tape and was now standing at the base of the tree:

'Okay, reel it in. Hold it. Right … okay, read it off there,' he said.

Tom pulled the tape taut and peered close at the numbers: 'Two hundred and eighty-nine feet, four inches,' he said into the radio.

The wind was really picking up again, so Tom dropped back down the rope to land on a rotten snag next to Guy and they shook hands for the camera. Our tree was thirty-eight feet shorter than Centurion in Tasmania, and 14 feet shorter than the tallest mountain ash on mainland Australia: a giant known as Big Ash One, growing less than a mile away from us in the same forest. At 303 feet tall – roughly the same height as the Statue of Liberty – Big Ash One had held onto its title by a clear margin. But any tree taller than 285 feet was still a very rare and special thing deserving recognition. Our tree could therefore take its place with pride amongst the top dozen tallest trees on the mainland.

Tom's radio crackled into life again: 'I've thought of a name for her,' said Brett. 'Roaring Meg.'

Roaring because of the howling storm we'd experienced during the night, but *Meg*? Only Brett knows the answer to that one, but it seemed to suit her perfectly.

Guy and Tom began their long descents back to earth, but I wanted to take a few moments to think about what we'd achieved, so I stayed behind, watching the tops of trees dancing in the breeze around me. The climb had been a success. Roaring Meg might not have been the tallest, but she was a beauty, and what an adventure we'd had sleeping in her branches. I'd also achieved a new personal best, having climbed over 285 feet in a tree for the first time in my life.

If I'd known then what was to come, I would have spent longer up there than I did, taking my time to savour that once-in-a-lifetime opportunity. But all too soon, I found myself abseiling back down to rejoin the world of schedules and long-haul flights. Meg is the one and only mountain ash I've ever climbed and I think I'd like to keep it that way: after all, she's a tough act to follow.

• • •

Roaring Meg died less than a year after our visit. In February 2009 the worst bushfires in Australian history raged through the state of Victoria. On 7 February, as temperatures in Melbourne reached forty-six degrees centigrade, north-westerly winds of up to seventy-eight miles per hour swept across the state, bringing down power lines to the west of the Hume Plateau. The ensuing fires spread through grassland to enter a pine plantation before heading south-east through residential areas and the national park, arriving at the town of Kinglake five hours later. The Kinglake fire complex, as it became known, continued to burn for a month before it was eventually contained in early March. By which time 820,000 acres had succumbed to its flames.

Meg was located in the Wallaby Creek catchment area inside Kinglake National Park, in the direct path of the inferno. When I spoke to Brett again recently he explained that Wallaby Creek 'would be unrecognisable now. A sea of eight-to-fifteen-metre-tall regrowth, with an ever dwindling cohort of light-grey eighty-metre dead towers above.'

Most of the tallest and biggest *Eucalyptus regnans* are now confined to the island of Tasmania. But who knows? Maybe in another two or three centuries' time there will be a giant tree carrying Meg's DNA standing in her place.

The Kinglake fire was just one of a whole series of multiple fires that merged and fragmented to rage across the entire region north-east of Melbourne in 2009. More than 1 million acres were destroyed in total and 1,200 homes were lost. Four hundred and fourteen people were injured and 173 lost their lives.

It's hard to lament the demise of a single tree or even an entire forest in the face of such terrible and tragic human suffering and loss. In a way, the trees are irrelevant. They will grow back. They already are. The forest will return. But what makes my heart bleed is the thought of what the local communities I'd briefly passed through on my way to the trees in 2008 must've endured during those terrifying weeks less than a year later.

Chapter 7

Ebana – Gabon

2008

Pulling on my harness, I took a moment to study the tree I was about to climb in more detail. The trunk was deeply furrowed and fluted, splayed out at the base like the foot of an enormous animal. Most of its buttress roots carried the unmistakable scars of elephant damage – deep tusk gouges that were slowly scabbing over as the tree tried to heal itself. Dark-brown sap was congealing into treacle to protect the living tissue beneath and the right flank of the tree was caked in dark-grey mud where it had been used as a rubbing post. Above this the tree's contorted trunk was reddish-brown and large loose flakes of bark gave it a shaggy appearance. I pulled one of the lower flakes off to reveal a patch of new, lighter bark beneath. The flake was brittle, like burnt toast, and smelt musty and pungent. Everything in this forest did. The air was filled with the slow-moving, heavy odours of rotting vegetation, fetid swamp and the unmistakable musk of forest elephants. Every now and then I felt the sluggish air shift and I would smell the sea. The muffled boom of waves breaking on a distant beach was a constant reminder that this was no ordinary forest.

This was the place where the dense forests of the Congo finally marched down to meet the Atlantic. A thin strip of white sand running along the shore for hundreds of miles was all that separated the world of trees from the world of water. That deserted no-man's-land was strewn with the sun-blasted deadwood of countless fallen trees. Enormous logs weighing several tons had been tossed up onto the beach with casual disdain by enormous Atlantic rollers. The Congo had met its match and an uneasy truce seemed to lie over the entire region, as if the forest was waiting for the day when the ocean would finally rise and sweep it all away.

I clipped my climbing rope into my chest clamp and pulled through the slack as I stepped up off the ground. The tree was growing on the edge of a vast inland lagoon and I floated out on the end of my rope to hang five feet above the black water. There were big crocs lurking out there and in a knee-jerk reaction I quickly climbed up another few feet to put more distance between me and its dark surface. The main trunk of the tree divided into three vertical stems fifteen feet aboveground. These continued up, eventually stretching out into a heavily branched canopy of immense size 100 feet above me. It was a classic Central African species of hardwood known locally as *ozouga*. A gnarled troll of a tree, with timber stronger than steel.

By the time I was thirty feet up I had already decided that this was the perfect tree for what I needed. The last three days had been spent creeping through this forest searching for a tree of sufficient strength and size, and I was relieved to have finally found it.

I'd been contracted by a TV production company to design and build the ultimate Tarzan-style jungle treehouse. The production team had chosen this wild stretch of forest on the remote coast of Gabon and at first glance it had indeed seemed perfect. It was virtually uninhabited by humans, a pristine mosaic of forest, savannah and inland lagoons home to elephants, gorillas, chimpanzees, buffalo, hippos and crocs. Upon closer inspection, however, the tree options had proven to be frustratingly limited.

This trip was a recce and what I needed was a tree of sufficient grandeur and presence to become a character in its own right. A jungle giant that could provide the perfect visual backdrop for the three TV presenters who would be spending a month living in its branches. It also needed to be incredibly strong and healthy. But this thin strip of forest sandwiched between ocean and lagoon had been hammered for centuries by the relentless coastal weather and was a dense, tangled riot of twisted lianas and broken trees. Every time a tree raised its head above the rest it was battered back down to size by the violent storms sweeping in off the Atlantic. There was a lot of deadwood hanging in the canopy and many of the larger trees were leaning at dangerous angles, struggling to maintain their grip on the loose sandy soil. All except the ozouga tree I was now climbing. It was no surprise that this tree was growing as far away from the sea as it could, right on the banks of the lagoon. It was sheltered by half a mile of forest to the west and had as much water as it needed. It was about 150 feet tall but what it lacked in height it more than made up for in sheer mass. Its three huge central stems would provide ample support for the treehouse's main deck. I could design a tailor-made structure to wrap around these enormous limbs and had no doubt that its timber was strong enough to support several tonnes of joists and floorboards. Things were looking up, so I shouted down to my two companions, James (the programme producer) and Joseph, (our forest guide) to let them know they could leave me to it for a while. They sauntered off into the forest chatting and I continued climbing until I was fifty feet up.

The three stems had now separated like giant fingers and I got out my notebook to scribble down a few ideas and potential designs. It was coming together nicely. I could spend the next two days surveying the tree in order to draw up plans that I could then use as a solid basis for construction. I hung there in my harness, imagining the house being built, taking shape around me.

My rope passed through a thin veil of leaves just above my head. I pushed my way through and entered the open canopy space above. At seventy feet up I was surrounded by a rambling network of huge horizontal branches. Several were over three feet in diameter and looked immensely strong. They snaked away in every direction and provided almost limitless options for design. I noticed a broken-off branch stub about ten feet above me that looked like it might be hollow. I decided to take a closer look just in case it revealed some undetected rot in the heart of the tree.

At that moment a solitary honeybee dropped down to hover in front of my face three feet away. It started zipping angrily from side to side and before I had time to register what was happening, it darted in to sting my right eyebrow. I quickly swatted it away and it flew off, leaving the sting behind. I tried to pull it out but my fumbling fingers only succeeded in squeezing the attached venom sac which pumped more poison into me. African honeybees pack a real punch and there was blood on the tips of my fingers. But they don't sting without reason and I realised that I must have blundered into a nest. A quick look up at the hollow broken branch above confirmed my fears. It was now erupting in a blizzard of small black dots. Having left its sting behind in my flesh, the dying bee had flown straight back to the hive, leaving an angry pheromone trail for the next wave of defenders to follow. Reinforcements arrived seconds later and came straight in on the attack. The first got me on my left eyelid while another crawled up my nose to sting me in the left nostril. I could feel several others trying to wriggle into my mouth. After stinging me, each bee was returning to the nest to gather yet more support, and the whole situation was escalating out of control quickly as I thrashed around, seventy feet aboveground.

One managed to prise its way through my tightly clamped lips to sting the inside of my left cheek. I ground it in my teeth and spat it out but another three crawled inside to do the same. I could feel my throat swelling and I was hyperventilating. An electric wave of adrenaline washed through me and my heart was accelerating madly. If anaphylaxis set in, my throat would swell to block my airway and the lights would dim pretty quickly after that, leaving me unconscious and stranded on my rope. By now, dozens of bees had crawled down the back of my shirt while others had squirmed their way in through the air vents on my climbing helmet to sting my scalp repeatedly. My head was swimming in toxins and I was losing my peripheral vision. Bright stars floated in front of my eyes and I knew there was only one way this could end if I stayed here.

I had to get down but I was still dangling seven storeys up, flailing around like a puppet on a string. I needed to change over onto my abseil device, which meant leaving my face exposed and undefended while my hands got on with it. I couldn't think straight and was losing consciousness but my hands knew the drill and operated on autopilot. Load rope into abseil device, step up in stirrups, disconnect chest clamp, sit back down, remove hand clamp and Go!

I was just about to black out when I pressed the handle on my abseil device as hard as I could and practically free-fell down the rope. The swarm followed me down, so I swung in to the bank, frantically slid my harness down over my hips to leave it hanging on the rope, and plunged straight into the safety of the lagoon. Crocs be damned. I submerged myself completely and couldn't believe that I was still getting stung by a few diehards while completely underwater. Taking off my helmet, I squashed all the remaining bees still entangled in my hair and inside my ears. I held my breath for as long as I could before scrambling up the tree's long twisted roots onto the bank. The main onslaught was now over. I wasn't going to hang around asking for more, though, so I stumbled into the forest to put as much distance between me and the angry swarm as possible.

After a few minutes I stopped to catch my breath. My ears were ringing and my hearing was muffled as if I was still underwater. I was relieved not to hear the angry buzzing any more but my breathing sounded ragged and shallow. Feeling as though I'd just downed a bottle of whisky, I had the urge to vomit, but as I didn't have anything to throw up, dry-retched into the leaf litter. I was left gasping for air with the effort. The only bees still with me were caught in the folds of my clothing where they writhed in slow agony, yellow entrails spilling out behind them. The air was thick with the bitter taste of venom, and a nasty red rash of toxin was spreading across the backs of my hands. I was experiencing an anaphylactic reaction, but having no medicine with me I concentrated on my breathing, taking slow, deep breaths in an effort to slow my heart and stop the poison spreading through my body. I desperately needed a heavy dose of antihistamine, so flicking the last remaining dying bees off me, I started to make my way back towards camp a mile away, stumbling forward and lurching like a drunkard. The initial tidal wave of adrenaline that had blazed through my body had evaporated to leave me feeling exhausted, confused, paranoid and trembling. I was not in a good way.

• • •

Several hours later I woke up on my bed in camp. It was dark and cool. I could hear rain outside and the occasional distant peal of thunder. An excited, high-pitched chattering came from the bats roosting in the hut's rafters above me. I fumbled under my pillow for my head torch and was immediately blinded by light bouncing back off the white mosquito net around me. Everything felt surreal and it took me several moments to get a grip on where I was and what had happened. James and Joseph had heard the attack. My yells of pain and shouts of warning had echoed through the forest and they'd rushed back to the ozouga tree. By the time they arrived at the scene I was already hauling myself out of the lagoon and had run past them in a blind panic. Realising what had happened, Joseph had quickly led James away from the danger zone and taken a shortcut to meet me a safe distance away on the game trail. From there they had both helped me back to camp, where they'd given me a large dose of antihistamine and put me to bed.

The swelling in my throat had completely subsided, thank heavens, but I still felt lightheaded and disorientated. I could now feel each and every sting. I counted at least forty on my head and arms alone, but several of these felt like stings on stings. My bottom lip was swollen up in a way I'd not experienced since being punched in the mouth at school, and my right ear was on fire. There were spots of dried blood on my pillow and I could feel heavy bruising on the edge of my eye sockets and the backs of my hands – the places where bone meets skin and there is little flesh to cushion the sting. All in all I felt like I'd just gone three rounds with a heavyweight boxer. But I was alive, and at the end of the day that was all that counted. It really could have gone either way.

The whole episode had been a bit of a nightmare. But there was something else that troubled me, something about the way in which the bees had behaved. They had gone straight for my face. These bees that had never seen a human before somehow knew that eyes, mouth and nose were the best places to focus an attack. I found the notion of such innate collective intelligence vaguely unsettling. I guess it made a kind of evolutionary sense, though, as they were used to defending their precious stash of honey from large primates with a sweet tooth. Chimp, gorilla, human ... I guess we all look the same to a bee.

I turned off my head torch and lay back down in the comforting darkness. The soothing sound of rain, mingled with the distant rolling boom of surf on the beach, helped me relax, and I lay there on the edge of sleep, chastising myself for not taking the first-aid kit into the forest with me. I had also failed to detect any signs of the nest before I climbed. I should have spent longer scrutinising the tree from the ground before I even fired a line up. I usually do, but I guess I was just so relieved to find a decent tree after so much time searching that my excitement ran away with me. I had been complacent and dropped my guard. I closed my eyes and sank down through soft foaming surf into a deep sleep.

· · ·

I was awake at 4.30 the following morning. I lay there for an hour or so, waiting for dawn, then took my mug of tea down to the edge of the lagoon to watch the sun rise through the mist. My joints felt stiff and I was aching all over, but the fog of toxins had lifted and my head was clear.

I wasn't mad keen to head back into the forest, let alone get back into my climbing harness, but we only had two days left in which to find a suitable tree.

Sneaking back in with Joseph to remove my ropes from the ozouga tree felt like some sort of therapy, like revisiting a past trauma or the scene of a crime. But I suppose it did me good. I didn't see or hear one living bee, but had no doubt that on such a fine day as this the colony would be very active. I found my harness still clipped to the rope, hanging slumped against the base of the tree. It was crawling with ants busily scavenging the curled-up carcasses of bees that had sacrificed themselves in defence of their nest. I took one last look at what should have been the perfect tree, then headed back into the forest to continue searching.

As luck would have it, two hours later we were standing at the base of another potential tree, again growing on the banks of the lagoon. Joseph tapped its base with the flat of his machete and said '*Ebana*.' I used my schoolboy French to ask whether ebana was a good, strong timber. His face lit up in a grin: '*Oui, oui, il est bon bois. Tres fort. Pas de probleme.*'

Joseph was the son of the chief of Sette Cama, the local village. He was the same height as me but broader across the shoulders and had a strange sense of humour. The first time I met him we went for a swim in the lagoon. He had disappeared beneath the dark water to grab my legs and drag me under before laughing hysterically in my terrified face. He then delivered a stern warning about the massive crocodiles to be found out here. We were treading water 100 metres from the shore at the time. His failure to mention this fact while we were still on dry land was a total mystery to me, but clearly of much amusement to him. I had liked him instantly.

Although it was also growing next to the lagoon, the tree standing in front of Joseph and me now could not be more different to the ozouga of the day before. Whereas the 'bee tree' had been hulking in appearance this ebana seemed graceful, almost delicate. Its bark was a lightly textured mottled grey and felt like the worn surface of old sandpaper. It too was regularly used as a rubbing post by the elephants, its stem cloaked in layers of mud – some of it still dark and wet. It split into three stems fifteen feet aboveground, each of which continued to branch into multiple others. The upper canopy – swaying gently in the breeze 100 feet above our heads – was a thick forest in its own right. Overall, the tree reminded me of an ancient beech pollard, the kind of tree I knew so well from the New Forest back home. I scrutinised it through the binoculars and couldn't see any cavities or damage, so I fired a line up to rig my ropes. The faint smell of bee venom that lingered on my harness made my heart race, so I took a deep breath and tried to focus on the job in hand.

I had rigged my climbing rope so that it led me up through the centre of the tree. Once above the main trunk I was hanging in a beautiful open colonnade of multiple stems that multiplied and grew thinner as I ascended. I swung across the central space to grab hold of one on the other side of the canopy. It bent and flexed under my weight before recoiling to knock gently against its neighbour as I let go and swung away. As I neared the top, I caught tantalising glimpses of the lagoon through the branches. I had run out of rope but still had another twenty feet of canopy above me, so I swapped onto my climbing lanyards and shinned my way up. At this height the canopy was about fifty feet across, and the multiple stems ran away from me to the right like the pillars of a cloister, before returning full circle on my left. I had a clear view across the lagoon far below. The surface of the water was sparkling like diamonds in the white-hot African sun, but up in the canopy the air was soft, green and cool. I had left the staleness of the understorey below and could taste the salt of the sea on the fresh breeze. The tree rippled gently with every breath of wind, each stem swaying in ever-increasing circles until they bumped together softly, almost apologetically, like people swirling on a dance floor. I looked back down into the heart of the tree, towards the main trunk eighty feet below me, where the numerous stems were slowly undulating like the tentacles of a giant octopus or sea anemone. I closed my eyes and felt everything ebb and flow around me, and as the fragrant air dried my sweat I knew that at last we had found our tree.

• • •

Two days later, James and I headed back to the UK to get things ready. Ten days after that, I was back in Gabon with several cases of tools and a whole heap of climbing gear. James stayed in the UK to finish writing scripts and I was now accompanied by Nick, a fellow tree-climber from Britain, who knew his way around a tree and understood how timber worked. We would build the house together. In my absence, Joseph had set about recruiting a small but solid team of men from his village to help, and we had three weeks to get as much done as we could before Christmas. It wasn't much time and the tree designs I had drafted were pretty ambitious. But as long as the timber we had ordered had arrived, we were good to go.

It hadn't. We'd purchased it from a small timber yard in Gamba, the nearest town of any size, located a four-hour boat ride away on the other side of the lagoon. Apparently the yard owner hadn't been seen for days and seemed to have disappeared off the face of the earth. Our schedule was tight. We had twenty-two days in total to get the house built and I became increasingly twitchy as each day passed without news. I told myself that it would be fine, that this was only a temporary delay and all would come good. But Central Africa often treats best-laid plans with utter derision and after six days my optimism seemed increasingly badly placed, to say the least. Even if the wood arrived tomorrow, we would still only have two weeks to build the thing. We were getting frustrated, and Nick and I decided to go for a run along the beach, followed by a swim in the sea, just to get out of camp and burn some energy before we both went mad. Like a couple of tourists we grabbed our towels and flip-flops and headed down to the deserted shore.

White sand swept away from us in a long gentle arc to disappear in a low mist of sea spray on the northern horizon. Surf was rolling up the beach to slowly collapse in a never-ending series of huge breakers and the sun-bleached carcasses of long-dead trees lay half-buried in the sand like fossilised dinosaurs. To our right sat the forest, a thick wall of looming vegetation. An occasional tree leant forward over the high-tide mark, but it was dark under the eaves, and no matter how hard I squinted I couldn't see through the gloom beneath the trees.

Putting my towel down on a fallen log I strolled up to the treeline to take a pee. I was fumbling around with my shorts when a movement caught my eye and I glanced up to see the dense jungle foliage in front of me being torn down by something big moving with incredible speed. Seconds later an enormous bull elephant exploded from cover and charged straight towards me. His huge black ears were flared and his trunk was screwed up tight in anger, but what really caught my attention were his tusks: six feet long and approaching at alarming speed. Maybe it was a bluff, but he certainly looked like he meant business. There was no warning, no bellowing, just a dreadful silent intent accompanied by the ominous crash of foliage as he powered his five-tonne bulk through the tree trunks and scrub as if they were grass. He was fifty feet away from me now and gaining fast. Spinning around, I legged it barefoot down the beach as fast as I could while still pulling up my shorts. I yelled at Nick and slapped him on the back as I passed: 'Elephant! Run!' He took a split second to register what was happening before sprinting down to dive into the surf next to me.

The bull chased us right down to the water's edge. He had been right on our heels but the beach shelved steeply here and he pulled up on the sand twenty feet away, where he bellowed at us in fury. The sound was deafening, even above the surf. A gut-twisting primordial scream of rage that I felt as vibrations in my chest even though I was waist-deep in foaming water. I could see straight into his open pink mouth as he held his trunk high and roared. He flicked out his trunk in a gesture of frustrated anger before lowering his head and fanning out his large, thorn-torn ears as if to charge straight into the sea. We backed further away into the surf, so he kicked a shower of sand at us instead. He was extremely angry, full of outrage at our presence. But I also detected a glimmer of childish pride in the way he now stood swinging his enormous head from side to side. A savage riptide began dragging us through the water parallel to the beach. The bull's body language spoke of smug satisfaction as he strutted along next to us, casting us the occasional sideways glance. He had certainly made it clear this was his patch. After shadowing us for a while he strolled back to the trees, leaving us to half-wade, half-swim our way back towards camp. I guess we'd got our run and swim after all, I thought peevishly.

Nick and I skulked back to our hut soaked to the skin, feeling like a couple of chastised kids. It was a good job Joseph wasn't there to meet us, or we'd never have heard the end of it. I poured us both a medicinal dram and we sat side by side in thoughtful silence, looking out over the lagoon. 'They didn't put that in the brochure, did they?' murmured Nick.

* * *

At six o'clock the following morning I sat with my mug of tea idly watching weaver birds collect grass from the edge of the water. These tiny black-and-red birds were flying up into the palm trees above our hut, trailing the long blades of grass like party streamers. There were dozens of nests dangling like baubles in each tree – a whole hanging garden of perfectly formed miniature treehouses. Each palm tree was a hive of activity. I watched them building with envy – I should've been up in my own tree by now, working on my own treehouse. I had just turned my attention back to the rising sun, when I caught the low drone of a distant engine. Nick strolled outside to join me just as a blue-hulled launch came into view across the lagoon, emerging out of the morning mist like a vision. It was stacked high with timber and sitting very low in the water. Planks and joists were piled across the gunwales, hanging ten feet out on either side. Joseph sat on top of the whole lot, shouting directions to the pilot. The boat swept round in a big arc towards the banks of the lagoon. Joseph was grinning broadly and we jogged down to guide the bow onto the bank as they coasted in.

We'd lost seven days waiting for this moment. A third of our total construction time had evaporated, leaving us just two weeks to get the thing built. On top of that, I now realised that this first delivery contained only roofing materials. What we desperately needed were the main structural joists. But I was beyond caring and a surge of relief washed over me as we unloaded it all onto the grass. It might take the rest of the day for the remaining timber to get here, but at least it had started to arrive. The timber merchant had been true to his word and I realised with relief that the following morning we would finally be able to get up into the tree to do what we'd come here to do.

• • •

The early-morning peace and quiet was violently torn apart by the chainsaw. A monstrous contraption hired in from Gamba, it was an old model with a blade well over four feet long, with no safety features whatsoever. After clearing its throat a few times it roared into life and Aubin, its barefooted operator, was immediately engulfed in a turquoise haze of exhaust fumes. He revved it till it screamed and placed it down on top of a plank where it sat idling before bouncing itself off into the leaf litter and cutting out. My ears were ringing and the smell of burnt chemicals lingering in the air jarred unpleasantly with the tranquillity of our setting.

We were standing in a newly cleared glade at the base of the ebana. The leaves above us were still dripping from the night's rain and everything was backlit, glowing emerald green against the early-morning sun. Shining ripples of reflected light bounced from the lagoon to float up and down the silver trunk of the ebana. A kingfisher flashed past us, taking a shortcut through the forest, while way out on the lagoon a flock of egrets glided over water that was as still and polished as a mirror. It felt like sacrilege to be making such a racket, but there was no other way. Our handsaws weren't able to get through the hard tropical timber of our main structural beams. We were utterly reliant on the rabid machine currently lying on its side smoking in the leaf litter at Aubin's feet.

Our first job was to get up into the tree and shout down dimensions, so that the joists could be trimmed to size by the team from Sette Cama. We'd struck gold with these guys, and one of them, Justin, was a natural carpenter. He adopted the role of foreman, keeping things rolling on the ground while Nick and I bounced around the branches above.

I pulled my harness on and took another close look at the tree in front of me. I threw my climbing rope up over a branch and pulled myself up to swing in against the mud-caked trunk. My eyes traced the dancing water reflections up the stem until I was peering into the living structure high above us. I felt a sudden unexpected pang of guilt. This tree had grown in perfect harmony with its environment. I had no idea how old it was but up until now it had been living peacefully in its own quiet corner of this forest, destined to grow old and die as nature intended. But now, for the sake of a TV programme, its fate was to be changed forever, I shook my head and made a vow to myself that whatever happened, the treehouse we built must not harm this tree. I was confident we could build the supporting platforms without the need for hammering in nails, but we would still be introducing huge additional loads, which needed to be distributed in a way the Ebana could safely tolerate. It also had to have a useful life that continued way beyond its contribution to a TV programme. The bottom line was that I didn't want to be responsible for ruining something so beautiful by cocking this whole thing up.

And so began two of the most intense weeks of my life. Each morning the team would stop by in the boat to collect Nick and me at sunrise from our hut on the banks of the lagoon. We would head straight to the tree and hit the ropes hard, getting as much done as we possibly could in those first few hours before the heat of the day smothered us like treacle and everything ground to a halt. I had designed the treehouse to hang suspended from steel cables anchored in the forks of branches high up in the canopy. The first thing was getting these installed. So by 6am on day one, Nick and I were swinging between the branches seventy-five feet up, until the cables – hanging down like steel vines to dangle twenty feet above the forest floor – were ready to be looped around the ends of the main load-bearing joists.

Soon the main deck began to take shape. The serrated howl of the chainsaw was accompanied by the incessant banging of hammer and chisel. Everyone was working flat out, throwing body and soul into it. This kind of work requires high energy levels and getting enough food into our bodies to fuel them soon became a real issue. There was no time to return to camp for lunch each day so at around nine o'clock each morning a different member of the crew would leave us to it and head out on his own in the boat, invariably returning a couple of hours later with half a dozen beautiful fresh fish in his bucket. The local lads from Sette Cama were all superb fishermen and while Nick and I swung on our ropes high above and the team on the ground cut timber and hoisted it up to us, one of them would prepare the most incredible stew over an open fire.

Lunchtime quickly became the most important time of the day for us all. Nick and I had long since run out of food supplies at our hut, so knowing we would not have supper, we loaded up on lunch until we could barely move. We would gorge ourselves then crawl off to find a patch of shade to doze for an hour or so. By two o'clock we'd be huffing and puffing our way back up into the tree to carry on hammering in planks, but by three, when the heat had finally gone out of the day, our energy levels would peak and we would be flying. Swinging around the tree and working like maniacs, getting the floorboards and joists in place faster than the team below could cut them to size. We stayed working up in the tree each day until it began to grow dark. The golden afternoon sunshine would recede further up the graceful silver stems above us until the whole tree was eclipsed by the forest to our west. The short-lived tropical dusk would suck colour from our surroundings and the hammers and saws would fall silent. As we packed away the tools and got into the boat each night we would hear the distant crack of branches followed by the low rumbling calls of elephants as they began to move through the forest towards their feeding grounds on the banks of the lagoon.

• • •

I lay on my back in the darkness. I'd been woken up by the grim sound of a rat being eaten alive by a snake somewhere in the rafters above me. The high-pitched screams seemed to go on forever and I could hear the soft creaking of the snake's coils and the desperate last scrabbling of the rat's claws before it eventually succumbed to the inevitable. Not a particularly pleasant morning alarm, for me or the rat. But there had been something else, another deeper sound, that had woken me. I'd felt a series of heavy thuds coming from somewhere out there in the darkness beyond our hut. All was now silent, but as I rolled over to go back to sleep it came again. A dull bang that shook the hut's foundations, followed by an avalanche of small falling objects like apples from a tree. I looked at my watch: 5am. Only half an hour before I had to get up anyway, so I crept out of bed to see what was going on. It was just beginning to get light as I cautiously stepped outside. A huge dull-grey shadow stood beneath the trees fifty feet away. It was the bull elephant. He was head-butting each of the palm trees with enormous force, causing a cascade of ripe fruit to fall to the ground with each blow. He would then shuffle around to pick them up one by one with his trunk, delicately placing them into his mouth like sweets. He must have sensed someone watching because he whirled around with surprising speed to face me for a moment before silently striding off into the shadows with his head held high and tusks glowing yellow in the dawn. Every bit as magnificent as I remembered him.

'Was that our friend?' asked Nick quietly as he stepped out to join me. He looked gaunt and tired as he stood there. A punishing schedule and not enough food were taking their toll on both of us. I didn't look much better. The last week had represented a slow but steady downward slide into squalor. We were working flat out from dawn till dusk, operating on one meal a day with no spare time to make the lengthy boat trip into Gamba to buy more supplies. Not that we had enough petrol for the journey or money for the food anyway.

With no time or energy spare to wash clothes or keep our hut clean things were getting pretty grungy. The cool clear water of the lagoon was a saving grace, but bathing at night in the light of a head torch while scanning for crocs wasn't exactly relaxing. On top of the hunger, tiredness and dirt, I'd picked up a skin infection. One side of my face was stained with a weeping rash caused by a parasitic worm dispersed through animal faeces. Charming. In addition, both Nick and I each had a healthy dose of crotch rot and chiggers. Chiggers are caused by small sand fleas that burrow under the skin of your feet, normally around the toenails, to lay eggs that gradually ripen and hatch to release adult fleas back into the sand. Several small patches of my flesh between my toes were slowly putrefying. I waited until they were ready to burst then dug them out with a hot needle and washed the wound clean. 'They didn't put that in the brochure either, did they?' Once again, Central Africa was taking its toll. Just what was it that kept calling me back to this part of the world?

As we stepped off the boat into the forest later that morning we were greeted by the strong smell of elephants. Their musky odour hung thick around the base of the ebana tree and there was a huge pile of fresh dung next to our timber stack in the centre of the glade. The sandy soil around it was drenched black by a gallon of urine that had already attracted a small blizzard of flitting yellow butterflies. There were three enormous, perfectly round muddy footprints on top of one of our planks lying next to the tree, and dozens more in the dirt around us. The ebana's stem had been newly plastered with wet mud. I couldn't believe it: despite all the noise we made during the day, the site had been visited by elephants during the night. Goodness knows what it must have smelt like to them. The acrid mixture of human sweat, urine and petrol fumes should have made them run a mile. But elephants are highly intelligent, curious creatures and I suppose they had simply popped by to see for themselves what all the noise had been about. Nothing was damaged and it must've been a magical scene as they stood in the silver dappled moonlight, rumbling to each other while contemplating the strange wooden structure above their heads.

• • •

I took a few minutes to look up at our treehouse and plan the day ahead. The main deck was all but finished now. Triangular in shape and thirty feet long, it jutted out over the water of the lagoon like the prow of a ship. Shaded from the direct heat of the sun by the dappled canopy above, it had become my favourite place to rest after lunch, lying on my back with the tree swaying gently around me.

By day twenty, our thirteenth day of construction, the smaller upper platform had also been completed, and was accessible via a ladder leading up through a hatch from the main deck. It floated within the open space of the middle canopy, with several of the tree's giant limbs passing up through its floor.

We would be back after Christmas to put the roof on and build another smaller platform in an adjacent tree, but for now we were finished. And as we floated back out onto the mirrored surface of the lagoon that evening, I could see the same quiet pride that I felt myself reflected on the faces of the team around me. We'd accomplished an incredible amount in less than two weeks. I just hoped that we would find everything in the same condition upon our return in a month's time.

• • •

New year back in England came and went and before I knew it I was back there in the treehouse, sitting on the floorboards in the darkness with my back against the tree. The soft evening air was full of the song of crickets, and the strange nasal honks of hammer-headed fruit bats drifted down from above. Water lapped against the lagoon shore below me and the whole treehouse was rocking gently in the breeze, creaking contentedly like a ship at anchor. It was a magical place to be. Taking another sip of whisky, I shuffled forward to stretch out on the rough timber. I let out a long breath and felt myself dissolve into the moment.

It was 10pm on the evening of 5th of February and the treehouse was finished. It even had a basic kitchen, and expedition provisions were stacked all around me. The three presenters were due to move in tomorrow. These included Guy (who I'd last seen in Australia when we climbed Roaring Meg together) and Julie, a primatologist. My friend Gavin, a cameraman I'd worked with often in the past, would also be joining them on-screen. For the next six weeks this would be their home, but for tonight none of them were here and I was celebrating in the best way I knew – by spending a night on my own. I had the house we'd built entirely to myself and soon drifted off into a deep sleep.

I awoke a few hours later. There had been a shift in the air, a sea change, and a steady chill breeze was rattling the saucepans hanging from the rafters above my head. I stood up and leant against the railing, peering into the darkness. The forest was suspiciously quiet. Even the crickets had stopped calling. Lightning flashed on the horizon and the first large drops of rain landed heavily on the thatched roof above my head. The breeze steadily increased until the whole structure began to creak and groan as if trying to break free of its moorings. The biggest threat to the treehouse was from the ebana tree itself, and a few minutes later I felt the first jolts and quivers as the huge limbs above me thudded against timber in the darkness. One of the saucepans clattered to the deck behind me as a wall of air arrived just ahead of the main storm. Air pressure plummeted and the sky directly above exploded in a flash of white and purple. The air tingled and thunder bellowed as rain whipped in through the platform's open sides. I ran round the deck to lower the storm blinds, but the turbulent air sucked the tarpaulin out into the darkness where it flailed around uselessly as the platform got utterly soaked. Each lightning flash revealed total chaos, as pots, pans, clothes and buckets were sent flying and bouncing across the floorboards.

The entire platform now heaved from side to side, accompanied by stomach-churning bangs. Some of the vibrations shook the structure so much that I was worried something would snap and everything would crash to the ground with me in it. The urge to bail out was almost overwhelming. But where would I go? An elephant-infested forest in the middle of a wild storm at night was no refuge. And besides, a squall like this had always been on the cards. This was the ultimate test for the treehouse: an essential rite of passage that I felt the need to share. Lying back down on the deck in the lashing rain, I relinquished myself completely to the power of the storm and eventually fell into an exhausted sleep. After a while, the rain softened and I knew the main danger had passed. It had been a rough ride, but my design had worked.

· · ·

Six weeks later it was time to go home. The filming had been completed successfully and ownership of the treehouse had been officially handed across to the World Wide Fund for Nature, here in Gabon. The wrap party on our final evening was an opportunity for everyone to let off a bit of steam and dance the night away. I was physically and emotionally drained and as wonderful as it was to be surrounded by the happy faces of so many new friends I had completely run out of energy by 10pm. The party was still in full swing. Everyone was dancing and whirling in the shadows of a huge bonfire of driftwood as I passed by into the night and headed towards an empty hut on the edge of the camp. Stringing up my mosi-net I lay down to sleep on the veranda. Looking up at the stars and watching the silhouettes of palm trees flicker in the glow from the fire, I sank into a peaceful sleep.

Several hours later I was woken up by a deep vocalisation rumbling in my chest, like the pedal note of a church organ. I opened my eyes, but it was utterly dark. The stars above were eclipsed by an enormous shadow looming right over me, and the pointed tips of two huge yellow tusks hovered four feet above my head. I lay perfectly still as the bull elephant gently pressed the tip of its trunk against the net inches from my face. It inhaled deeply and I heard the giant lungs inside his massive chest inflate above me until I thought they would burst. I could actually feel the air being sucked up into his trunk as he smelled me. I barely had time to register what was happening before my eyes were forced shut again by an avalanche of air as he exhaled. I could smell the grass fermenting in his stomach as my mosi-net filled with the moist air from his lungs.

I thanked the heavens that he was in a better mood than he had been the first time we'd met. He must have been watching, waiting in the eaves of the forest for the party to finish and the fire to die down, before stepping out into the clearing to feed beneath the palm trees. He had stumbled across me sleeping and decided to take a closer look. Despite lying directly beneath five tonnes of elephant I was feeling surprisingly calm. He could have already trampled me in my sleep if he'd meant any harm, and besides, I had nowhere to go. To say he had the upper hand would be an understatement. He let out another deep rumble that sank through me, before gliding quietly away into the night. I felt like I'd passed some kind of test. The stars reappeared above and I noticed a pale glow on the horizon beyond the lagoon. It was the start of another day but it was time for me to leave Central Africa – just as I was beginning to feel accepted by the locals.

Chapter 8

Kayu Besi – Papua

2009

Taking a small lead weight from my chest pocket I placed it snugly inside the slingshot's pouch. I'd attached the catapult to the top of a nine-foot pole and the thick black elastic now creaked softly as I pulled it all the way down to the ground. It was stretched to the limit and a quick glance at its old, pockmarked rubber warned me not to take too long. Breathing out slowly I waited until my aim was steady then let go. The rubber recoiled with a loud crack and the fishing line whisked off its reel with a dry hiss. To my relief, the shot was on target and the weight sailed over the branch 150 feet above me with ease before plummeting back down and embedding itself in the thick jungle leaf litter. No sooner had it landed than the young lad next to me sprinted off to retrieve it – yelling out in triumph when he found it a few seconds later.

Turning around, I was greeted with broad smiles and a murmuring chorus of approval. A small audience of Korowai warriors had gathered to watch this strange ritual, and even Aliom and Anom, two of the tribal elders, had momentarily dropped their stern countenance to grin back at me with twinkling eyes. I was just as surprised as they were that I got the shot first time, but a bit of audience pressure goes a long way and I was happy to have put on a good show. Nasé, one of the younger men, celebrated the moment by jumping up and down on the spot, calling out in high-pitched whoops as his hornbill-beak penis sheath bounced up and down. Everyone fell about laughing and I was reminded of just how welcoming the tribe had been since I had arrived in their village three days ago.

Several of the Korowai were carrying longbows, and even though they'd never seen a slingshot before they had grasped the notion of what I was up to immediately. They now came forward to inspect the catapult closely, turning it over in their hands and tentatively pulling at the strong elastic. We were on common ground, and it felt good to be connecting with them despite the language barrier. I handed the catapult to Anom then headed into the forest to start hauling up my climbing rope. The young Korowai lad watched closely as I fumbled to untie the small lead weight with clumsy, nail-bitten fingers. Taking it from me, he deftly unpicked the knot in a couple of seconds before placing it back in my palm with a grin.

These were good people despite their mysterious, even fearsome, reputation, and looking back at the others I watched as they sat down on a log to chat and share a smoke. Aliom retrieved a ball of baccy from his habitual hiding place behind one ear and wedged it into the end of his long bamboo pipe. Lighting it from a glowing ember wedged in a forked stick, he then passed it down the line as they embarked on an earnest group discussion. The rhythm of their conversation was refreshingly polite and measured, with each having his say before keeping quiet to let the next speak his mind fully.

Anom took a huge drag, bowed his head in a cloud of dark-blue smoke, then lifted his face to scrutinise the branches of the tree towering above us. They had carefully selected this particular individual to be the tree in which they would build a traditional Korowai house. But this would be no ordinary treehouse. It would teeter in the slender branches of the tree's upper crown, well over a hundred feet aboveground, and be big enough to sleep ten people. I was part of a small crew sent here by the BBC to film them building it. But whereas I had ropes, harnesses and all the other paraphernalia of a modern climber, they had nothing more than what the forest could provide. I couldn't wait to see how they did it. Just getting up there without ropes would be an incredible feat, let alone building a house in its branches ten storeys aboveground without the use of nails and largely without metal tools. But I had already learned not to underestimate these incredible people and had no doubt that the next two weeks would be as exciting as any I'd ever experienced.

Walking over to them, I took a seat to one side and listened to the ebb and flow of talk. Wayu, a strong man with fierce eyes, carrying the tribal scarification of a warrior across his chest, seemed to lead the discussion. But eventually, one by one, everyone fell into silent contemplation as they surveyed the tree. Lifting his hand, Wayu traced the shape of its branches with his fingers while deep in thought.

This tree had been chosen for its strength. I recognised it as a type of ironwood. As the name suggests, such trees have some of the toughest, most durable timber on the planet. There are many different species of ironwood – or *kayu besi* – throughout Indonesia, and to this day I have no idea which one this was. But what I can vouch for is the extraordinary feeling of resilience and strength it radiated when touched. As if carved from living stone. The Korowai had made an excellent choice; it was the perfect tree to build a house in.

Climbing trees in the tropics isn't like climbing trees back home, where you know exactly what species the tree is and can judge what to expect from its timber. Britain has barely a handful of tree species compared to a tropical rainforest. Stand in the New Forest and you might have half a dozen different species growing around you. But in the tropics you can multiply this by ten, many of which will be complete unknowns to a climber, in terms of timber strength and reliability. So to know that this tree was an ironwood was a huge advantage. The reputation of these iconic trees went before them, and as with English hornbeam or yew, I had 100 per cent faith in its strength.

But I'd learned not to be complacent and scrutinised it closely. Its fluted base was wrapped in a coat of bright-green moss, but above this the slender trunk was clean and free of vines – gracefully rising for eighty feet before spreading out into an open canopy. Its long, slender branches stretched almost vertically into the sky. Even from down here I could tell from their slow-grown, crooked shapes that these branches were phenomenally strong. I made a second inspection – this time through binoculars. No hornets' nests, cracks, cavities or fungi. No broken branches or hanging deadwood. It was in fantastic condition and about 180 feet tall, making it slightly taller than most of the trees around it.

I'd seen similar trees in Borneo and Sumatra over the years, but ironwoods of this size and maturity were becoming rare. They sit at the top of the illegal logging hit list, fetching very high prices on the international market. The tree towering above me was simply beautiful – the perfect embodiment of natural grace and form. To plunge a chainsaw into it would be sacrilege. But timber as strong as steel is a desirable thing, and sadly – just like elephant ivory – it will always be coveted by people with more money than sense.

Thankfully, of course, the Korowai had no intention of felling it. But I was still saddened by the realisation that it would never again look as beautiful and perfect as it did in this moment. Just like our ebana tree back in Gabon, the fate of this kayu besi would now be influenced by human agenda. The building of the house wouldn't kill it, but once again I somewhat regretted that it wouldn't be left to live out its life untouched.

The men were still deep in discussion, but I was keen to get up into those strong branches as soon as possible. The limb my rope passed over was 150 feet aboveground, around thirty feet below the very top of the tree.

By the time I'd anchored the end of my rope around the base of a nearby tree and pulled on my harness, the guys had again come in for a closer look, standing silently with arms folded, scrutinising my every move. I handed them a karabiner to look at. As far as I could tell there were only two metal items owned by the entire clan: a machete and an axe, nothing else. All their other tools were made of wood, stone or bone. No cooking pots, watches, coins – nothing of metal seemed to exist here, other than the machete and the axe, so the form and function of a karabiner were completely alien to them. They handed it around with mild curiosity, but showed no discernible interest in what its function might be. To them it was an abstract piece of technology. Unlike me, they were perfectly capable of climbing the ironwood without such trinkets, and I was suddenly aware of the huge cultural gulf stretching between us.

Once my full weight was on the rope, I focused on the climb ahead. A few men answered a distant yodel and picked up their bows to head off back to the village. But the rest sat back down on their log, lit another pipe and settled in to watch the entertainment.

My rope was dangling ten feet away from the main trunk and I began to spin gently as I climbed. Arriving level with the ironwood's first branch I took a moment to immerse myself fully in the canopy; soaking up its atmosphere like a sponge. I've done this hundreds of times and every time feels as sensational as the first, because every forest is subtly different. But the rainforests of Papua are particularly special. The air is full of animal calls, which seem familiar until you remember they are made entirely by birds. Papua has no primates and other than its shy endemic marsupials it has very few mammals. So birds reign supreme and have flourished to fill almost every niche. Every outlandish screech, bark or howl comes from a bird of some kind, and far from feeling empty in the absence of large mammals, the forest is brimming with life.

After a few minutes I carried on up to the top of my rope, 150 feet aboveground. The ironwood's branches were now within reach and felt reassuringly strong. My full weight was hanging from a limb no thicker than my arm. I'd made sure my rope also passed over a second branch, but I needn't have worried. I might as well have been hanging from a steel beam. The dynamic forces exerted on the timber as I bounced my way up the rope were nothing to this tree, and the branch supporting me barely flexed under my weight.

The bark up here was thin and flaky, with a mottled russet and ivory colour. Every movement I made dislodged small flakes that fell spiralling to the ground like sycamore seeds. I was now higher than most of the surrounding trees and although the view wasn't three-sixty, I could see to the horizon in places. The forest presented a seemingly endless swathe of green. Flat, mysterious and enticing for as far as the eye could see.

Looking back down into the heart of the crown I easily imagined where the house would be built. A sturdy cradle of giant limbs reached up beneath me to provide the perfect support. Transferring onto my lanyards I moved across onto another vertical stem, then slid down into the very centre of the tree. A spider the size of my hand darted up the stem next to me with lightning speed. It was perfectly camouflaged, blending into the tree bark to disappear entirely every time it stopped. There was plenty of life up here and my attention was caught by a thin column of ants winding its way up another branch to my left. A solitary worker stood off to one side, poised and motionless. Something about it looked slightly different to the others, and peering closer I realised it was a tiny praying mantis, an ant-mimic the same colour and shape as the insects streaming past it. With lightning speed it lunged in to drag one of the others out – eating its meal alive, while the doomed ant twitched and writhed in the tiny fastidious jaws. The tropical canopy really is another planet sometimes.

Having familiarised myself with the tree in which we'd be filming I headed down. A few moments later it started to rain, and by the time I'd reached the ground all of the Korowai were gone and I was on my own. I was already soaked through, so as there was little point rushing off to find shelter, I took my time stashing my harness in its bag at the base of the tree.

It had been a good day. The ironwood was a joy to climb, radiating nothing but good vibes the entire time I was up there. Some trees have personalities and I've climbed plenty that have been a pleasure from start to finish. I've also been thwarted by just as many – trees that didn't seem to want a human anywhere near them. I've no idea why some trees are like this, they just are. And rather like people, appearances can be deceptive: it's not always the obvious ones that turn out to be trickiest.

• • •

I'd wanted to visit the Korowai ever since seeing a photo of their treetop houses in a copy of *National Geographic* many years ago, so it felt surreal to actually be here with them. Their jungle home was a very long way from England, but it wasn't just the miles that made this place so far removed. Just like the Congo, this land truly felt like another world, as if I'd stepped through a portal into another dimension. As I slogged through the mud on my way back to camp, my mind wandered back to the astonishing moment I'd met my first Korowai warrior. I now knew him as Anom, but on the evening we met he'd seemed to walk straight out of the mists of another world.

The journey out here from Bristol had been nothing short of epic. A week of travelling that included seven flights and a day's boat ride. The crew and I had eventually reached a small village called Yafufla, perched on a high escarpment overlooking the Becking River in south-east Papua. Yafufla was on the southern edge of Korowai territory, and our last night's lodging before arriving at the tribe's village deep in the forest.

Our hut teetered on wooden stilts three feet aboveground and wobbled like a jelly anytime someone shifted in their sleep or got up to go outside for a pee. There were six of us scattered around the room: Gavin the principle cameraman, whom I'd just been working with in Gabon; Rachel and Tom from the BBC; Jim, an American anthropologist; and Bob, our Indonesian fixer. A good bunch of people, but it soon transpired that one of them concealed a terrible secret: our hut swayed to the rhythm of some world-class snoring and my heart sank at the prospect of having to listen to that racket every night for the next few weeks. But in the absence of any personal space or privacy we would all need to be super-tolerant of each other, and besides, I'm not always the easiest travelling companion myself. I talk in my sleep, get ratty when hungry and whistle under my breath too much.

Eventually I dozed off, only to wake again at 3am. The snoring had been replaced by a low murmuring of hushed voices coming from the hut's entrance. The soft glow of firelight flickered through gaps in the wooden walls, so I pulled on my shorts to see what was going on. Emerging onto the small balcony, I found Bob sitting next to a fire opposite two men the like of whom I'd never seen before. Their eyes flicked towards me and they fell silent as Bob turned round and subtly gestured for me to sit down beside him. Making myself as inconspicuous as possible, I leant back to study Bob's companions from the shadows. I hadn't seen these men before. Everyone we'd encountered so far had worn Western clothing courtesy of the missionaries downriver. But these men were dressed in traditional Korowai clothing, which is to say they weren't wearing much at all.

Anom was the older of the two and Bob quietly explained that he was here as ambassador from the Korowai, to officially guide us into their territory. Small, dark-skinned and sinewy, Anom was in his fifties but had the taut-muscled physique of a man half his age. He wore a woven fibre headband and a necklace of tiny white shell fragments. Two hoops of rattan were looped round his waist and his manhood was covered with a seedpod. But his most striking adornments were a piece of sharpened white bone stuck through his septum, and a tiny cowry shell embedded within a hole drilled in the end of his nose. His face was craggy and his hair wild. He could have been a distant relation of Keith Richards. Behind him – its black polished surface gleaming like oil in the firelight – stood a seven-foot-tall longbow. An immensely powerful weapon that I had no doubt he was master of. Beside it stood a sheaf of arrows, some tipped with wide bamboo blades, others with vicious-looking barbs delicately carved out of bone. None were fletched, and they were four feet long: more like spears.

His companion was younger but dressed in much the same way, with the addition of a long slender cassowary-bone dagger tucked into his woven belt. A thick warrior's necklace of pig's teeth hung in a white crescent across his dark chest and his sinewy muscles flexed as he slowly rocked back and forth smoking one of Bob's cigarettes.

The men's shadows danced in the firelight as I sat and listened to the soft cadence of a language unlike any I'd ever heard. Not as clunky as Indonesian and far more fluid than English. Like the gentle murmur of leaves in a forest. I was spellbound.

After a while they lay down to doze next to the glowing embers, so I went back to bed, where I lay awake thinking about what that morning might bring when we made our final trek through the jungle into Korowai territory.

• • •

Climbing into the ironwood for the first time had been a fantastic way to stretch the long journey out of my muscles. I wanted to keep this momentum going by getting back up there the next day to rig some camera positions. The following morning, however, was a write-off. Other than Costa Rica, I've never been in such a wet jungle. By mid morning it had been raining solidly for seventeen hours, a relentless heavy downpour that leached all colour from the forest and drowned out all attempts at conversation. We Brits think we know all about rain: we don't. British weather, however bad, generally sweeps through quite quickly. Large tracts of lowland rainforest behave very differently. Rain squats over the same patch for days on end. The trees themselves create it by releasing compounds into the air that encourage water molecules to coalesce into clouds. Trees mould the environment around them, and anything else wishing to live in a jungle needs to deal with getting soaked through on a regular basis.

Gavin the cameraman and I were sitting under a tarpaulin near the ironwood, watching sheet water guillotine down to create a moat in the mud around us. The long-drop toilets back in camp had flooded overnight and our base was now awash in a slurry of mud and human excrement. To cap it all, one of the tribe's pigs had crawled into one of the toilets to die. Not a very auspicious start to the day, so we'd decided to head into the forest in the hope of getting up into the canopy the moment the rain stopped. Anom had joined us and cackled loudly as Gavin and I bickered over the best way to light a fire to boil water for tea. It was the first of many times we'd see him laugh at our strange ways, his wild appearance enhanced by a solitary yellow tooth.

It was afternoon by the time the rain eased off into a drizzle and we felt able to begin work. I had my eye on a tall, slender tree adjacent to the ironwood, and set about rigging a rope in its branches. By this time we'd been joined by several Korowai men and women. I got my climbing rope stuck in a high fork, so one of the men offered to shin up and free it. Before I could tell him not to worry, he'd free-climbed eighty feet up and solved the problem. He used hands and feet to maintain three points of contact at all times and moved with graceful poise, careful not to shock-load or jolt any branch. Some of the best free-climbing I've ever seen. These people were clearly born to the trees, but this display was merely a taste of what was to come.

Once my ropes were rigged I climbed into this adjacent tree to get a new perspective on the ironwood. I was rewarded with the perfect view of its canopy, level with where I presumed the house would be built. Looking back down to the ground a hundred feet below, I saw forty Korowai systematically clearing the jungle around the ironwood's base. Women tackled the smaller trees and saplings with stone axes, while men laid into the larger stuff.

Despite the fact that they only had one steel axe between them, it wasn't long before big trees were coming down left, right and centre. Men took turns using this precious metal tool, swinging it left-handed with brutal force to make the directional undercut, while another used a traditional stone axe to attack the timber from the trunk's opposite side. It was amazing to see stone and metal used side by side, and while the steel axe was undoubtedly faster, the stone versions were still capable of felling large trees surprisingly quickly. The air was filled with the shouts of people and the rhythmic *thwack* of chopping as one by one the trees between mine and the ironwood were laid low. Their leafy canopies sighed through the air as gravity tugged them down to the ground. None of them were as big as the ironwood, but they still came down with a wallop, and each impact was accompanied by a chorus of triumphant calls from the Korowai.

Several toddlers stumbled amongst the fallen timber, playing with toy bows and arrows. My heart was in my mouth as tonnes of wood rained down around them. Amazingly no one got hurt, but the rainforest was taking a phenomenal hammering and by the end of the following day, the kayu besi stood alone and adrift amidst a sea of destruction. Its exposure served to accentuate its size. I still couldn't get my head around how these guys were going to get into its canopy without the use of ropes.

Many of the fallen trees were being stripped of their bark for use as flooring, and the smaller trees were being lopped into poles and thrown into bundles at the base of the ironwood. The men were now hard at work using these materials to build a series of wooden scaffolds and ladders up towards the ironwood's first branches. They worked with incredible speed and dexterity, wrapping bare legs around the uprights as bundles of poles were hoisted up on the end of long rattan ropes. I filmed them from my perch opposite, hanging on safety ropes while they free-climbed around the wobbling scaffold fifty feet aboveground, with nothing to catch them but thin air should they fall. They swarmed over the structure like ants, working together as a team to ensure their best, most experienced climbers had everything they needed to keep pushing up as fast as they could. By sunset they'd reached the ironwood's first branch and built a level platform of sticks around the tree's central stem. This seemed to be the launch pad from where they would make a break for the canopy and establish the foundation beams of the treehouse itself.

As dusk approached I was left alone in the clearing to look down on the scene from my perch high above. The end result of the day's labour was a hectare of forest that looked like it had been blasted by artillery – a rugged mess of chest-high stumps. It was astonishing: within twenty-four hours two acres of primary rainforest had been reduced to a mangled heap of twisted trunks and snapped branches. Okay, there was a steel axe knocking around, but for the most part this speedy clearance had been done by forty people using stone tools. As an experiment in practical archaeology it couldn't be more thought-provoking: the forests of Neolithic Britain clearly hadn't stood a chance.

● ● ●

That evening as usual I headed down to the stream with the others to wash in the deep black water flowing sluggishly out of the surrounding forest. Each evening Bob, our Indonesian fixer, whose tent lay right next to the path, had the dubious pleasure of watching a line of half-naked Brits in flip-flops trying to jump the large puddle next to his tent without dropping towel, torch or soap. He'd respond to the routine chorus of 'Evening, Bob' with his customary 'Evening, BBC, look out for the crocs.'

That night I paused to ask him about something that had been playing on my mind. I just couldn't work out why the Korowai cleared the forest around their treehouses so extensively. A few trees here and there, okay. But was it really necessary to clear-fell two acres? It seemed to go way beyond any practical demand for building materials. The felling I'd witnessed had appeared almost fanatical. I'd also detected a desire amongst the Korowai not to be caught out by nightfall; a determination to make sure that everyone, particularly the children, were safely back inside their own treehouses before sunset.

Bob explained that the Korowai have been the traditional victims of headhunting raids from neighbouring tribes for centuries. I knew this. 'But surely that stopped way back,' I said. In most regions, yes, Bob explained, but old habits die hard and the legacy of this insecurity was mistrust of any dense cover that might conceal a surprise attack. Fair enough. But Bob then went on to explain that the Korowai also live in perpetual dread of a more surreptitious threat: witchcraft.

Khakhua are sorcerers inhabiting the guise of fellow clansmen, who take control of that person, commanding them to commit violent acts. An alleged Khakhua implicated in a crime, either by the victim or by general consensus, is then put to death and dismembered with their body parts distributed to adjacent clans to be eaten in cannibalistic rituals. The Korowai believe that this is the only way to vanquish the Khakhua's evil spirit forever. Accusations of sorcery can be levelled against anyone at any time, and everyone within Korowai society lives with this threat hanging over them their entire lives. People have been forced to hand over close relatives to the kin of victims making the accusation from their deathbed. They are powerless to prevent the grim killing and ritual consumption of their loved one that then follows.

'These and other spirits like them live in the jungle around their houses, and cutting back the trees stops them from sneaking into the family home unseen,' said Bob.

Dark stuff, and it was easy to see why the Korowai took refuge in the trees themselves to escape such threats.

Running all this past anthropologist Jim over our meal of beetle grubs that evening, Bob added: 'Aliom is the resident shaman: it's his job to protect the tribe from such spirits.'

This didn't surprise me at all. Although I respected Aliom and had even grown quite fond of him, I found him deeply unsettling at times. He was a bit older than Anom, the other tribal elder, and had some form of skin condition that gave him a greyish, almost spectral colour. Although he was sinewy like the others his skin sagged in strange creases, as if it was a size too large for him. He had extremely quick, darting eyes and a heavy brow often crumpled into a frown, while his mouth hung in a habitual lopsided, left-handed grin.

A humourless wolfish grin that gave the impression he was studying us in a quizzical fashion, as if sizing us up. A rattling cough ripped his chest apart every few seconds, but other than that he remained silent, content to watch us furtively, passively shunning the glance of the camera and largely ignoring our attempts to communicate.

There was a distinctly otherworldly air about him and it didn't surprise me to learn that Aliom had almost certainly partaken of cannibalism in the past.

'As, I'm sure,' Jim was quick to point out, 'have most of the other older guys here. Captives taken in battle were also sometimes given the same treatment.'

I wasn't quite sure what I thought about that, but as fond of them as I was, it was now impossible to look at the older warriors – including Anom – in the same way as before.

• • •

The next morning, Gavin headed up onto the scaffold to film some close-ups of the men, while I went back up into the neighbouring tree to film the whole scene from a distance. A woman in a grass skirt and dog-tooth necklace arrived, carrying smouldering embers wrapped in a leaf with which to make a communal fire. I watched the thin trail of blue smoke rise into the air behind her as she balanced barefoot along a fallen tree then hopped down to join the other women already sitting beneath a canopy of palm leaves. The smoke from the fire slowly filled the clearing and the morning sun broke through in solid beams, adding incredible beauty and atmosphere to an already timeless scene. It felt like forever since we'd seen the sun. This was our first day without rain and everyone was in high spirits, making the most of it.

Most of the men were already up on the tower. Some carried bundles of sticks on their shoulders as they climbed the rungs, while others shouldered long, snake-like coils of rattan. The whole scene was alive with activity and I was reminded of the moment in *Gulliver's Travels* when the Lilliputians tie Gulliver down with ropes. A similar army of tiny figures was now working quickly to enmesh the kayu besi's giant form within a tangled web. The Korowai were relentless, working without rest, as if worried the tree might suddenly wake up and stride away before it could be properly restrained.

By mid morning the tower was ninety feet high and had entered the ironwood's enormous crown. From here the whole construction took on a new lease of life and soon galvanised into an ingeniously constructed lattice that seemed to engulf the tree's canopy like a wicker basket. An eight-year-old boy, climbing up higher to get in on the action, was told to get back down by an older, experienced guy. The boy dropped back onto the rungs below and spent the next ten minutes gallivanting around like a lunatic. As precarious as this looked to my eyes, I reminded myself that the Korowai learned to climb trees from the day they could walk. Nevertheless I was encouraged by the inexperienced lad's dismissal. There was no room for complacency. The men at the top fully understood the consequences of a hundred-foot fall, even if the kids didn't. So I relaxed a bit and enjoyed the experience of watching the whole construction materialise in front of my camera lens.

By the following morning the latticework had engulfed over half of the ironwood and it was time for Gavin and me to get up into the ironwood alongside the Korowai. This would be my first time back in the tree since climbing it a week or so ago. It had been changed beyond all recognition, and although my ropes still hung down its trunk they were now redundant as I prepared to clamber up via the new network of ladders. Weighing around four stone more than most of the Korowai, I made my first foray into their wicker world very carefully. A couple of rungs slipped a few inches before coming to rest on their rattan lashings, but I was amazed by how strong the whole thing felt. It flexed and moved, but this was deliberate. The kayu besi was a dynamic living thing that would move all over the place in a storm, and anything built in its canopy would need to do the same to avoid being ripped apart. The main ladder connecting the first landing stage to the upper canopy was set at forty-five degrees, which meant I had a fantastic view down through the rungs to the cleared forest 100 feet below. I could see kids and dogs running around down there, and took great enjoyment from the feeling of being this high in a tree without having to rely on ropes.

The top platform was cradled snugly within the tree's middle crown. This would provide the foundation for the house yet to be built. From here the ground was entirely hidden from view, and knowing this a gang of teenagers was lounging around on the platform, chatting and smoking in peaceful seclusion from their mothers and sisters far below. Some things don't change.

Having made it up here I was keen to take a good look at the view, but as empowering as it was to be free from ropes, it seemed sensible to install a couple of safety lanyards around one of the stems for Gavin and me before edging out along a horizontal pole. As I placed my hand in the fork of a stem next to me, I noticed a faint rope-rub in the bark. I was now standing in almost exactly the same spot I'd been hanging in my harness while watching the spider during that first climb. This meant we were now around 120 feet aboveground. It seemed impossible that this could be the same tree. It's beautiful canopy had been changed beyond all recognition. Entire stems were missing, hacked off and discarded to make way for the house. Where there had been long, elegant branches was now an ugly thicket of amputated stumps, and the open space beyond the ironwood's ragged limbs bore no resemblance to the pristine canopy that had hung there before all neighbouring trees had been felled. But as ugly as this was, the Korowai had very good reason for thinning the ironwood's crown. Leafy canopies present a sail-like wall of resistance to the wind and are the main reason why tall trees thrash around so much in a storm. Since the treehouse would add weight and rigidity to the top of the tree, it made perfect sense to reduce the canopy's load as much as possible. Removing surplus foliage lowered wind resistance and helped maintain the ironwood's overall balance. Being inside a house made of sticks at this height while it was torn apart by the tree in a storm wasn't anyone's idea of fun. Our Gabon treehouse had been built much lower down, but it had still taken a kicking from the ebana's thrashing stems. This one, in the top of kayu besi would have to tolerate far worse.

Turning away from the view, I noticed an elderly Korowai warrior in the far corner on the platform behind the others. He was far older than anyone else here and neither Gavin nor I had seen him before. Several people had recently arrived from neighbouring Korowai clans to help with the build, but it was still surprising to meet someone completely new for the first time at the top of the tree. He sat cross-legged, gripping the poles beneath him between his toes while using long strips of rattan to lash the floor together. He seemed a bit unsteady and had a particularly wild look about him, even for a Korowai. Like many of the older warriors he had a tiny cowry shell embedded in the end of his nose and wore a headband. He was painfully thin and his cheeks were sunken hollows beneath a short grey beard. As I sat down to watch him work, he broke into a beautiful high-pitched song. A series of repeated phrases that jumped octaves like a yodel rang out over the canopy as clear as a bell. He could probably be heard from the neighbouring clan's territory. He stopped singing to peer up at the teenagers playing like gibbons in the very top of the tree above us. They were shaking the crown all over the place and the slight furrow in his brow said it all. Then, seeming to notice me for the first time, he leant forward to peer into my face, our noses almost touching. Both his eyes were clouded over with cataracts. I couldn't believe it: a sixty-year-old man, barely able to see five inches in front of his face, was clambering around in the branches 120 feet aboveground. These people were amazing.

Things were moving quickly now, the platform of sticks upon which the house would stand was almost completed and additional materials to build its walls and roof were being hauled up in large bundles that spun slowly through space on their long rattan ropes.

The old man again looked up at the lads skylarking in the branches twenty feet above us. They were balancing on twigs no thicker than my fingers, gripping the wood with their toes while they surfed the bouncing foliage, arms waving above their heads. Ironwood is strong stuff, but there are limits. Nasé told them to stop fooling around and get down so he could get on with thinning the branches out. One of the boys ignored the command, so Nasé struck the base of the branch with a stone axe. An idle threat, but it got the point across and the boy came shinning down in the blink of an eye. In fact the cutting of ironwood was way beyond what a stone axe could cope with, so Nasé handed the clan's one and only metal machete up to Wayu, who proceeded to lay into the timber with a series of resounding metallic rings. It sounded like a sword fight, with the dense ironwood parrying the blade, flicking it off at great speed in unpredictable directions. But Wayu cracked on and as he finally severed the limb, the familiar whooping call was sent out by Nasé to warn those below. The bushy branch tipped over the edge of the platform, righting itself vertically beneath its parachute of leaves to drop slowly down to the forest floor with a gentle swish and a distant thud.

The men whistled incessantly as they worked, an ongoing chorus of shrill phrases repeated over and over again as they sat cross-legged, lashing the poles to the scaffold.

'And I thought your whistling got annoying,' said Gavin to me. 'It's like being surrounded by a gang of postmen.'

By mid afternoon the following day the house was almost complete: walls of wooden poles lashed together with rattan, a pitched roof thatched with sago palm leaves, and a floor of tree bark laid down to cover the gaps in the supporting platform. Gavin had captured some wonderful, rare footage of the structure materialising around us.

Before the final touches were even in place it was being visited by women and children. Many of them had net-bags slung from their shoulders containing piglets and puppies. By the time Anom made his first visit there were two fires crackling in mud hearths and kids and animals were tearing around all over the place. Sitting down on the house's small balcony, he smoked his pipe and admired the view over the surrounding jungle with evident pleasure.

In fact everyone was looking happy, and with good reason. What had been accomplished was nothing short of phenomenal. The finished house was like nothing I'd ever seen before, made entirely from four basic materials provided by the forest: vines, tree bark, palm fronds and poles – nothing else. And when it was finally abandoned and allowed to collapse, it would fall back to the ground and return completely to the earth. The ironwood would survive, branches would regrow and I had no doubt that kayu besi would live on for many decades, even centuries to come.

• • •

The building of a house like this was clearly a big social event, a culturally defining act for the Korowai. They took huge pride in their work, and their ability to operate confidently in such an extreme environment seemed to form an essential part of their identity. Building high up in the canopy is what they *did*, and they did it better than anyone else on the planet. I just hoped we weren't witnessing their swansong. Missionaries were creeping upriver towards the Korowai's lands and some clans had already forsaken the forest for a life in government-built settlements of dreary wooden huts.

The Korowai clearly have a complicated and intensely intimate relationship with the forest around them. Trees provide them with almost everything they need: materials, fuel, refuge and culture. Even their staple daily food comes directly from them. Sago palm provides both carbohydrates (in the form of cakes baked from its starchy pith) and protein, via the large squirming beetle grubs that spill out from the stem like jelly beans.

There were so many questions left unanswered. I wondered whether their relationship with trees might also be spiritual. It was almost inevitable that trees should play a huge role within their folklore and religious beliefs, but what were those roles exactly? Did the Korowai deify them, or were trees simply to be feared as the hiding places of dark spirits? Or both, since fear and deification often go hand in hand?

Although I occasionally caught people looking up at kayu besi with wonder in their eyes there appeared to be little room in daily Korowai society for sentimentality. Trees weren't coddled or romanticised and it made me question my own attitude. Was my affection for trees simply a projection of my own spiritual needs – a way of filling a void left by a modern distrust of formal religion? I don't know, but if I should ever be lucky enough to meet a Korowai again I will be sure to ask them more about the way they *feel* about trees and how they *relate* to them in a spiritual sense. Even though I know this would be like asking a fish about water, or a bird about the air through which it soars.

Chapter 9

Fortaleza – Venezuela

1987

Simon and I were sitting on the carpet of his mum's lounge. We were twelve years old and had just come back from crawling through the New Forest watching deer. 'Check this out,' he said, selecting a VHS tape from the teetering stack next to the video player. He pressed play and the flickering screen resolved into an image of lush tropical jungle. The tape was a copy of a copy and the colours bled into each other, but I could make out the silhouette of someone climbing a huge tree. The camera zoomed out to show him dangling on a rope at least a hundred feet aboveground. He used mountaineering clamps to slowly inch-worm his way up the thin line, and for some strange reason wore a motorcycle crash helmet.

He looked exposed and vulnerable. I could just make out a vast tree canopy looming in the mist high above. Enormous black branches underexposed against a milky-white tropical sky. Each branch was the size of an entire English tree and carpeted in dense forests of shaggy ferns and vines, and the tree trunk that supported this hanging garden was bigger than any I'd ever seen. The tree dwarfed the climber, made him look like a child.

Just as I was wondering what the crash helmet was for a huge feathered shadow swooped down from the canopy above to punch the climber hard on the shoulder. The force of the impact sent him spinning – arms and legs flailing uselessly in space while he twisted round, frantically trying to see where the next attack would come from. But the enormous bird was gone. In the blink of an eye it melted back into the shadows and all the man could do was quicken his pace and press on for the sanctuary of the branches high above. A minute later the huge bird struck again, approaching swiftly from behind to wallop him hard on the back of the head. A stunning blow that explained the need for a crash helmet.

Simon was obsessed with birds of prey, a walking encyclopaedia of Top Trump bird facts, and I asked him what on earth the bird was. It looked like some sort of massive eagle. 'Yep, it's a harpy eagle,' he replied, and rewound the clip so we could watch it again. 'The guy's climbing up to film its nest, and they are really secretive, aggressive birds,' he explained, and pressed the pause button the instant the eagle next appeared. I shuffled closer to the TV to take a better look at the juddering image on screen. The harpy was in full strike pose, with huge wings fanned out like a cape. Its long legs were held out in front of it, ready to rake the climber with fists full of sharp talons. The name suited it well; it looked like some demonic creature of myth and legend. The video was more like a sci-fi movie than a wildlife film. With a huge wingspan, the bird was much bigger than the cameraman it was attacking. But I also gazed in wonder at the colossal tree that towered over man and bird to dominate the entire scene. The film's narrator told us it was a kapok tree, growing deep in the jungles of Central America, and I could see the eagle's nest it supported, a huge eyrie of branches built in a fork at the top of the kapok's main stem. There was probably a chick in that nest, which would explain the eagle's aggression towards any intruder. It was the perfect tree for such an impressive bird to nest in: a living fortress. Totally unscalable without ropes.

Simon pressed play and the harpy disappeared in a streak, to leave the tiny climber swaying out of control on his rope once more.

The rest of the film revealed the secret life of a harpy's nest. The cameraman perched inside a hide built in the kapok's uppermost branches. It was magical. Yes, he'd taken a kicking from the eagle, but the rest of his film stood testament to what a bit of determination and a lot of patience could deliver. To a twelve-year-old already obsessed with trees and wildlife the film was a revelation.

It would be another few years until I got to climb my first big tree alongside Paddy and Matt in the New Forest, but

Simon's video had just planted the seeds of an obsession that would slowly shape my life. And with the characteristic naivety of a twelve-year-old schoolboy, I hoped that one day I'd be lucky enough to meet a harpy while dangling on a rope in the canopy of a kapok.

2010

I walked into camp, slumped down in a chair, cracked open a warm beer and took the offered cigarette. Adrian was already inhaling deeply from his and I followed suit. It had been quite a morning. The nicotine and alcohol were most welcome, despite the fact that it was barely 10am and I didn't smoke. There was blood trickling down my neck and my ears were ringing. I was soaked with sweat, my back was covered in bruises and my hands were shaking. We sat in silence, lost in our own thoughts, while trying to piece together the events that had led to this moment. I stared at the tar stain on the end of my cigarette filter while absentmindedly flicking the ring pull on my beer can. I drained it in one and Adrian silently handed me another. I felt my body relax and a deep exhaustion crept through me. My bones felt like lead and I slid off the seat to lie down on my back in the dirt and stare up into the clear blue Venezuelan sky.

What had just happened? My head was reeling, so I stubbed the half-smoked ciggie out in the dust next to me and let my mind rewind to trace the chain of events leading up to this moment. Closing my eyes, I took myself back to the day three months earlier when I had first entered this forest. Back to the day I had first stood below the giant kapok tree and squinted up at the harpy nest we had come here to film for the BBC.

* * *

Stepping from the sun-blasted open into the cool, dark jungle for the first time had been bliss. Like diving into a cool lake on a hot day. The sounds of the forest had enveloped me and it took a while to grow accustomed to my new, darker surroundings. Every rainforest has a different atmosphere and this one felt particularly full of life from the very moment I set foot in it. Flocks of parrots raced noisily across the early morning sky above. Hummingbirds hovered and dodged amongst the lush vegetation and I had just met a long black snake while crossing a stream. It'd come questing towards me through the water, head raised and tongue flicking. I'd stood still to let its sinuous seven-foot-long body pass between my legs on its way downstream, the staccato warnings of birds betraying its location long after I'd lost sight of it amongst the dark ripples and eddies.

Stepping out of the water, I was faced with a short but steep hill to climb. My rucksack was heavy with ropes and my boots slipped in the leaf litter. I took my time; my breath was laboured and ponderous as my lungs expelled the last of the stale air-conditioning inhaled during the long journey to Venezuela from England. Reaching the top of the slope, I took a moment to catch my breath and look around.

The surrounding forest was lush and vibrant. Young saplings grew beneath a dense upper canopy of mature trees.

Patches of bright sunlight dappled the forest floor and back-lit cobwebs hung across the path, telling me I was the first person to walk down the trail that morning.

The forest smelt incredible. An earthy aroma of leaf mould laced with delicate citrus scents from unseen flowers. Pockets of different smells hung in the cool air without mingling, so I was greeted by a succession of enticing odours as I walked through the clinging spider silk.

Adrian the producer had told me how to find the harpy tree.

'You can't miss it, it's by far and away the biggest tree round here,' he'd added, after sketching a map in the dirt as we drank coffee in camp.

Keen to crack on as soon as possible, I had left him sorting a few things and headed into the forest on my own. I was under no illusion about the challenges we were up against, and wouldn't be able to relax until I'd seen exactly what I had to deal with. Climbing a fully grown kapok tree to install a remote camera within an active harpy nest was an exciting challenge, but not to be taken lightly.

I continued along the trail, turning right at a junction to follow the path along a ridge. A few minutes later I arrived at another junction and followed the trail down a gentle slope to the left. According to Adrian, the kapok was down here somewhere, growing in the lee of the ridge. But I couldn't see it. I stopped to get my bearings. For a massive tree it was proving pretty elusive.

Looking down the slope into the gloom, I realised that the stand of trees growing close together at the bottom of the hill was in fact one huge tree trunk. The base measured at least thirty feet across and sunlight and shadow played across its smooth grey bark. My eyes tracked up its colossal stem until it disappeared from view behind other branches in the foreground. Lifting my gaze yet further I saw it reappear above the surrounding forest canopy. Only then did the kapok unfurl its giant limbs to stretch out like an enormous parasol and dominate the other trees beneath it. It was one of the broadest, biggest canopies I'd ever seen. It wasn't the first kapok I'd met, but it was by far the biggest – a real bruiser of a tree. I stood there taking it all in, remembering the first time I'd seen an image of a kapok, twenty-three years ago at Simon's house. And here I was, at last – about to climb one.

I walked closer. The lower trunk flared out in a wooden avalanche of buttresses. Giant roots seemed to spill over the ground like molten wax before disappearing into the earth. I noticed subtle detail and texture in the bark, horizontal creases following the contours of roots, like stretch marks on skin, and patches of mottled green algae revealing where moisture lingered. Several of the buttresses were so tall, sunlight couldn't penetrate the narrow gaps between them. I gave a root a tap with my boot. Two tiny bats flew up past my face to flit around for a few seconds before tumbling back down to roost. Peering over the root I saw them hanging upside down from tiny ridges in the bark, chattering excitedly to each other. I put down my rucksack and stepped back to get a proper look up at the rest of the tree.

Its trunk rose straight up for 120 feet before splitting into four giant limbs. These continued on rising, dividing again and again to support the immense canopy. Down at the base I was still standing in morning shadow, but high above me the foliage shone in bright sunlight. Each glowing leaf was the size and shape of an open hand. The foliage was dense but largely confined to the tips of branches. Inside the canopy was an open, airy space crisscrossed by huge grey branches, many of which appeared to be covered with large thorn-like spikes. These would add yet another dimension to the climb, and I'd have to rig carefully since they could easily rip through the soft nylon of my ropes. I was still contemplating this new challenge when something higher in the canopy caught my eye and I glanced up into the unfaltering gaze of an adult female harpy eagle.

She'd been there the whole time, silently watching me as I walked around in the gloom 200 feet below her. She stood at least three feet tall on her thorny perch, and had a grey, surprisingly owl-like face. Her upper chest was a deep charcoal that contrasted beautifully with the snow-white plumage of her breast. Her enormous folded wings were slate grey and her flanks were barred black and white. But what really drew my attention were her massive legs. They were bright yellow and as thick as my wrists. Her feet were as large as my hands and each one carried four jet-black, murderous-looking claws. I raised my binoculars for a closer look. The two rear talons in particular looked like real killers about five inches each in length. I guessed she used these thumb talons to kill her prey on impact, driving them forward like knives to puncture the body of a sloth or monkey.

Despite her sublime beauty she was also intimidating. She exuded a palpable aura of power and intent. Having realised that I'd now seen her, she leant forward to return my gaze and scrutinise me even more closely. Her head bobbed slowly from side to side and I had no doubt that she was registering every bit of my appearance. Being the object of such focused intent was unnerving, a feeling that increased when she slowly raised the dark feather crest on top of her head. The crest waved gently in the breeze like a headdress, and I had the uncanny impression she knew exactly what I was there to do and was fully prepared to prevent me from doing it.

It's never a sensible idea to anthropomorphise animals, but in those first few moments I just knew that she could tell I was there to climb her tree. And it *was* 'her' tree. The kapok dominated the forest, but she owned the kapok. This tree was her fortress – her *fortaleza*, in Spanish – and it was clear to me that she would do anything she could to defend her nest.

This nest itself lay hidden somewhere beneath her. I couldn't see, but it was obvious that it contained something important to her from the manner in which she stole glances at it. Growing bored of me, she eventually unfolded her dark wings and glided across to the other side of the kapok where she perched looking out over the forest. It seemed my first audience with a harpy was over.

Walking back up the slope towards the ridge, I searched for an angle from which I could see the nest. I eventually found it cradled between huge limbs at the top of the tree's main stem, safe from the elements and away from prying eyes. I wondered how such a massive thing could've remained so well hidden from the ground. It was ten feet across and five feet deep. Big enough for me to comfortably sleep in. Now *that* would be a night to remember, I thought, as I headed back up the trail to collect the rest of my climbing gear from camp.

• • •

Back outside the forest, everything was shimmering white-hot and painful to look at. Walking back into the shade of camp was a relief. I could hear chatting. Adrian, and Graham, the cameraman, were filling their water bottles. They pulled up some chairs and the three of us sat down around the makeshift kitchen table to discuss our options.

We'd talked it all through so many times already. How to install the nest-cam had been the topic of conversation for days now. First and foremost, above all else, was the need to ensure the absolute safety of the birds. Rigging cameras on nests is an intrusive process and getting one onto a harpy nest was about as tricky as it got. Every step had to be carefully planned to minimise disturbance. Smashing an egg or harming a chick would be totally unforgivable. As would stressing the parents out to the point where their defence of the nest caused them to injure themselves. They could easily snap a talon, buckle a feather, or even break a wing while trying to drive us away. I for one didn't want a failed harpy nest on my conscience.

We were right to be nervous, but we were also confident that it could be done without causing harm. We just needed to think it through step by step. It was possible that we'd be confronted by the adult birds at some stage. But before we'd even left England we'd agreed that our defence in the face of an attacking eagle must be as passive as possible. Even trying to ward off or deflect a blow could injure the birds.

Our original plan had been to sneak in under the radar and get the camera on the nest without either of the parents noticing. But the female's behaviour that morning had made it obvious that this wasn't going to happen: she was keeping close tabs on everything that happened in the vicinity of her tree.

From the manner in which she'd been regularly glancing down at something hidden in the nest it was obvious there was either an egg or a chick up there. Either way, we wouldn't be able to keep her off the nest for too long. Without mum there to look after it, any egg or chick would quickly chill or overheat, depending on the time of day. Neither outcome was acceptable, and the clock would start ticking the moment she flushed off the eyrie at our approach. I decided to get the ropes up that afternoon, leaving the birds to settle down again before climbing up to install the camera.

• • •

I knelt down in the leaf litter and pulled the catapult's thick elastic down as far as I could. I'd mounted the large, metal Y-shaped head to the top of a tall wooden pole to give me as much power as possible. The target branch was 140 feet up, well within range, and I wouldn't normally have needed to pull the elastic back so hard. But it wasn't a clear shot. The throw-bag had to get through a series of tiny gaps in the foliage and I needed the catapult's full power to punch it through any leaves that got in the way. The kapok was in the prime of life, its canopy thick and healthy, with no hanging deadwood. (This lack of deadwood was a great relief. The last thing I wanted was to dislodge something heavy onto the nest.)

I still hadn't seen the smaller, less aggressive male harpy, but the formidable female was back on her spiky perch above me, shoulders hunched and crest raised. She was balancing on one foot with the other held up in front of her as she slowly clenched it in obvious irritation. I was glad to see her so clearly as it meant there was no danger of accidentally hitting her with the catapult. I was more concerned about accidentally hitting the nest. A throw-bag could easily smash an egg or injure a chick. I chose my shooting position very carefully and from this angle the nest was completely protected by one of the kapok's giant stems.

I aimed slightly above the target branch, pulled the elastic down the last few inches, slowly breathed out and released. The bag shot clean through the gaps in the canopy, over the branch and carried on to finally wrap itself gently around a few leaves in the very top of the tree. It was a good shot. I waited until the bag stopped swinging before pulling it gently back through the leaves to drop it over the big branch.

The harpy glared at the small blue throw-bag the whole time. She glided across to take a closer look at it. Having satisfied her curiosity, she then turned back around to face me again before flying off to a different branch, out of sight.

I hauled the climbing rope up into position. By the time the tree was rigged the afternoon was getting on and I was keen to give the birds some space. Stashing my kitbags in the leaf litter at the base of the kapok, I turned for camp.

Reaching the ridge, I peered back up at the kapok, which was glowing in the early-evening sunlight. Its vast canopy seemed to shine from within. It really was a beautiful tree, rising above the forest like an enormous mushroom. From this shallower angle I could see just how massive the lower limbs were and how much open space there was between them. The birds had chosen their nesting site well; they had a clear view of everything that happened both in the tree's canopy and around it. There would be nowhere for us to hide once we climbed above the lower canopy.

• • •

The following morning I slipped a heavy Kevlar stab vest on over my climbing shirt and did the straps up tight. It was comforting to know it could stop a knife blade, but had it ever been tested against an irate harpy? I pulled on a pair of arm greaves, then bent down to pick up the heavy riot helmet lying at my feet. It was dark blue, with a scratched perspex visor and a thick padded neck guard. I turned it over in my hands to read the word 'Police' in faint letters across the front, before putting it on. Its thick foam padding muffled my hearing and destroyed my peripheral vision so that I had to turn to face anything I wanted to see clearly. I pulled down the visor, which instantly steamed up and heightened the cramping sense of claustrophobia.

We'd brought this second-hand body armour out with us from Bristol. Climbing a tree in it wasn't going to be fun. But it was probably better than being ripped open by an angry eagle. There was still a good chance it wouldn't come to that though. Every harpy is different and this pair might be content to monitor our progress from a distance. But we wouldn't know for sure until we got up on the ropes, by which time of course it would be too late. Better to be safe than sorry, I thought, remembering that video of Simon's.

• • •

By 5.30 the following morning, Graham, Adrian and I were standing amongst the enormous roots at the base of the kapok. Graham was preparing the nest camera while Adrian and I got suited-up ready to climb. Fitting the nest-cam was a one-man job, but four eyes were better than two, so Adrian would climb up with me. Graham would film our progress from a canopy platform in an adjacent tree. He could concentrate on the birds from there and radio through a warning if necessary. This was really important, since it might not just be the female harpy that we had to contend with. I hadn't seen her mate yet, but had no doubt that the male had seen me plenty of times, and we had to assume that both adults were watching us right now.

I peered up at the thin white ropes. They were hanging in open space twenty feet away from the tree trunk. I gave them a gentle shake to free them from snags. A thin veil of mist gave the scene depth and emphasised how high we had to climb. One hundred and fifty feet above us the first glimmer of sunlight was catching the kapok's leaves, and above this I could see a pale-blue sky that promised another hot day ahead. Time to get going.

I put the nest-cam in a small bag and hung it from the back of my climbing harness then clipped myself into the rope. The riot helmet was stifling. I could already feel my core temperature rising and I had barely left the ground. The combined weight of the helmet and stab vest was making me top-heavy, pulling me backwards off balance. This, along with the rope's elasticity, made it hard going and almost impossible to get into an efficient climbing rhythm. I was in a negative space and struggling to get my head right for this climb. It just all felt so wrong. Without being able to see or hear properly, I felt totally disconnected from the tree I was climbing.

But there was nothing for it. Yes, it was going to be tricky, but I reminded myself that no one was forcing me to wear this gear. It had been my own decision, so I might as well get on with it. We had chosen to wear the body armour for good reason and if we were attacked by the harpies then any amount of discomfort would be worthwhile.

I watched Adrian bouncing up his rope three metres away from me. Our plan was to keep pace with each other, to climb side by side and watch each other's back. But we were slowly spinning, at the mercy of the ropes' natural twist, and without peripheral vision I could only see Adrian when he was right in front of me. I would spin, he would appear with his back to me, and then he'd be gone as I carried on spinning.

It was all pretty surreal and as I climbed upwards my sense of unease increased. We were being watched and I could tell from Adrian's body language that he felt it too. Both of us were stopping occasionally to peer round in a vain attempt to see where the birds were.

Fifty feet aboveground we broke through the dense understorey foliage to enter the open canopy zone above. However vulnerable I'd felt climbing up was nothing compared to how exposed I felt now. For the next seventy feet we would be dangling without cover and I was suddenly relieved to be wearing all the gear. The idea of doing this without body protection was verging on suicidal. My heart was racing and I fully expected to be winded by an unseen attack any second. My imagination was running away with me, so I reined it in and focused simply on climbing the rope.

The tree trunk next to us was still massive, even at this height above the ground. I looked up towards the nest: another forty feet to go. It was almost entirely hidden behind an enormous creeping plant that I now realised with surprise was a huge cheese plant, like a vastly enlarged version of the one my parents used to have at home in the 1970s. So this is where they come from, I thought – how bizarre to see one here.

'Look out, she's coming!' I was suddenly brought back to my senses by Graham's voice over the radio.

I twisted my head round just in time to catch a fleeting shadow pass fifteen feet away, on its way out of the kapok. Spinning round, I watched her fly across to perch in the top of a neighbouring tree. She ruffled her feathers, raised her crest and adopted a half-crouching position to watch our every move.

I pushed on towards the kapok's canopy as quickly as I could. Adrian was a little below me and still very exposed. I looked back at the eagle watching us from a hundred feet away. Suddenly she pitched forward and plummeted silently off the branch. With head hunched between powerful shoulders, she was coming in fast and low, straight towards Adrian.

'Adrian, lower your visor, get ready. Lower your visor!' I shouted.

He flicked the perspex down but still had his back to the approaching bird. Then at the last moment she veered away with astonishing speed and landed on a branch fifteen feet above us. She glared at us with fierce eyes. Seeing her alongside Adrian had given me a true sense of her incredible size, and both of us had been set swaying on our ropes from the downdraught as she'd put the brakes on to twist away. She had given us fair warning: a shot across the bows. I wondered how she would react when we finally got up to the nest itself.

Keeping a close eye on her, we pushed on as fast as we could. A few minutes later I arrived level with the huge platform of branches and swung across onto its edge. I could now appreciate just how massive the nest really was. It was three metres wide and two deep. Some of the branches were dead, some still had green leaves, but they were all big and heavy. It was an impressive construction, strong enough to take the weight of several people. And there at my feet, nestled deep in a small, bowl-like depression, were two delicate ivory-coloured eggs. They were almost round and about the size of goose eggs. So the female harpy was still sitting. The chicks hadn't hatched after all. I looked up at her, still close by on the branch above us, and I kept my eyes on her until Adrian came up alongside. She flew back across to the other tree, where she was content to remain while studying us.

This uneasy truce held for the whole time it took me to install the camera. Attaching it to a branch next to the nest was a fiddly process. Once it was done, Adrian headed back down to the ground 140 feet below us. I followed a few minutes later, slowly abseiling down while stopping at intervals to attach the camera's long power cable to the tree. Halfway down I felt a movement in the air, but I couldn't see anything when I twisted around to look.

It was a huge relief to finally arrive back on the ground amongst the kapok's huge twisting roots.

'Did you see her?' asked Adrian as I touched down.

I took off my helmet and looked at him. 'What do you mean? When?'

'The female harpy, she buzzed you a few minutes ago,' he explained.

'No. No, I didn't.' The shift in the air I had felt must have been her. An eagle weighing nine kilos with a seven-foot wingspan travelling at fifty miles per hour had passed within three feet of me and thanks to the bulky helmet I hadn't even seen her.

It was a relief to have the camera in position but I wouldn't be able to fully relax until we could see an image. Graham joined us and we all crouched around the tiny LCD monitor balanced on a tree root. We turned it on. The screen went blue for one nerve-wracking instant before revealing a lovely wide-angle image of the entire nest. On the right-hand side of the frame were two white eggs nestled within their scoop. In the background was a sweeping panorama of the surrounding forest. It looked great.

Adrian and I pulled down the ropes and carried our gear back to camp. Graham joined us there an hour later to report that the female had returned to incubate her eggs within minutes of us leaving the tree. This was great news. So far, so good: our mission had been a success. With luck we would now be able to capture intimate, rare footage of one of the world's most impressive yet secretive eagles raising its young.

But we were asking a lot of that little camera. Harpy chicks take a long time to fledge – six months, in fact, and that was a very long time for our small nest-cam to stay functioning in such a hot and humid environment. The thought of having to go back up there to fix it didn't appeal to any of us very much. Once the chicks hatched, their parents really *would* have something worth defending, and the more they invested in raising them, the more the bond would strengthen and the more aggressive they would become in their defence. But for now everything seemed fine. The camera was working, the birds had taken the disturbance well and all was going smoothly. With a bit of luck the next time I climbed the kapok would be to derig the camera after the chicks had left the nest. Without the need to wear the body armour, I'd have a chance to freely explore this magnificent tree.

It was a nice thought, but somehow, the moment my phone rang with Adrian's number several months later, I knew instantly that something had gone wrong with the camera.

• • •

It seemed like only yesterday that I had last stood at the base of this massive tree. But three months had now passed and a lot had happened since. The nest-cam, though still broadcasting, had completely fogged up and the image was unusable. It needed to be fixed, which meant climbing back up there, onto a nest which was now home to a very large harpy chick. I could see its fuzzy white outline stumbling around like a drunkard in the back of shot. It was several months old and growing fast on its diet of monkeys and sloths. Its parents were hunting around the clock, bringing food in regularly to meet their offspring's rapidly growing appetite.

This was the busiest time for a harpy nest and the parents had invested a lot of time and effort in their chick since it had hatched. They had a lot more to lose this time round, and there was no way they'd sit back and watch me climb into the nest alongside their one and only chick. They were going to react, for sure. But there was no way to predict how extreme this reaction might be until I was actually up there.

So once again I knelt down in the leaf litter, took careful aim with the catapult and released the elastic. The throw-bag flew true, straight over the same branch as before. Dropping the catapult, I made a grab for the thin fishing line accelerating up into the canopy. But just at that moment there was a sharp tug and the line was ripped out of my hand, taking the skin off my fingers. I looked up to see the female harpy grappling with the throw-bag, trying to carry it away in her talons. She was hanging upside down from the swinging bag, spinning around with huge wings flapping. There was a real risk of her becoming entangled, so I made another lunge for the line and for a brief moment we were locked in a tug of war before she let go and dropped away to glide out of the tree. I looked around but couldn't see her anywhere. She'd arrived like a bolt of lightning then simply melted back into the forest. Completely vanished. All was still again and the only sound was the soft patter of lead shot falling on leaves. She had ripped open the thick canvas throw-bag with her talons and left my fingers bleeding.

None of this boded at all well for how she was going to react to me being up there. I was left in peace to finish the rest of the rigging but my head was full of doubts and fears. By the time I arrived back in camp I'd decided to make additional body armour. The riot helmet, stab vest and arm greaves were a comfort, but that still left my lower back and legs exposed. I needed to find some additional padding to protect kidneys and thighs and remembered with an air of resignation how much I'd grumbled at wearing just the vest and helmet the first time round. But I had a horrible feeling that this morning's show of aggression was merely a taste of what lay in store. Tomorrow would come soon enough.

• • •

I awoke in the darkness. The night air was filled with the sound of insects and I could see the faint neon glow of a passing firefly through the thin flysheet of my tent. In the distance the haunting sound of howler monkeys told me that dawn wasn't far off. I checked my watch: 4.30. Realising that I wasn't going to get any more sleep, I pulled on my clothes and wormed my way out into the cool night air. Trees loomed black against a sky filled with stars.

Pulling on my boots I headed over to the kitchen hut to pour myself a strong black coffee from the thermos on the table. I sat there for half an hour trying to get my head into the game. It was obvious I was going to get attacked by one if not both of the harpies. I could deal with that, I had my armour and who could blame the birds for defending their nest? It was a price that had to be paid in order to fix the camera. But what really worried me was the thought of accidentally injuring one of the adults during the fray. I'd have to stay as passive as possible and try not to provoke them. But the instinct to defend yourself is hard to suppress and would try my patience. As a last resort, I'd have to know when to retreat if it all got out of hand.

An hour later the three of us were standing together beneath the kapok. Adrian had found some strips of rawhide from somewhere and was taping them around my waist with a roll of gaffer tape. This provided good protection for my lower back, effectively closing the gap between stab vest and climbing harness. I wrapped my thighs in more of the same while Adrian went to help Graham put on similar armour. To minimise disturbance, we had only rigged one set of ropes this time. So I would climb up first, transfer onto a temporary anchor and free the main ropes up for Graham to join me. This would leave me unable to retreat if attacked, but one person could work on the camera while the other kept watch. Getting up there one at a time in the first place was going to be a challenge though, since we wouldn't be able to watch each other's backs during the climb.

The riot helmet smelled of mould and rancid sweat. I pulled it on and did up the chin strap. I clipped the rope into my climbing clamps then pulled the slack through. With my radio firmly attached and switched on, I began to climb. There was no sign of the birds, but they would be watching.

The riot helmet's narrow field of view kept me blinkered and its heavy padding muffled all sound. My breathing was loud and laboured, but everything else was clipped and distant as if underwater. Unable to see or hear much, I concentrated on the rhythm of climbing. Arriving at the top of the dense understorey, I pulled down my visor in preparation for breaking cover. The scratched perspex instantly steamed up, leaving me blind as I wriggled my way up through the tangle of branches.

I entered the open space above and it was now only a matter of time until I was spotted by the eagles. The race to reach the protective canopy seventy feet overhead had now begun, and until I got there, I was fair game. Sweat trickled into my eyes, stinging like acid, and my muscles burned. I drove myself up the rope as fast as possible.

The first warning I had was an ominous shadow barrelling down fast from the left. With head hunkered low between her wings, the harpy presented a streamlined profile until she got to within ten feet of my face, where she pushed her enormous talons forward to attack. But realising I'd seen her she veered away at the last second. The rush of air from her immense wings sent me swinging on the rope and my back was now towards her. Climbing blind again, I continued my dash upwards as fast as possible, with heart pounding loud in my ears.

Within seconds the radio crackled into life: 'Watch it, she's coming back in.' By the time I'd twisted round she was a hundred feet away, powering towards me with deep strokes of her huge black wings. She was accelerating with terrifying speed. All I could do was watch her get bigger and bigger as she came in hard and fast straight towards my face. Thirty feet away she fixed her wings into a rigid glide and twisted to one side at the last instant to kick me hard in the kidneys with both feet as she shot past like a missile. The makeshift armour worked. Her talons didn't penetrate, but she'd delivered a powerful punch that left me bruised and spinning on the rope. There was nothing else to do but press on climbing at full speed.

Swaying around all over the place, I could feel myself spiralling up the rope in dizzying circles. The heat, sweat and blindness left me feeling sick. I flipped up the visor to take a breath, only to see her rushing in towards my face no more than twenty feet away. The twist in the rope span me round again, there was a whoosh of air and a heavy impact – this time she got me square in the middle of the back. I caught a fleeting glimpse of her broad rounded wings and huge fanned tail as she scythed away with those enormous talons dangling beneath her like knives.

A few minutes later she reappeared above me, landing on a branch next to my ropes. There was no clear flight path between us so I took the opportunity to push myself up as fast as my burning muscles would allow. I was approaching the top of my rope and had now entered the kapok's canopy. The harpy was right there, leaning towards me, her black eyes staring me down and her giant hooked beak open to reveal a reptilian tongue panting in time with her rapid breathing.

Her powerful yellow feet gripped the branch hard, those formidable rear talons resting on their needle-sharp points. It was obvious she was waiting for another chance to attack. Without taking my eyes off hers, I squeezed myself up through a tight fork in the branches then balanced precariously to stare up at her. After a minute or so she seemed to relax a bit and sat up straight with her crest raised.

Now came the tricky bit. In order for me to free the ropes for Graham's ascent, I needed to rig another anchor. I'd have to take my eyes off her for a few seconds to do that. There was no choice but to give her the benefit of the doubt, in the hope that she wouldn't press home the advantage.

The next thing I knew I was spinning on my rope seeing stars. My ears were ringing and I could feel a searing pain at the base of my skull. I scrambled back onto the spike-covered branch as quickly as possible and placed my hand on the pain. The left-hand side of my neck between collar and jaw was numb and when I took my hand away there was blood on my fingers. She must have seen the gap between neck guard and stab vest and gone for it. I felt like I'd been hit with a baseball bat, and I turned my head a few times to check there were no broken bones. But blood wasn't good, and I tried to stem the flow by pressing hard with my fingers, which only made me feel more lightheaded and giddy.

I shouted down to the guys: 'I'm okay, but that's it – I've had enough. I'm out of here!'

Graham's voice drifted up to me from far below: 'Stay there, James. I'm on my way. I'm coming up to you!'

I just had time to disconnect and attach to the neighbouring branch before I felt the climbing rope below me begin to stretch and bounce. He was on his way.

But seconds later she flew at me again, stooping fast, with talons stretched out towards my face. This time it didn't seem that merely turning to face her was going to deter the attack, so I shouted and waved my arms. She swerved and veered to land on a branch ten feet away, where she leant forward to study me again with wings half-cocked, ready for action if the opportunity arose. To turn my back on her now or look away momentarily would clearly invite another attack. I wasn't going to make that mistake again. So while she craned her neck to get a clear view of me I did my best to maintain eye contact while using an adjacent branch for cover. We were at an impasse – our eyes locked. This was her home turf and I was the outsider.

Risking a quick glance down the ropes, I saw Graham just emerging from the understorey. The harpy must have noticed him as well, because she leant a little further forward to peer down. Just when I thought she was going to swoop down on Graham, the male harpy appeared out of nowhere and came arcing in beneath me towards him. I raised the alarm but Graham had already seen him and lifted his feet up in front of his body to ward off a blow. The eagle realised he'd been rumbled and banked off to the side at the last second, to leave Graham swinging. He pressed on up the rope regardless, and within a few minutes arrived next to me on the branch. I had collected my nerves a bit and the bleeding seemed to have stopped. So with Graham keeping a close eye on the female only feet away, I had my first opportunity to take a proper look at the nest behind us.

Where three months ago there had been two small white eggs nestled in a delicate bowl, there was now one big angry chick. It was the size of a large chicken, with grey wings, a white head and two enormous yellow feet. It was leaning back on its haunches, talons raised towards me. Its beak was open in defiance and every few seconds a pale nictitating membrane slid in a cold reptilian fashion across its fierce dark eyes.

The surface of the nest was covered in a thick layer of leaf litter and strewn with the dismembered remains of half-eaten carcasses. Bloated green flies swarmed over mangled flesh and pale rotting meat seethed with maggots. The chick edged back away from us. We had to be careful not to scare it out of the nest, so I only went as far as I needed in order to reach the camera. Graham and I spent the next thirty minutes cleaning the splattered eagle dung from its lens and wiping away three months of accumulated grime. By the time we'd finished, the chick seemed surprisingly relaxed with our presence, but a quick look back over my shoulder at its mother was enough to remind me not to get complacent. Graham and her were eyeballing each other and the truce was holding – just. But I knew that in a moment one of us would have to abseil back down, leaving the other here to deal with her on his own. I offered to stay, and watched Graham lean back off of the branch then drop into the void, to be swallowed by the thick understorey vegetation seventy feet below. She remained perched, glaring at me and Graham escaped unscathed.

Now it was my turn and I knew what was coming. I fixed her with a stare and jumped off the branch while cranking the handle of my abseil device as hard as I dared, but there was no avoiding it: with wings tucked in beside her she stooped straight down on top of me and swerved round to strike me one last time in the shoulder before disappearing into the forest. I'd well and truly had enough, and dropped like a stone down the rope to the safety of the forest floor.

'Mate, your neck's bleeding,' said Adrian once I'd landed and discarded the riot helmet. 'Looks pretty bad ...' He came closer to take a proper look. 'The collar of your shirt's all ripped up, there's a slice in the neck guard and it looks like she got a talon right down into your neck next to your jugular. Yep, a bit to the left and you'd be in trouble.' She'd made a deep puncture wound with one of her talons. Who knew what bacteria live on the claws of a harpy? It was going to need a proper scrape-out and clean, but at least the bleeding had stopped.

We gathered round the small LCD monitor to look at the image of the chick sitting on the nest, sulking at the camera.

A few minutes later the mother bird landed back in shot. She stood motionless, staring at her chick. Then she dragged a scrap of monkey carcass towards her, and with short sharp tugs began tearing off small strips of meat with her beak. She leant forward to offer the scrap to the chick, which came shuffling towards her with wings flapping weakly. With infinite tenderness she delicately placed the tiny morsel into the chick's waiting mouth. It was a fantastic sight and we couldn't have asked for better proof that all had gone well and we hadn't caused any lasting disturbance.

I looked up at the huge silver branches shining in the sunlight high above. It was a different world up there in the harpy's fortress. What a privilege it was to have visited it.

'Let's get back to camp. We've got to clean that wound out,' said Graham. I didn't need telling twice. It was only 9.30 in the morning, but I really needed a beer.

Chapter 10

Idyl – Morocco

2013

Loose shards of limestone clinked like broken crockery under my feet as I made my way slowly up the mountainside. The ground was a tinder-dry jumble of exposed bedrock. Thin layers of soil lay between shattered boulders, and dry wispy grass grew in patches where it could. It was a wonder that anything could grow here at all, let alone thrive, and I marvelled at the enormous trees rising straight up from the bones of the earth around me.

These were Atlas cedars and the clear mountain air was laced with the spicy scent of their resin, a wonderfully evocative smell that seemed to float down from another century like incense. Looking up, I could see their topmost branches bathed in bright sunlight, while down here amongst the shadows I was surrounded by their wide trunks standing amidst a spartan understorey of holly and maple.

It was mid October in the Atlas Mountains of Morocco. Red berries in the branches of thorn trees confirmed that autumn was here, and although the day was warm there was a flinty edge to the mountain breeze that whispered of a harsh winter ahead. Baked to within an inch of its life by the fierce North African summer sun, then plunged into sub-zero temperatures and blanketed in deep snow during winter, this forest was a place of extremes. Anything growing here needed to be hardy and resilient to survive. The gnarled cedars around me certainly were. Unlike the younger trees growing in sheltered spots further down the valley, these massive veterans had real personality. The grove I was standing in was huddled on a steep ridge, like a regiment of soldiers making a last stand at the end of a battle. Each one was totally different from its neighbour, and their body language seemed defiant against the ravages of time and weather. Branches snapped off by winter snowfall, trunks scorched by summer fires: each tree was a living record of its days, with epic stories laid bare for anyone to read.

Selecting a space between two roots, I sat with my back to a trunk and looked down the slope I'd just climbed. It looked steeper from here and I was now level with the upper canopy of several big cedars. Their layered, horizontal branches were backlit by the morning sun, and their delicate evergreen needles were tinged with silver. Sunlight bounced up from the forest floor to illuminate the underside of branches, and their enormous scaly trunks glowed chestnut brown. Foliage sighed in a gentle breeze under a clear blue sky. The forest had a feeling of ageless serenity about it.

• • •

My dad and I had arrived in the bustling Berber town of Azrou, here in the Middle Atlas range, two days ago. It was a favourite place of ours since we first visited it sixteen years ago. I'd been living and filming in the deserts of southern Morocco at the time, and as much as I loved the stark beauty of the northern Sahara, I'd missed being around trees. So when Dad came to visit we took a road trip and discovered this gem in the heart of the mountains. Azrou is the gateway to some of the most wonderful forests I've ever seen, and I've continued to return whenever I can, although nowhere near as often as I'd like.

The Atlas cedar is one of the most beautiful trees on the planet, in my opinion. But like all living things, they need to be seen in their natural environment to be fully appreciated. Each one displayed the breathtaking balance of form shared by all wild things growing in harmony with nature. Maybe it's to do with the wonderful smell of their sap or the meditative solitude of their mountain home, but for me, just spending time around these ancient trees helps soothe the soul.

Happily, cedars are also a total joy to climb. They aren't the tallest, but with strong timber, horizontal branches and (in older trees) a flat-topped canopy that allows you to stretch out and admire the view, they are hard to beat. Dad was down in the souk doing what he loved best, bartering and haggling with the traders for carpets and fossils, which left me to spend the day doing what I loved best: searching the forested hillsides above for the perfect tree to climb. My plan was to return the next day to climb it and spend a night in its branches. I'd climbed plenty of cedars, but never slept in one, and I felt the need to get as close to these magnificent trees as I possibly could.

A movement further down the slope drew my eye to where a troop of Barbary macaques moved through the trees, turning over rocks and foraging under logs for morsels to eat. They were a sudden reminder that despite the mountainous terrain of these coniferous forests, I was still in Africa and up until very recently these remote valleys had also been home to a whole variety of other mammals unique to this continent.

Africa's only species of bear survived here until the mid nineteenth century and the last of Morocco's wild Barbary lions lived in these mountains until the 1940s. There had once been large, healthy populations of both. In fact, most of the lions that met their end in the sand of the Roman coliseum came from here.

I tried to imagine what it must have been like to see a Barbary lion in this landscape. Famous for their large size and the thickness of their shaggy black manes, they must have been an incredible sight, prowling through the snow on a still moonlit night, gliding silently between the deep-blue shadows of enormous cedars. Although the lions are gone, the forest remains, and as I looked at the ancient trees growing on the ridge around me, it was wonderful to think that such a cat might have scratched its claws on the hard timber of any one of them as it passed. Maybe even the one I was now leaning against.

Another intriguing thought is that there might, just *might*, be a remnant population of the Barbary leopard still here. Though it is thought by many to be extinct, some local shepherds believe they still roam the forests, and I vividly recall the spotted pelt I saw for sale in Azrou souk fifteen years ago. Thick, luxuriant fur like nothing I'd ever seen in sub-Saharan Africa. I'm a hopeless romantic when it comes to such things and I wanted to believe they were still here, somewhere. If any big cat can survive without the outside world knowing, it's a leopard.

The call of a raven brought me back to this century. Taking a sip of water, I stood up to move further along the ridge in search of a tree to climb.

I was beginning to see a pattern. These older trees grew together in pockets – distinct groves in the very heart of the forest. And unlike many other trees, which tend to grow best in the fertile alluvial flats adjacent to rivers, these trees seemed to reach their zenith on the rugged upper slopes of the mountain where the soil was at its thinnest. It was a mystery to me, that only added to their allure. They were defiant, almost rebellious trees, which seemed to march to a different rhythm.

Cresting the ridge, I was met with a beautiful sight on the flat space beyond. Mature cedars stood in an open colonnade, like the arches of an enormous high-domed mosque, and the sun had broken through to illuminate this space with shafts of light. Each beam that hit the forest floor contained a resident pair of dancing butterflies. With brown wings covered in large creamy spots, they looked like the species called speckled wood. Soft clouds of dust swirled in the turbulence from their tiny wings. I stood entranced, watching them spinning and spiralling round each other as they rose up through the pillars of light towards the canopy above. I'd walked into a glade of heaven.

My eye was drawn to a splash of colour amongst the stones at my feet. Bending forward, I realised it was a wild crocus. I'd never seen one before. Its six lilac-coloured petals were held in a vertical crown that seemed to glow in the dappled sunlight. The orange threads of its three stigmas were clearly visible. These stigmas were collected and dried in the sun to become saffron. I thought about the expensive crimson spice I'd seen piled high in cedar-wood bowls in Azrou's souk. The crocuses and cedars seemed unlikely companions, but were clearly linked in a delicate partnership of some kind. For such a seemingly rugged environment, these forests are surprisingly fragile, and I was reminded of the serious environmental pressures they face.

In 2013 the International Union for Conservation of Nature completed a periodic review of the status of conifers worldwide. The Atlas cedar was upgraded from *least threatened* to *endangered* overnight. Declines of 75 per cent occurred in the mid twentieth century and the cedars have been experiencing prolonged episodes of severe drought since the 1980s. These forests once stretched right across the mountains of the Maghreb, but with Algeria's contingent all but gone, Morocco now contains around 80 per cent of what's left. The main issue – inevitably, in such a seasonally dry environment – seems to be global warming. The forests around Azrou lie on the northern slopes of the Atlas Mountains and have historically benefited from Atlantic moisture, but much drier conditions arriving from the south are exerting their influence. Southern slopes are now dotted with the poignant white skeletons of cedars killed by drought, marking the trailing edge of a forest that is retreating north. Since the Atlas cedar only occurs naturally at elevations of 4,000 to 8,000 feet, the forest is caught between a rock and a hard place. It has nowhere to go. And additional pressures from illegal logging, overgrazing and soil erosion make the situation even more precarious.

Generally I'm a glass-half-full kind of person, but even I struggle to remain optimistic about the long-term future of the Atlas cedar within its natural range. Individual trees can be grown very well in Britain, but forests are obviously so much more than the sum of their trees. We may be able to preserve genes for ex-situ conservation in the future, but that's not a patch on a cedar – or a Barbary lion, for that matter – thriving in its natural environment.

I touched the crocus delicately with the back of my finger. Its petals were so soft I could barely feel them. How could something so fragile survive here? My gaze returned to the butterflies, so ephemeral in their courtship, and then to the huge cedars around me. What a magical place this was.

• • •

'So did you find your tree?' asked Dad when I made it back to Azrou that evening. I'd found him watching the sunset from his favourite table on the steps of the Hôtel des Cèdres overlooking the marketplace. He was sipping a glass of *nous-nous* and I marvelled at his ability to drink nuclear-strength coffee at any hour of the day. Pulling up a chair, I told him that I had found the perfect one and couldn't wait to climb it. There was a bag of freshly purchased trinkets by his side and it seemed he'd had just as good a day as I'd had. He'd retired from the London antiques trade a few years ago, but old habits die hard and his satisfied expression spoke volumes. I just felt sorry for the traders in the souk.

The call to prayer went up into the clear evening sky and the smell of tagines cooking over charcoal drifted through the narrow streets. A three-quarter moon was visible above the forest-clad hills and I realised with a smile that the next time I saw it rising would be from the comfort of a hammock suspended a hundred feet aboveground in the canopy of a cedar.

• • •

It was almost noon the next day. But while the barren mountain slopes higher up baked in the fierce dry heat, the forest here was shaded and cool. The now familiar smell of cedar resin filled the air as Dad and I picked our way between the boulders. We were making our way along the slopes of a wooded valley towards the tree I'd chosen to climb. I'd recorded its position in my GPS, which somehow felt a little like cheating and certainly detracted from my enjoyment of the forest as I blindly followed the trail of digital dots on its LCD. But I was keen to get there as soon as possible, with the intention of being settled in my hammock at least an hour before sunset. Dad was keen to camp out too, so I'd brought a second hammock for him to rig at ground level somewhere nearby.

The chosen tree stood on the far side of the butterfly glade, just before the small plateau dropped back down into the next valley. It wasn't the tallest cedar I'd seen, but was growing in the best position by far. From the moment I had spotted it I knew it was the one. Having finally made the choice, I couldn't wait to get up there.

Once we got to the base, Dad strolled off to find a place to camp while I took a few minutes to get acquainted with the tree I was about to climb.

It was a beautifully proportioned specimen. The trunk measured six feet across – not too massive – and rose straight up towards the canopy in a beautiful column of knot-free timber. The first branch didn't emerge until seventy feet up and was nothing more than a twisted dead stump. But the main canopy above that was perfect: huge horizontal branches spreading out in every direction, offering endless hammock-rigging possibilities. The tree's location at the edge of the plateau, high above the next valley, promised fantastic views. To cap it all, it faced west, which boded well for sunset.

Wasting no more time, I set up my catapult and fired a line over the lowest solid branch I could see. I hauled up my rope, planning to use it to get above the sheer trunk into the lower canopy. From there on I would climb up through the rest of the tree from branch to branch. My lanyards would be there to catch me if I fell, but I felt it was important to climb the tree itself, rather than a rope. I didn't want to be transported to the very top of the canopy via a rope connecting it to the ground in one long pitch.

The distant clinking of rocks told me Dad had found a campsite and was clearing a place for a fire. So stepping into my harness I pulled it up onto my waist and removed any extra karabiners and kit I wouldn't need. Tying the end of the rope onto a rucksack containing camping gear, food and water, I clipped in and pulled through the slack. Climbing in dry Mediterranean weather made such a pleasant change from slogging up through the searing heat and humidity of a tropical jungle. It was nice not to be drenched with sweat within thirty seconds of leaving the ground, and refreshing not to be harangued by biting insects.

But I'd spoken too soon – although I remained blissfully insect-free, the sweat was soon flowing. Halfway up the trunk I entered the sunlight and felt my skin instantly prickle with heat. Arriving in the shadow of the canopy a few minutes later, I stopped to take a breather. My sweat evaporated into the dry air to cool me down and within a few moments even the dark patches of moisture on the front of my t-shirt had completely disappeared. I peered up the trunk to see how much further I had left to go.

The rope passed up through a gap between the tree and a huge dead branch just above me. The gap had looked much bigger from the ground and now I was beginning to wonder whether I would fit through it. It would be a squeeze, for sure. It would have been easy enough to bypass this bottleneck by transferring onto my other lanyards, but I decided instead to have a go. Inevitably, it turned into a proper little grapple, which nearly left me irretrievably wedged. Too many tagines, it seemed, and when I eventually did emerge back into the open above, my arms were covered in angry scratches and a mixture of tree sap and dirt. Flakes of dry bark adhered to the sap in places, and I managed to rip a few hairs out picking them free. But the smell of the resin was out of this world and I couldn't resist dabbing my finger in it for a taste. I'd like to say that in doing so I discovered an amazing new elixir, some sort of secret natural potion guaranteed to create a sense of eternal wellbeing. Rather disappointingly, however, it turned out to be extremely bitter and unpalatable, although there was an underlying sugary spiciness to it that made me try it again just to be sure. Nope, still horrible – so taking a swig of water I carried on climbing until I reached the top of the rope, where I sat back to take a proper look around at my new surroundings.

I laughed out loud with spontaneous pleasure at the view that greeted me. The forest canopy hung around me in floating terraces. Horizontal layers of thick foliage suspended at different heights within neighbouring trees. Everything was backlit, glowing bluish-green in the afternoon sunlight. The sun itself was eclipsed by a branch, but the surrounding needles shone in a halo of silver, and long threads of gossamer shimmered in the air as dozens of newly hatched spiderlings floated down through the canopy around me.

The position of my tree on the edge of the escarpment meant I was now level with the very tops of others growing on the slopes below. They looked close enough to leap into through the clear mountain air. The forest rose up the opposite side of the valley to peter out on an open plateau beyond, and high on the horizon, above everything else, floated the enticing silhouettes of mountains. All I could see were mountains and Atlas cedars, the loveliest trees on the planet. It made for an idyllic scene.

The very top of the tree was another thirty feet above me, but the spot I was hanging in would do just fine for my light-weight hammock. I hauled up the rucksack and hung it from a branch next to me. The hammock was brand new and wrapped up in a tight ball. It unravelled to hang down below me, and grasping one end in my teeth I swung out on my rope along a large branch to attach it. I then swung across to another limb ten feet away to pull the hammock taut, before letting myself fall back into the middle, where I dropped down onto my new bed. I'd sort out the sleeping bag later on, but for now it felt great to lie back and watch the sunlight dance on the underside of the canopy directly above.

The sun was still a hand's breadth above the horizon and I had plenty of time to just lie there, so I closed my eyes and listened to the forest. The day was cooling and air was on the move as the sun dropped towards the horizon. A gentle breeze whistled softly through the cedar needles around me and somewhere down in the valley, where shadows were already gathering, a tawny owl called once and then was silent.

I could still hear the occasional clinking of rocks from Dad – heaven knows what he was doing down there, constructing some sort of wall to keep out the wolves, by the sound of it. But for the most part it was utterly silent. In fact, *silent* wasn't quite the right word: it suggests an absence of sound.

Peaceful, is a better description, or even *tranquil*. It's hard to describe. But the hour I spent gently swaying in my hammock 120 feet aboveground in that cedar, while watching the sun slowly descend over the Atlas Mountains, was one of the most serene of my life so far.

After a few minutes I opened my eyes to see a tiny spider dangling on its thread a foot above my face. It seemed to be dropping in line with my nose, so just before touchdown I gave it a gentle blow. It dropped faster in response and I caught it by the silk just before it landed on me. Re-anchoring its thread to the branch next to me, I peered over the edge of my hammock to watch it continue its epic head-first descent through the canopy. The forest floor was 120 feet below and I couldn't believe a spider that size could produce enough silk to make such an epic abseil. Since I had nothing more pressing to do, I estimated that if the tree was enlarged to dwarf me, as it dwarfed the spider, I would need a rope more than 69,000 feet long to reach the ground from this hammock. The tree would measure almost seventeen miles high overall, placing its topmost branches somewhere in the stratosphere. Amazing. Just trying to visualise what a sixteen-mile-high cedar would look like made me smile. As I watched, a gentle breeze blew the spider in towards the tree. It landed on the trunk ten feet below me, detached itself from the silken thread and scurried off across the bark. I guess I wouldn't discover how much silk is inside a spider after all.

I'd have to remain attached to my safety rope while I slept, which also meant keeping my harness on. So in a bid to make myself as comfy as possible I removed all my extra karabiners and hung them out of the way. Unrolling my sleeping bag, I removed my boots, pulled on a woolly hat and lay on my side to watch the sunset. Fire rolled across the sky and the blood-red sun slid slowly down behind the mountains. *Salat al-maghrib*, the evening call to prayer, drifted up on the edge of the wind from a distant mosque hidden in the folds of the mountains, then all was silent.

A few hours later I woke up cold. I'd fallen asleep on top of my sleeping bag, so slid down inside and listened to the sounds of the night. The waxing moon was rising through the trees but it wasn't yet high enough to shed any light, so the forest around me was inky black. Stars glittered in the canopy and tawny owls were calling. Their plaintive notes reminding me of that first night I'd slept in Goliath, back in the New Forest all those years ago. I fell back to sleep, wondering what the owls were saying to each other.

The next time I awoke, the moon was high in the sky and the forest around me was bathed in its soft glow. There was a waxy sheen to the cedar foliage, but the huge branches twisting around me remained in shadow. Looking out over the valley below, I could clearly make out the tops of the taller cedars reaching up into the moonlight. I rolled over in my hammock and peered down. The trunk below me was dappled with beautiful silver shadows. Its scaly bark looked prehistoric and timeless, and I wondered how old this tree was. It felt as though it had been here, keeping watch over the valley below, forever. It was certainly several centuries old and could easily be half a millennium or more. Five hundred years was a long time to live in these mountains and my brief visit would barely register on the timeline of this cedar's life. But that's one of the alluring things about trees, isn't it? They seem almost eternal figures of reference in the landscape, reminding us to make the most of every passing day in our all-too-brief lives. A tawny called again from the tree next to me and I drifted back to sleep.

By the time I stirred again it was seven o'clock in the morning. I opened my eyes to a different world. Colour was seeping back into it and the moonlit night felt like a passing dream. The pale eastern sky heralded the coming of the sun, and the breeze already carried the enticing smell of resin, but for now the forest around me was still in shadow. It was cold but not frosty, and I lay there trying to muster the energy to swing out of the hammock and start climbing. My plan was to greet the rising sun from the very top of the tree, which was only thirty or so feet above me. The ladder of thick, strong branches would lead me there. I wriggled out of my sleeping bag and swung my legs over the side of the hammock to pull my boots on.

Taking in the slack on my sliding knot, I pulled myself up on the rope, stood in the hammock and stepped off to swing in towards the trunk. Landing with my feet against the stem, I adjusted my harness properly then reached up to hang from a branch by my hands to stretch out my back. The coldness had settled in my bones and I felt a couple of clunks as the weight of my body straightened my spine ready for the climb.

Pulling myself up, I gave myself plenty of slack in the rope and moved quickly from branch to branch without stopping, until I was crouched beneath the topmost layer of foliage.

The branches here were smaller, more gnarly and weather-hammered. Lichen grew everywhere and dust drifted down when I touched the tree. Several branches had lost their bark to reveal intricate lacy grooves where beetle larvae once lived. The topmost layer of branches had woven around each other to form a dense horizontal matt – a flat tabletop of foliage. Above this, I glimpsed blue sky. Repositioning my safety anchor to the branch just below me, I again gave myself plenty of slack in the rope, ready to take the next few steps. Pushing my hands up through the bristling needles, I emerged into the space above.

My torso was now completely above the canopy, just in time to see the first rays of sunlight burst through the crown of a neighbouring cedar. The warmth of the sun was instant. I felt the rays sink deep into my bones and I sat there with eyes closed basking in its glow for several seconds. Aware of a soft buzzing sound, I opened them again to find myself surrounded by dozens of honeybees peacefully foraging in the canopy around me. Hundreds of slender, yellow, finger-like cones stood erect on the branches. These were the tree's male cones, which had matured over the summer months ready to release their pollen now that it was autumn. The bees were cashing in en masse. The cedar's needle-like foliage also stood erect, growing in little clusters atop short woody stems. Thick waxy cuticles gave these needles a bluish-green colour, and picking a few I rolled them between my palms to release the heavenly aroma I'd grown to love.

Looking further afield I saw that my tree was one of a line of mature cedars of similar height and age standing on the edge of the crescent-shaped escarpment. Turning around to face west I looked out over the valley towards the distant High Atlas mountains on the horizon. The escarpment's shadow fell flat across this landscape like an enormous sundial, and although the top of my tree was now bathed in full sunlight, those below me were still in darkness. As the sun rose higher, I watched the leading edge of this shadow shrink back in towards my ridge until everything was in full sunshine. The trees growing below the shelter of the ridge were some of the tallest I'd seen in these forests. The books tell us that Atlas cedars rarely, if ever, exceed 130 feet in height. But I can say for a fact that the one I was standing in was at least 150 feet tall and I'd happily eat a karabiner if those in the valley below me weren't pushing 165 feet.

It was an incredible view. But further down the valley to the south, a spectre loomed. Many of the mature cedars there were dead. Large trees like the one I was in, presumably with many more years to give, had been killed in their prime. Their sun-bleached carcasses still stood over the surrounding forest, looming like ghosts. Trees die all the time, of course, and these may have been the victims of natural causes. But they definitely hadn't succumbed to old age, and to see an entire grove of them standing dead and lifeless seemed ominous. I'd bet prolonged drought was the cause. A thick understorey of evergreen holm oak had now grown up beneath them, and it seemed extremely unlikely that any cedar saplings would be able to compete with them for light in the future. Not that I'd seen any young cedars growing anywhere in the forest so far. The large roaming herds of domestic sheep and goats had presumably seen to that.

Despite the sight of those dead trees, I felt my spirits rise when I took in the rest of the view one last time before climbing back down. The vast majority of trees around me were in a fine state of health. Even those that had lost major branches or had their crowns snapped out by high winds were still growing vigorously, and clearly had many more decades left in them.

By the time I derigged my hammock and abseiled back down to the forest floor, Dad had packed up and was waiting for me. Smoke still curled from the hot embers of his campfire and I was a little peeved at having to pour the last of our drinking water on them to prevent the forest from burning down around us. But as he pointed out with a smile and a shrug, there was plenty of mint tea waiting for us in Azrou.

We decided to follow a more direct compass bearing back, rather than the winding route suggested by my GPS, and after half an hour or so we came across a low fence running through the trees. It wasn't designed to keep people out, so stepping over it we continued on our way. Patches of brambles grew here and there and the understorey vegetation of silverthorn and Italian maple seemed thicker here than anywhere else we'd seen. Grass grew higher and crocuses were more common.

We'd clearly entered a protected area and the low fence had been erected to keep livestock out.

It was then that we encountered a miniature forest of tiny green cedar seedlings, directly beneath a particularly ancient multi-stemmed cedar. A couple of hundred were growing up through the bone-dry leaf litter around us, apparently self-sown by the enormous tree towering above. It was a reassuring sight: our last day in these forests and we'd finally found evidence of natural cedar regeneration. Here, sprinkled around us, was hope for the future. Two hundred seedlings docs not make a forest, but it was a start. Sixteen years ago when I lived near here, there had been no protection in place. But this livestock fence showed that measures were being taken to turn the tide and these forests were now being given a fighting chance. All nature needs is to be met halfway; it'll manage the rest.

Taking off my rucksack I lay down on my stomach amongst the parched twigs and debris of yesteryear to take a closer look at the seedlings. No more than two inches tall, each was a delicate cluster of soft green needles atop a slender chestnut-coloured stalk. They looked impossibly fragile and I could see how a hungry sheep would make short work of them. These were the little green titbits and morsels that would get nibbled off straightaway. Resting my chin on my hands in the dry soil, I looked up past the seedlings towards the massive tree above them. It was a real mother of the forest, many centuries old, and once again I was struck by the seemingly impossible way in which such huge organisms start out. It just beggars belief that a fragile little wisp of life no bigger than a toothpick can grow into one of the great trees of the world, and the Atlas cedar truly is one of the great trees of the world. It's certainly one of the most beautiful. I just hope they are still to be found growing wild in those mountains where they belong for many millennia to come. And who knows? Maybe one day the cedar forests of the Atlas will be the haunt of lions and bears once again.

Epilogue

I am sitting in my hammock, eighty feet aboveground, halfway up Goliath. To my right is a swooping branch thirty feet long. To my left is Goliath's huge trunk, the thick red bark swirling in patterns as it flows up towards the top of the tree, ninety feet above me.

The early-spring sunshine is streaming through the delicate foliage and the air is alive with birdsong. As I write this, firecrests flit through the branches around me searching for titbits, and a treecreeper is hopping up the trunk next to me. To sit back and watch the natural world carry on around you as if you weren't there is one of the real joys of being in the canopy. Mornings like these are what the New Forest does so well.

I first climbed this tree twenty-six years ago – although I didn't quite make it to the top that time. In three days I'll turn forty-two, although I don't feel it. Well, not mentally anyway. Various minor injuries have taken their toll on my ability to run up trees in quite the same way as I used to, but I'm still the kid who loves to get up into the branches and idle away an hour looking at the view. I guess I must have changed a lot since I first sat on this branch 9,500 days ago, but that's the thing about getting older, isn't it? You're always the last to know, thank goodness. Besides, I have no intention of hanging up my harness for many years to come. Not with so many other wonderful trees in the world to climb and explore. The canopy, and filming the wildlife within it, has lost none of its fascination for me – quite the opposite in fact. Next month I'll be heading out to film birds of paradise in New Guinea, followed by four weeks with orangutans in Borneo. I can't wait, although leaving my family for such long lengths of time doesn't get any easier.

Goliath is now several feet taller than when I first met him, and the faint, healed-over rope burns on the branches around me stand testament to the fact that two and a half decades is also quite a long time in the life of a tree. Cambium savers, designed to protect bark from rope abrasion, hadn't been invented back in 1991, so our ropes left friction marks around the base of branches as we hung from them to abseil. These days, things are different. Climbers take a lot more care not to damage the tree they are in. Generally speaking, I feel that people are now much more aware of how their actions might affect nature and the countryside around them. When I was growing up here, the thought of seeing an otter in the forest, or hearing a goshawk chanting from the depths of a wood, was a wild fantasy. Buzzards were rare and you had to go very far afield to catch a glimpse of a peregrine or a raven. Yet only this morning I was greeted by the strident '*Kek-kek-kek*' of a goshawk as I walked through the trees with the ropes on my back, and then watched the feathered black silhouette of a raven fly directly above Goliath as I started to climb.

Despite all the controversy and negative press surrounding environmental issues, I actually believe we are now living in a time of great hope for British wildlife. I'm not saying we should get complacent, but the uproar with which the public greeted the government's 2010 attempts to sell off protected woodland into private hands was a heartening example of just how much people do care. As long as the trees still stand, it seems, there is hope.

As I've suggested before, trees are often the constant by which we measure the passing of years and the events of our own lives. We project our own memories onto them, and looking down through the branches below me now, I can still see my grandfather, my father and I standing there, looking up, and can almost hear the excited yapping of my dog, Buster, as he is hoisted up to me by my mates, with head poking out the top of a kitbag. (He greeted me with enthusiastic kisses and wagging tail, then tried to climb out onto a branch, at which point I realised he was much better suited to a life on the ground and lowered him quickly back down to safety.)

The year I finally made it to the top of this tree for the first time – 1994 – was also the year that I met my wife-to-be.

Yogita and I were on the same course at university in Derby, and I can still remember the first time – the very first moment – I ever saw her. Twenty-three years, three children and a lot of joy and some sadness later, we are closer than we've ever been, but she has yet to climb Goliath with me. In fact, when I'm not working in some jungle somewhere, I now do most of my climbing on my own. Alongside my job as a wildlife cameraman I also run my own company training others how to climb trees. I love it. But the incessant deskwork that goes with running a small business would soon suck the joy from the job if I wasn't able to escape back to the trees regularly. Thankfully, Yogita seems to know what's best, and happily banishes me to the canopy, knowing full well that when I return I'll be more relaxed and easier to be around. Risk assessments, emails, accounts and all the rest of it make James a dull boy.

So I arrived here in the forest at dusk last night. Getting out of my van and placing my feet on forest soil was like reconnecting to everything that had gone before. I was on home ground and surrounded by memories as I walked through the gloaming towards Goliath; passing by the huge Sitka spruce I've been promising myself I'd climb since I was seventeen, and the Douglas fir I so clearly remember climbing in my early twenties. Stepping out into the open, I was somehow relieved to see Goliath still standing where he had always been – silhouetted against the dark-blue western sky. Just as silent, lofty and stoic as ever. What a tree.

As I got closer I noticed that someone had carved their initials on the trunk at breast height. The letters had been crudely slashed into the laminated red bark with a long-bladed knife. At first this made me angry, then disappointed, then just plain sad for the person who'd done it. The bark was way too thick for a knife to hurt the tree, and the letters would soon be lost to time as the thick cambium healed over. But it got me thinking about why someone would do that in the first place. It struck me as a rather desperate act of insecurity. But then maybe this is the point: human beings are fundamentally insecure creatures by our very nature. Most tree graffiti, however mindless, can usually be seen as a crude attempt to graft part of ourselves onto the future of another organism that is almost guaranteed to live far longer than us.

Elsewhere in the forest there is an old beech tree that carries the poignant inscription 'T. B. James', followed by a US military star and the date '1944'. The tree has done its best to heal the wound, but the silver-grey skin of a beech is a lot thinner than a sequoia's spongy bark, and the letters were still legible after more than seventy years. They had been carved into the tree with a knife, or perhaps the tip of a bayonet, by an American soldier stationed in the area on the eve of D-Day. Now *that* I can understand. And whether he made it through the landings alive or not, his memory is entwined with the tree which has, in my mind, now come to symbolise an individual's hope for the future and the immortality of self-sacrifice.

• • •

I shot my line up into Goliath's branches as the last of the light was fading, then returned at dawn this morning to climb, reaching the very top just in time to watch the sun rise above the

Solent and kiss the tops of the tallest trees around me. Wrapping my arm tight around Goliath's neck, I felt the rays dispel the chill of a night spent in my van, and watched sunlight – glorious, golden, sparkling sunlight – flow out across the canopy, while listening to Bach's 'Prelude' from his Cello Suite No. 1 on my headphones. The first time I listened to that piece of music in a tree I was moved to tears; this time I closed my eyes and swayed gently with the rise and fall of the cello, opening them again to look out over the forest in time with the final soaring cadence. I felt like I was flying, swooping down from Goliath to skim across the tops of the oaks far below. Floating like a bird.

This view from the top of Goliath is still my favourite of any tree I've ever climbed. A few years ago I visited California to climb redwoods on their native soil. Some of those trees were exceptionally tall, growing on a different scale to any others I'd ever climbed. More than twice the height of Goliath, almost a hundred foot taller than Roaring Meg even: just magnificent. But even the view from the top of a 350-foot-tall coast redwood couldn't compare to the one I experienced this morning from the top of a tree that held so many wonderful memories for me.

As I looked out over the New Forest, I remembered the time I found myself climbing another, very different tree, which turned out to be the favourite of someone else, someone far more illustrious. That too had an extraordinary view from its top branches.

In the grounds of Buckingham Palace stand two beautiful London plane trees growing side by side, close to the Queen's private apartments. They were planted by Queen Victoria and Prince Albert and were given their names accordingly, although I have no idea which is which. What I do know, however, is that they are both absolutely stunning – just beautiful trees, with the strong, open-limbed canopies so characteristic of mature planes in their prime. While climbing one of them to rig cameras for a documentary, I happened to glance up at the palace. The Queen was reputed to be away from home that morning, so I was more than a little taken aback to see an extremely familiar silver-haired lady standing by the net curtains of her balcony window watching me intently. I had just reached the top of the tree and stuck my head out of the leafy canopy, and there she was, less than a hundred feet away, just staring at me in disbelief. I had no idea what to do or how to react. Resisting the temptation to smile and wave, I suddenly became very self-conscious. Her Majesty's rather stern expression spoke volumes and it was immediately obvious that no one had mentioned anything to her about what I was up to.

After ten of the most surreal minutes of my entire life, the palace door opened and a small pack of corgis bundled down the steps, accompanied by a smartly dressed man in a gold-buttoned waistcoat and pinstriped trousers. Realising I had better explain myself rather sharpish, I abseiled down to be greeted by the corgis yapping up at me from the base of the tree.

'The boss would like to know what you are doing in her favourite tree,' the man asked while reining in the dogs.

Apparently no one had mentioned to the royal household that they might expect to see some random bloke clambering around in the canopy outside their windows. I made my apologies and reassured him I wasn't there to hurt the tree in any way, but it just goes to show how much certain trees are cherished by people from all walks of life. Even Queen Elizabeth II has her favourite, and I find this heartening for some reason. It seems somehow symbolic of the depths of emotion trees are capable of generating in all of us – whatever our backgrounds.

The other day I tried to count up how many trips I've made to rainforests since 1998. I lost count at seventy six, ranging in length from two weeks to three months. That's around eight years so far. But even after all that time in the jungle, Goliath has come to represent everything that is wondrous about tree-climbing for me. In truth, he is an easy climb. But then, for me, this is the whole point: the older I get, the less I want to be scared witless. Comfort and familiarity have taken the place of adrenaline-fuelled thrill-seeking, and I now place far greater emphasis on nurturing one-to-one relationships with the trees I climb.

The most gifted tree-climber I know, a friend called Waldo, has his own special tree near his childhood home in Dorset. Although it is a beautiful tree, it isn't a particularly hard climb, nor particularly tall or challenging. But the point is that Waldo feels at home in its branches. Feels free to let his mind wander as he swings around from limb to limb, arriving back on the ground somehow rejuvenated, and all the better for it. Most tree-climbers are just like this – most of us have a favourite tree tucked away in our back pocket, ready for the days when we feel the need to spend a little time rediscovering ourselves and a few precious hours beyond the reach of other intrusions.

So in this respect, Goliath for me is still a place of refuge. I also found that becoming a father for the first time nine years ago heralded an almost overnight aversion to taking extreme risks. We have very little control over many events in our lives, but in the instances where I felt I had a choice – particularly while at work in the rainforest canopy – I have deliberately shied away from doing dangerous things. Life is full of enough unexpected challenges without going out and intentionally courting disaster. And with regard to tree-climbing, I now try to pick my battles very carefully, endeavouring not to drift unconsciously into risky situations if I can help it. As much as I love them, trees are extremely dynamic living structures, and there are never any guarantees that branches won't fail or that there aren't any hidden dangers lurking up there.

* * *

Near to our home in the South West of England is an ancient, gnarled yew tree that could easily be a thousand years old. It stands in a quiet corner of a long-forgotten wood and looks out over a beautiful valley. When times get tough I leave my ropes at home and climb into its upper branches to sit there thinking, watching the world go by far below. Sometimes this is enough and after a while I climb back down to the ground, feeling calmer of spirit and somehow all the better for having spent time in its branches. On other occasions I begin to talk.

Not necessarily to the tree, more to the world in general. I voice my sorrows, fears and concerns, letting the wind carry away what it can as it flows through the canopy around me. I'm not saying this always works. Some sorrows run too deep to heal completely. But it certainly helps by offering somewhere calm to retreat to – a space beyond the borders of busy modern life within which I can reflect on what's been lost, or focus on what lies ahead. As living entities trees have their own energy and yews in particular have a power that is hard to describe. Spending time in those branches, surrounded by this energy often helps me to cope with life's challenges. When things grow almost too dark to bear – as they can for anyone on occasion – it helps me on the journey towards coming to terms with events, and a little better able to offer the support and help my family needs to move forward.

That yew tree is where I go to look for answers when things grow rough, but also where I go to say thank you for everything else that is wonderful and positive. There is so much to be grateful for in this life, and I feel that to give gratitude for the good times is just as important as mourning one's sorrows, if not more so. Life is there to be celebrated and I find that a few minutes spent focusing on the positive goes a very long way towards maintaining a personal balance.

I have an extremely open mind when it comes to spirituality. The more I travel, the more I realise how little I know and how much there is to learn from other people's beliefs. I grew up Christian, lived for two impressionable years in a devout Muslim society, and married into a loving Sikh family. Over the last two decades my travels have brought me into close contact with dozens of different religions and philosophies, all of which contain profound elements of truth that I respect very much. But I have also come to realise that spirituality is where you find it, and I myself find it most easily when up in the trees.

Looking to the future, our boys will soon be of an age when they can start exploring the wonders of the canopy for themselves. They are already swinging around the branches of the oak in our garden, so it won't be long until they accompany me on a proper climbing trip somewhere. A dream is to one day return here to the New Forest and climb Goliath alongside all three of them. Perhaps in another twenty-five years' time. Although I expect I'll need to take things a little slower by then.

Acknowledgements

This book would not exist without the creative visions and hard work of two key people: Sarah Blunt, senior radio producer at the BBC in Bristol, and Jamie Joseph, senior commissioning editor at Penguin Random House.

It's been my pleasure to work with Sarah on numerous natural-history-based radio programmes over the years. Her skill and ability at turning my tree-climbing thoughts and ramblings into radio that people might want to listen to is a source of constant wonder to me. Jamie happened to tune in one day and contacted me out of the blue to suggest there may be a book about climbing trees in there somewhere.

Jamie has been absolutely instrumental in getting this book under way and championing the idea to make it a reality. Without his call (or tweet!) this book wouldn't have happened and the stories contained here would never have left the pages of my diaries. Both Jamie and Sarah took a punt on me and I am humbly grateful for the opportunity to work with them both.

• • •

Many of the chapters in this book recount exploits experienced while filming in the jungle canopy for National Geographic, the BBC and various independent film companies. Many people are involved in such productions and each have an important role to play in helping those projects become a reality. I am extremely grateful for the opportunity to have worked with you all along the way. Thank you in particular to the following people (many of whom appear in this book), for helping to make each trip to the jungle such a wonderful and memorable experience: John Waters, Genevieve Taylor, Michael 'Nick' Nichols, Dave Morgan, Brian Leith, Ralph Bower, Huw Cordey, Mike Salisbury, Sean Christian, Justine Evans, Rupert Barrington, Rebecca Cecil-Wright, Mirko Fernandez, Kevin Flay, David Roubik, Guy Grieve, Melanie Price, Tom Greenwood, Brett Mifsud, James Smith, Nick Dunbar, Bob Pelage, Rachael Kinley, Jim Hoesterey, Tom Hugh-Jones and my childhood friend Simon Holloway. A special thanks to Adrian Seymour and Graham Hatherley for having my back during our harpy eagle adventure and – of course – to Sir David Attenborough, whose enthusiasm and passion for the natural world has been a major source of inspiration for millions of us over the years.

Thank you to the fantastic team at PRH, including assistant editor Lucy Oates, publicist Kealey Rigden and freelance editor Will Atkins, whose insightful comments and suggestions were instrumental in helping the narrative flow. Thank you also to Alistair Carr, Helen Macdonald and Justin Marozzi – three hugely experienced and talented writers – for giving a complete novice like me encouragement and invaluable advice on how the publishing world works. Alistair – your generous personal advice and support has been particularly inspirational and appreciated. Thank you.

Thank you also to Andy Page and Jayne Albery of the New Forest Forestry Commission for giving me permission to clamber around the forest's treetops for the purpose of publicity photos. Many of these trees are nationally important specimens and I appreciate their trust in granting me access to their branches.

Gratitude is also due to all those free-thinking tree-climbers and friends who I have had the pleasure of spending time with in the canopy over the years. There have been many from all corners of our planet, but my particular thanks and respect goes to Ben Jones and Waldo Etherington, for being constant sources of positive energy and fun to be around while up in the trees. You both have a natural generosity of spirit, brightening the lives of all who are lucky enough to call you friends.

• • •

Very special thanks to both Paddy Graham and Phil Hurrell for getting me off the ground in the first place. Paddy – your infectious enthusiasm for climbing trees while we were growing up in the Forest was a source of constant fun and inspiration. Thanks for giving me my first rope and harness, and for introducing me to an incredible canopy world that few had ever visited. Phil – you will always have my humble gratitude for helping me get a footing in the wildlife film industry, and for providing such generous advice, support and friendship at every turn. You are a legend.

Likewise, thank you to cameraman and friend Gavin Thurston, for letting me camera assist him for so many years. Some of my enthusiastic assistance in the early years would probably qualify as 'negative help', but I learned an immeasurable amount along the way and every trainee cameraman needs someone to look up to.

• • •

My enduring appreciation, love and gratitude go to my mother Alison and my father Chris, for their unfailing support in helping me follow my dreams. I don't really know where to begin – there being a million reasons to be grateful – but my heartfelt thanks goes to you both for forking out for all the printing of those endless photos I took of trees, squirrels and deer as a kid (in an age before everything was digital) and for giving me free rein to explore the woods for days on end. This book owes its beginnings to you. Thanks to Liz for being – well, my sister really. Sisters have to put up with a lot.

• • •

Finally, there's no way I could have written this book without the support, patience and love of my wife Yogita and our boys Rohan, Tarun and Eshan. Eshan – our youngest – arrived half way through the writing of this book, so to say this last year has been a wee bit intense would be to fall spectacularly short of the truth. Yogita – I am in awe of you. Not only did you give birth to our wonderful third son, but you also somehow managed to give me the time and space I needed to write this book. It would not exist without such unconditional love and support from you. The next 300 school runs are on me! And lads, now the book's finished, we can spend our weekends visiting trees, museums and castles again – oh, lucky you!

• • •

For all those who may wish to find out more about what you can do to help preserve the remaining rainforest, I could do far worse than suggest you pay the following websites a quick visit. Thank you!

Greenpeace
www.greenpeace.org.uk

World Land Trust
www.worldlandtrust.org

Global Canopy Programme
www.globalcanopy.org

Borneo Orangutan Survival Foundation
www.orangutan.or.id